For
BUCKEYE
FANS ONLY!

Wonderful Stories Celebrating the Incredible Ohio State Fans

RICH WOLFE

Published by Lone Wolfe Press, a division of Richcraft. Distribution, marketing, publicity, interviews, and book signings handled by Wolfegang Marketing Systems, Ltd.—But Not Very.

Chief researcher: the wonderful Eric Hansen
Layout by The Printed Page, Phoenix, AZ
Author's agent: T. Roy Gaul

Rich Wolfe can be reached at 602-738-5889

ISBN: 978-0-9729249-8-6

Printed in the United States

Chat Rooms

5. THAT'S ENTERTAINMENT

6. HOME SWEET HORSESHOE

Chapter 1

Ya Can't Be Famous Unless You're a Buckeye Fan

Buckeye Fever—No Cure

SHORT FIELD GOALS AND LONG DOGLEG PAR-3s

JACK NICKLAUS

Long before the 73 official tour titles, the 18 victories in golf's four majors, the eight milestone victories on the senior circuit, the 20 holes-in-one . . . Jack Nicklaus used to make like legendary Buckeye kicker Tad Weed in his backyard and dream about following him to Ohio State. Nicklaus did end up at OSU, but Woody Hayes coaxed the Golden Bear in a different direction. Even so, Nicklaus' love of kicking a football lived on and so did his affection for Hayes.

I first met Woody Hayes when I was a freshman in high school or maybe a little before. It was really nothing that unusual as we lived in the same town, Upper Arlington, Ohio. While Woody was perhaps the most famous man in town, he never thought of himself that way or acted any different.

> **"I first met Woody Hayes when I was a freshman in high school"**

We were Midwesterners—we try to treat everyone the same. He had heard about me and knew my dad, so he asked about me and my plans. We saw each other a few times. I loved Ohio State football and was around it a lot. Woody was active around all Columbus sports, including the high schools. Not just football, all sports. He was looking for the best athletes to join each of the sports played at Ohio State. He was also a regular at my dad's pharmacy.

My dad, Charlie, had gone to OSU and the pharmacy school. After college, he played for the Portsmouth Spartans, which became the Detroit Lions.

From the time I was 6 years old until I was 20, I missed only one Ohio State home football game. Then it was because I played in the World Amateur Team Championship and for the Eisenhower Trophy at Merion **GOLF*** Club. Even then, I got the Ohio State-Southern Cal game on the radio. I walked around the golf course, carrying the radio and listening to the Ohio State-Southern Cal game while I was playing in the tournament. I shot 66-67-68-68 and won the individual title. So I shot 68 that day. If I hadn't been carrying around the radio, maybe I would have shot another 66.

The only game I missed prior to that was, I believe, 1947, when I was 7 years old. Pandel Savic threw a pass to Jimmy Clark for a touchdown and made the extra point to beat Northwestern, 7-6. They only won two games that year. I think they beat Missouri, 13-7, for the other victory.

I had a scare when I was 13. I actually had polio but didn't know it at the time. I was sick, but it was flu symptoms, nothing unusual. By the time they figured out that it was polio, I had it for only a couple of weeks. I probably gave it to my sister, who had it much worse than I did. She was hospitalized, had to wear a brace, has one leg shorter than the other. Of course later, the vaccine was developed. I was very lucky, especially when you consider that I went on to have a career as an athlete.

One of the things I really enjoyed growing up was kicking a football. I kicked just about anywhere I could—at school, in the neighborhood street with the other kids, but mostly on the football field. When I was little, I would kick balls in the backyard. We had a couple of tall trees at the end of the yard, I can't remember what type. I used to use those as targets, as pretend field goals, and kick balls through them.

I really enjoyed kicking as a kid, in high school, even in college, though I didn't play on the team. I even taught my kids and grandkids how to kick. I've always found that part of the game fun.

My experience at Ohio State was probably like a lot of people who attended the university. I did all the usual things. Sure, I played a lot of

While playing ***GOLF** in 1567, Mary Queen of Scots was informed that her husband, Lord Darnley, had been murdered. She finished the round.

sports, I just loved sports. The golf team was a big part of my life and growing in importance. Like a lot of kids, I went to the football games and other sporting events. I enjoyed my fraternity and the friends I had. We had a lot of fun.

I had a relationship with Woody while I was in school, but nothing much different than we always had, except now we were closer together around the sports facilities and school. Every now and then, I would go over to the football practices and join the kickers and kick with the team. Woody always had time to say hello or chat a little. That was the kind of man he was.

"I would go to the football practices and join the kickers and kick with the team."

I was lucky to have enjoyed a relationship with Woody over the years. He's a man I always respected, not just because he was a great coach and I love Ohio State, but because he was a great man, a man I respected. The way he cared for others and helped others—he was extremely selfless.

These feelings come after Woody somewhat broke my heart. I dreamed of playing football at Ohio State. I played football, basketball, ran track, played golf growing up. But when he and my father spoke, Woody recognized a greater talent for me and greater opportunity for me in golf.

Woody Hayes played a significant role in my career as a golfer, helping put me on that path after my father introduced me to the game. He always stayed in touch with me and my family. I can even remember when he came out to support me when I was playing in the U.S. Amateur Championship in **DENVER***. He would call back to the Columbus paper and report the results. He was there at my father's funeral. He would do anything, he was always giving. Trust me, he taught me and a whole lot of other kids a heck of a lot more about life than he did just about football.

Arnold Palmer designed the Bear Creek Golf Club in *DENVER. Above the urinals in the men's locker room is a picture of Palmer relieving himself against a tree at the club.

That's why when I was asked to dot the "i" at the OSU-Minnesota game in 2006, I decided I would wear a cap and tip my cap to the crowd. And the cap I would wear would be a black hat with an "O"—just like Woody's. It was my little way of recognizing and paying tribute to a man that meant so much to Ohio State and to me personally.

Ohio State is special to me, mostly because I grew up in Columbus. If you grew up in Columbus, it was a big part of your life, probably the same as for the alumni and fans of Southern Cal, or Notre Dame, or any school. I love sports and Ohio State. I still love going up for games.

I see more Ohio State games in person now than I really had a chance to in years past. Not just the big games and the national championship games, sometimes it's just a regular home game. But I love the opportunity just to go up and be a part of it, the whole atmosphere and experience. There's nothing like it.

But there was one other big milestone, life-changing event that happened while I was at Ohio State, and it wasn't golf or football. It was meeting Barbara Bash and walking her to class one day. A couple of weeks later, we went out on a date. And as they say, the rest is history. If it weren't for meeting Barbara and that walk to the chemistry building, I doubt I would have ever achieved half of what I did. Most importantly, I would have never enjoyed the greatest thing that ever happened to me—our marriage, our children and our grandchildren.

The Professional Caddies Association (PCA) has 2,800 members and is headquartered in Palm Coast, Florida. Until 2002, the PCA's Hall of Fame was located in founder Dennis Cone's Winnebago.

IF FOOTBALL'S A RELIGION, WHY DOESN'T INDIANA HAVE A PRAYER?

LEE CORSO

He was the jester of the Big 10 when Woody Hayes was king, but Lee Corso, now a longtime college football analyst with ESPN, and the legendary Buckeye coach found common ground, mutual respect and a lasting friendship. That is, after Corso had a little fun with an oddly timed team picture taken during an Indiana-OSU tussle in Bloomington, Indiana.

The whole idea had its origins long before that day in 1976. It was 1951. **INDIANA*** beat Ohio State, and Woody Hayes walked across the field. He said, "That football team will never beat me again—ever."

It's now 1976, and I walk across and say, "Hi Woody. How are you doing?" He growls at me. I say, "What the hell are you mad at me for? I was 10 years old when those guys beat you." He just throws his hat and laughs at me.

The game is at Bloomington, now. You've got to understand that. We win the toss, and we move the ball down and throw a pass in the left-hand flat, and an Ohio State guy picks it off and goes about 80 yards for a Buckeye touchdown. They miss the extra point, so the score is 6-0, which ain't too bad because the game just started.

Then, we get the ball, and we move down the field on a really great

By winning percentage, ***INDIANA** ranks 12th in all-time Big Ten football standings behind the University of Chicago.

drive and throw a post-corner touchdown. Boom. Kicked the extra point. Indiana 7, Ohio State 6. I walked across the field to the official and said, "We quit." He said, "What?" I said, "We quit. We ain't playing no more." He said, "You can't do that." I said, "Why?" He said, "You're going to get beat." I said, "We're going to get beat anyhow. I quit. We're not going to play anymore." He said, "You can't do that."

I said, "OK. Time out." I said, "Photographer, team, hurry up." We ran to the right, down underneath the scoreboard, which said, "Indiana 7, Ohio State 6," and took our team picture. Woody takes his hat off, and he throws it at me. He's yelling at me across the field. The crowd is going crazy. There was a full house, because all the people from Columbus came down to Bloomington, and it's crazy. The referee says, "What the hell are you doing?" I said, "You know what, mister, it's been 25 years since Indiana has been ahead of that S.O.B., and I want a picture to prove I'm ahead of him."

After the game, the photographer comes to me and says, "Lee, do you want another picture?" I said, "No, 47-7 don't look too good." He beats me 47-7.

That was a spur-of-the-moment thing, really. I've never done anything as a coach or in television that was contrived. Everything is spontaneous. It's a hell of a lot funnier.

I tried to bring humor to my coaching. Once, I went to do my **TELE-VISION SHOW***. We got clobbered that day. It was Halloween. Right next to my set, there was this big coffin. I was getting ready for my coach's show. I said, "I've got an idea." So, I got into the coffin. The show opened. I cracked the coffin open just a little bit, and I said, "Hello, folks. This is Lee Corso. We ain't dead yet. We'll be back." I did the show sitting in the coffin.

Here's the problem. I always felt that society paired intensity with strength, and humor with weakness. A perfect example was Bob Knight and I. Stern-strength—Knight. Humorous—Corso. I was more competitive than anybody else you ever met. You ask the Purdue people

The first coach with his own *TV SHOW was Bud Wilkinson at the University of Oklahoma in 1952.

about that. I made that an obsession to beat them more than they beat me at the end of my career. I was obsessed with surviving at Indiana. I lasted 10 years. They ought to put me in the Hall of Fame just for being there 10 years.

I was more intense than anyone ever would believe. I never thought that having a sense of humor was a sign of weakness. I still don't. There's nobody, I don't think, more intense and knowledgeable about college—I've been involved with college football for over 50 years. Hello! That's a while. You don't do that without having a passion for the game. I still feel that a sense of humor is your best weapon to get through tough times and to entertain people. They want a sense of humor. I never considered it one of my weaknesses, although people sometimes criticize me—"he's not intense." That's ridiculous. Nobody was more intense than me.

When we took that picture under the scoreboard, my players thought I was crazy. I always did crazy things. I brought them in for their first game without the warm-up in the stadium and brought them in on a double-decker London bus. The first game I ever coached at Indiana in 1973, I promised the fans they'd see the best pregame warm-up in the history of football . . . the best new uniforms.

The place was packed, against **ILLINOIS***—55,000. I didn't show up for the pregame. Illinois coach Bob Blackman was walking around. His team was on the field. The people were all buzzing. "Where the hell is Indiana?" Can you imagine? A team warming up on the whole field—and the other team not there?

Five minutes before the ballgame, I come over the hill there in Bloomington, right behind the scoreboard. I had my team in a red double-decker English bus, with a fire engine in front of it. They took us down to the middle of the field. My team comes roaring out of the bus. The crowd was going crazy. We won the toss. Went down and scored—7-0. We got beat 28-14. Reality set in. But, I did exactly what I said—a splash! The teams were used to doing a bunch of things.

> **The Chicago Bears wear blue and orange because those are the colors that team founder George Halas wore when he played for the University of *ILLINOIS.**

My time at Indiana was facing Woody and a little bit of Earle Bruce's time there. I had an advantage because Woody liked me a lot. I had a lot of respect for him. What happened is my first time at a Big 10 luncheon meeting, Woody makes this impassioned speech about General George Patton. I mean, it was the greatest speech you ever heard. He was crying. He was talking about Patton and how much he loved Patton. I'm sitting there. Whoa!

The next summer, my wife and I go to Germany. We go to Luxembourg. I said to my wife, "Betsy, just a second. General George Patton is buried here. He's the only American general buried outside of American soil." We went to Patton's grave. Betsy took a picture of me kneeling at the cross of Patton. The next year, I brought it back and gave it to Woody. I said, "Woody, this is your picture." He said, "What is it?" I said, "I'm saying a prayer to General Patton for you right at his grave." He never beat me bad after that. He said, "Thank you so much." He had that as one of his treasured gifts—me praying at Patton's grave for him. I said a prayer to Patton for Woody Hayes. He loved that.

> **"That's how I got all the great players from Ohio to come."**

Woody used to get me in recruiting. I would meet him every August at the Jai Lai Restaurant in Columbus, out on Olentangy River Road. We'd sit and have lunch, and I'd learn from him. He would tell me, "I'm going to tell you the guys whom Bo (Schembechler) and I are going to take, so don't screw around with these guys. Go for the other guys. Don't worry about beating me and Bo, 'cause you're not going to do it. You beat those other seven guys, and you'll last at Indiana."

I used to take his list and go right past these guys and go to the next guys. That's how I got all the great players from Ohio to come. All my good players, my captains—Tim Clifford was the most valuable player in the Big 10 in 1979, only the second player in the history of Indiana to do that. I had Timothy McVay. I had all those guys. Scott Arnett, the quarterback from Columbus that beat LSU. All those guys.

McVay was a two-time captain. Terry Tallen was a two-time captain. Mike Harkrader—the first freshman running back in the history of the Big 10 to make 1,000 yards. Ever. He was right there from Middletown. I had some great players. Mike Harkrader was the guy who broke two legs. He ran into the tuba when we were playing at West Lafayette, broke his leg into the tuba, played a little bit more into the fourth quarter, broke two legs and still played.

When Woody Hayes was fired, Earle Bruce had a tough job. He was taking over for a legend, which is hard to do. You really want to take over the guy that gets fired after the legend. That's the basic principle. From 1976 on, we had some great games. I wasn't as close to Earle, although I had really one of the best games I ever coached in my life with a big win. When Earle was at Tampa, I was at Louisville, and we beat them. It was a great football game. He had some great teams at Tampa, and I had some really wonderful football teams at Louisville. We had a relationship, but it was not like with Woody.

I never had an opportunity to coach at Ohio State. I had two job offers when I was at Indiana. One was Stanford in '79. From my memory, I beat LaVell Edwards in the **HOLIDAY BOWL*** in '79, and then the Stanford job opened, and LaVell Edwards had the job offered to him. He recommended me. They called me from Stanford, but, at that time, I had just won a bowl game, and we were one of the top-ranked teams in the country. We lost to Michigan on that play that they screwed me on. So, we were really at the top, and I talked to my family and said, "I can't leave now. These people were good for me my first three years there."

As I moved into television, the ESPN *College GameDay* trips into Columbus were wonderful. In fact, that's where me putting the mascot head on my head started. Brutus the Buckeye. I used to pick games, and Brutus walked by. I said to Kirk Herbstreit, "You know, I'd like to get that head and put it on and have some fun." He arranged it. The next day I put the Brutus the Buckeye head on, picked Ohio State to win with Brutus on my head. Holy s---. The crowd went wild. The people in the truck went wild. I said, "Yo! I think I've got myself a shtick here."

The ratings went up. Everything went crazy this last 30 seconds of the show, because I'm sitting there with this Brutus head on. All of a sudden, wow! You can't believe the reaction. That's when I started putting the mascot heads on—right there in Columbus, with Brutus the Buckeye.

In the 1983 ***HOLIDAY BOWL**, Brigham Young University quarterback Steve Young <u>caught</u> the winning touchdown pass in a 21-17 victory over Missouri.

When we do our *GameDay* shows, you have to be objective. Kirk is the same way, even though he played at Ohio State. On our shows, I can't be a Florida State graduate. I can't be an Italian. I can't be a Catholic. You can't be nothing. You can't be nothing when you're on television, because you're going to make somebody mad if you are. Like when I'm putting the heads on. The worst time I ever had—picture this—there are 85,000 people, Miami's playing **FLORIDA STATE*** in Tallahassee. Five minutes before the game, we're in the stadium. They're putting up on the TVs all around the stadium who I pick . . . and I put the Ibis head on. Holy s---. The place went crazy. Yelling and screaming.

That was a perfect example. I thought Miami would win because of Ken Dorsey, and they did. You can't be a homer. You won't last in this business. I'm fortunate this is my 20th year. One of the reasons I'm still there is because I try not to ever be anything except honest and passionate.

Which takes me back to Woody Hayes, who was exactly that. The first person to call me after I got fired at Indiana was Woody Hayes. The first person to call my wife, Betsy, was Anne Hayes. If I could say something to Woody Hayes right now, I'd just say, "Thank you, Woody, for your friendship and your love."

When Lee Corso attended ***FLORIDA STATE** University, his roommate was Burt Reynolds.

NOW LET'S MEET THE QUARTERBACK OF YOUR OHIO STATE BUCKEYES ... NUMBER 15, JOHN HAVLICEK

JOHN HAVLICEK

He is a burger king now, or more precisely the owner of three Wendy's restaurants in Westchester County, New York. The former 13-time NBA All-Star and key cog in eight Boston Celtics NBA championships also has a hand in a food company, Lakeview Farms. And today at age 67, John Havlicek can reflect happily that the two-sport thing with the Cleveland Browns and Celtics never quite worked out and that Woody Hayes never was quite able to convince him to suit up at quarterback. (Though it would have been fun at the time and might actually have nudged Hayes out of the three-yards-and-a-cloud-of-dust mentality before it went out of fashion.) Here he is pictured in his high school football team photo.

I almost never get asked about my days as a football player anymore, but what a lot of people don't know is that I was recruited more for football than basketball. I visited Ohio State four times—three for football. Woody Hayes was the coach there at the time, and I was an all-state quarterback. Later, he would introduce me as "the best quarterback in the Big 10—only he doesn't play."

I grew up in a little town called Martins Ferry, Ohio. A lot of recruiters found their way to that small town in eastern Ohio on the Ohio River. I had a lot of offers. I played baseball in the spring, and we always played on weekends so I never visited a lot of those schools. I did visit West Virginia, Ohio State and Cincinnati. I had offers from the University of Florida, Miami, Georgia Tech, the Ivy League schools, Southern California and a lot of the Big 10 schools. I might have gotten an offer from Michigan, but it didn't enter into my mind that much about Michigan.

I was from a small high school, Bridgeport, and was unsure of how much I was going to be required to do academically. I didn't want to screw up and take on too many activities and not be able to do the schoolwork. My first thought was "I like basketball more than the other sports, so that's going to be my primary focus." Had my favorite been football, then basketball would have been secondary, and I don't know if I would have played. I just liked basketball better.

That didn't stop Woody. He spoke at our high school all-sports banquet. He recruited me very hard. He said, "OK, if you're not going to come to play football, I want you to come and play basketball at Ohio State." So, he was helping basketball coach Fred Taylor recruit me. Fred Taylor played Major League baseball, so he knew about playing multiple sports.

> **"I played in the Ohio-West Virginia football all-star game, and Woody came down to see it."**

I played in the Ohio-West Virginia football all-star game, and Woody came down to see it. He thought I played well. He never gave up that I would eventually play for him, even though, at that time, I had decided to play basketball. It was one of those all-star games after your senior year in high school, and it was in August. I already knew I was going to be playing basketball at Ohio State, but he still came down to the game. I'm sure there were other people he was interested in, too. In fact, one of the running backs did play at Ohio State, so he was looking not only at him, but he was thinking maybe he could talk me into football.

The football program was something I'd followed quite a lot, because they had been to Rose Bowls. You didn't hear much about Ohio State's basketball program. Most of the people that I thought about basketball-wise were the people at West Virginia University, because I lived in that area, right down on the Ohio River. Hot Rod Hundley and Jerry West were there. They were a nationally prominent team, whereas Ohio State really wasn't at that time.

I lived in the same town as the Niekros of baseball fame. We grew up right across the street from each other. *PHIL NIEKRO was one year

Hall of Fame Pitcher *PHIL NIEKRO lost only one game in high school. The winning pitcher was Bill Mazeroski.

older than I, and Joe, who just passed away in November, was four years younger than I was. Phil played one football game at the end position. His parents really wouldn't let him play, but his senior year, he said, "I'm going to play." He went against all their wishes. One of the first times he got into a game, he really got whacked and hurt his back and had to have a back operation. That was unfortunate, because he wanted to do all sports. He did play basketball. Joe was like the little tag-along brother. He was in the eighth grade when I was a senior, and Phil was already one year out of school.

I enrolled at Ohio State in the fall of 1958 and I ended up playing a couple of years of baseball at Ohio State, in addition to basketball. My senior year I didn't play, because I was drafted by the Boston Celtics. My thing about baseball was that I really enjoyed baseball, but I wouldn't get out for the team until early April, because our basketball team was always in the Final Four—three years in a row, winning the NCAA championship in 1960. By that time, the baseball team had already been to Florida on their spring trip. They'd been working out indoors since the first of January. The season was basically over in one month. At about the time I was rounding into shape, the season was over. I played first base and often batted clean-up.

Baseball went away, but football didn't. The Cleveland Browns drafted me in 1962 in the seventh round, based, I guess, on my high school ability and what they were able to see as I played basketball. I had speed and quickness and good hands. I was a quarterback in high school, and the Browns tried me out as a quarterback but they had another quarterback there. While he was throwing, I was running pass patterns, and while I was throwing, he was running pass patterns. They became more impressed with my ability to catch, plus I hadn't played since high school, so they figured they'd make a wide receiver out of me. I ended up being up being the last receiver cut that year.

They asked me back to training camp six years in a row, but I said, "No, the Good Lord's trying to tell me something." I didn't pursue it anymore. The reason I wanted to play football is that I was going to try to play both football and basketball professionally. The football season ended around the first or second week in December. I would have only missed somewhere around 12 Celtics games. I figured I was going to try and do both. Fortunately, I ended up just playing basketball, and that turned out to be a good thing.

The fact that I was from Ohio and the Browns had really great teams back then made trying football all the more appealing. All through college, there'd be 50 guys in a dorm room sitting watching **JIM BROWN*** and Bobby Mitchell and those Browns play. I just felt if I could do both, that would be pretty neat, and I just loved the games.

While I was at Ohio State, I went to all the home football games. My sophomore year, I thought about trying to play football, too, because I really missed it, and I enjoyed the game. I don't think I ever reached my peak in high school, and I was a pretty good player, so I figured I could do a lot more. Woody had plans for me to be the quarterback and Tom Matte to be the halfback and Bob Ferguson to be the fullback. Then, when I didn't sign on to play football, Tom Matte, who was a running back, became the quarterback.

I really liked Woody. He was one of the most interesting people. You could have a conversation with him, and it was always so interesting. He was just a great human being to talk to. He always had a lot of good things to say and reasons behind what he was saying. I took his football class at Ohio State, and he was a great teacher. He could really teach. I think, even though it was a football class, he was one of the best instructors I ever had.

In football, everyone talked about "three yards and a cloud of dust," and that type of thing. Woody would say, "Well, if you can get three yards—the length of a football is eleven inches—and add the length of a football, you're only one inch shy of a first down. He was just so thorough about everything. Everything he designed had a purpose, and it was so thorough. He just felt that the percentages of not passing the football were greater when you ran it as far as achieving yardage and turnovers. I think if he had me, he would have thrown it a little more, because that's what I was—a passing quarterback.

In college, it would have been interesting to think about what might have been had I played football. In the pros, I probably would have gotten banged up somehow, so I think I really made the right decision.

The only person to score back-to-back fifty-point games in the history of Long Island High School basketball is ***JIM BROWN**, the NFL legend . . . Jim Brown was selected in the 1957 NBA draft by the Syracuse Nationals.

1968:
IT WAS ABOUT PRIDE
IT WAS ABOUT WINS
IT WAS ABOUT TIME

LOU HOLTZ

Lou Holtz once said of his first college head coaching job, at William & Mary, that "there were not enough Williams and too many Marys." He would have liked to have gotten a little more Woody Hayes than just the year and a half he experienced. Still, the ESPN college football analyst and retired coaching legend counts his short stint as an OSU assistant coach as the most influential segment of what turned out to be a brilliant coaching career. And it almost was enough—not once, but twice—to lure him back to Columbus.

The big break of my coaching career came about without me knowing a lot about it. Ohio State had a bad 1966 season and had some bad moments still in 1967. Purdue had them 35-0 at halftime that year in an eventual 41-6 rout in Columbus. I only knew one guy on their staff at the time, and that was Esco Sarkkinen.

After that season, Harry Strobel retired as offensive line coach, so Woody Hayes—who was the head coach—decided to move Earle Bruce to the offensive line and hire a secondary coach. Well, Esco Sarkkinen puts my name on the board, but at the time, I don't know this. I go to New York to the coaches' convention. I record the minutes for the American Football Coaches Association. They have a dinner after, and they ask me to stay.

Woody Hayes was at the dinner. He's not like anyone else. Woody's gonna go look up the janitor or somebody—he isn't going to high-falute with everybody else. He comes over, and I introduce myself, and the name must have registered with him. For about four hours, through dinner, after dinner, he's talking to me about secondary play. I don't even know he's interviewing me. I'm just talking about things I believed in. The next day, my birthday, January 6, 1968, he called me and offered me the job as defensive back-field coach at Ohio State.

The same day I was offered the defensive backfield job at Georgia Tech under Bud Carson, who had just replaced Bobby Dodd. I had a decision to make. I was probably going to go to Georgia Tech, because the offer was much better than Ohio State.

> **"Initially, my desire was to coach against a team that beat Notre Dame."**

But my relatives found out about it, and they're all from Ohio and big Ohio State fans. So I went up there to interview or to see whether I wanted to go or not, and that's how it ended up.

The only time I had ever been around Woody was when he and Bo Schembechler spoke at the Virginia Coaches Association in 1961. He had brought his son, Steve, down there. He was nice enough, but you hear all these crazy stories about Woody Hayes. I knew he was volatile. At the same time, you have respect for a guy who had accomplished what he had.

Growing up in East Liverpool, Ohio, I followed three teams pretty good growing up. Notre Dame, obviously, because all my relatives were Catholic. Then, of course, you followed Ohio State at that time because you're from Ohio. Our high school coach, when we had a great football team my junior year, took us to see Ohio State play Purdue down there in the stadium. He took the whole team down. Vic Janowicz and Tad Weed and Hopalong Cassady and all those people—yeah, I followed them.

The other school I followed was University of Pittsburgh, because the main paper in our city was the *Pittsburgh Sun-Telegraph,* which later combined with the *Post-Gazette.* I remember in the late 1940s, Bimbo Cecconi handed to Jimmy Joe Robinson and they ran the Single Wing under Mike Milligan. I was pretty abreast of those three teams.

When I began to have head-coaching aspirations, initially, my desire was to coach against a team that beat Notre Dame. The reason was because up until they hired Ara Parseghian in 1964, Notre Dame had never hired anything but an alum. Up until then, my thinking was

"I'm not going to ever coach at Notre Dame, because they don't hire anything but alums. You want to go coach at Ohio State, because you aren't going to coach at Notre Dame."

"He rips my shirt pocket off. I took the check and ripped it up."

It turned out my first chance to be a college head coach came after just one year as an assistant coach at Ohio State, the 1968 national championship season. When I got the chance to go to William & Mary as head coach, I jumped at it. I knew I wouldn't get very many chances to be a head coach.

I was 32 years old. They called me and offered me the job over the phone 'cause I'd been an assistant there before. I told Coach Hayes. He got upset. I said, "Well, Coach, the people I hurt the most are the ones who made this opportunity for me, and it meant a lot to me, but if you're going to be that way, then OK."

He calmed down and said, "OK, take it. I'll tell you what I want you to do. I want you to write a chapter on pass defense for my book, *Hotline to Victory*." I said, "OK, I'll do that." So I write the chapter for *Hotline to Victory*. I take it up to the North Complex, where he was. This was in late June. I give him the chapter. I stand there. I've got on this coat. I've got on a shirt and tie. He reads it. Doesn't say anything.

Finally, he says, "Mmm-hmmm." Takes out a checkbook, writes a check and gets up, comes around and gives me the check. And I give it back to him. I said, "Coach, I don't do this for money. You've done so much for me." And he says, "No. You take it." And he started cussing. I said, "No, I'm not going to take it." He takes it and tries to stuff it in my shirt pocket. He rips my shirt pocket off. I took the check and ripped it up. I said, "Now I don't work for you anymore. I can rip this check up quicker and easier than you can write them." He started laughing. He said, "OK." We shook hands and laughed.

The thing I regretted when I walked out of there was not that I tore the check up—I wish I would have looked to see how much he thought that chapter was worth. Was it worth $5 or $5,000? I don't know. I do know I didn't have a lot of shirts, and he ripped the pocket off my shirt.

You know what, the first game I coached as a head coach at William & Mary that following September was against Cincinnati in Cincinnati. Coach Hayes came down to the game and brought his quarterback.

Ohio State was to open up the following week. He came in and talked to our team after the game. We lost a tough one, 26-18, and we lost late in the game. It was just that he cared enough to come down and talk to our team and see me! He was a special guy.

Little did I know I would be hearing from him soon after. Woody Hayes tried to hire me from William & Mary when he lost assistant coach Lou McCullough. He said, "Come back to Ohio State—as the defense coordinator, recruiting coordinator—and you'll replace me as head coach when I retire." Now this was 1970. I said, "Well, how much longer are you going to coach?" He said, "Two or three years."

My wife wanted to go back in the worst way. I said, "If I'm going to end up at Ohio State, I'll end up there because they want me and not because they're sort of forced to take me." I told Woody, "You can't guarantee that, Coach." He said, "Well, I'll just resign in August. They'll have no other option but to hire you." But I stayed at William & Mary.

The funny thing is, Woody didn't retire in two or three years. After they let him go following the 1978 season, I heard from Ohio State again. This was my chance. But what happened was I'm at **ARKANSAS***. We'd beaten Oklahoma in the Orange Bowl, and the next year we're playing in the Fiesta Bowl against UCLA when the job opened up.

I went over to coach in the Hula Bowl, a college all-star game. Hugh Hindman, whom I have great respect for, was the Ohio State athletic director. He was the tackles/tight-end coach when I was at Ohio State as an assistant. I knew him very, very well. He called me and said, "We'd like you to apply for the job at Ohio State." I said, "How many people are you going to interview, Hugh?" He said, "Probably six, but you're certainly one of our leading candidates."

I said, "Hugh, couple of things. No. 1, there isn't anything you're going to find out in an interview that you can't find out from NC State, from William & Mary, from Arkansas. Plus, I coached there at Ohio State. You know me. I've got a track record." Arkansas really had as good a program as Ohio State had at that time. I said, "For me to go interview at Ohio State, and then something else happen, it would be totally

When Lou Holtz was coaching *ARKANSAS, his personal attorney was Bill Clinton.

unfair to the people at Arkansas. I'm not going to do that. You know me. You know everything about my background. If you want me to coach at Ohio State, chances are I would probably take the job. I can't say that, but I'm not going to go through the interviewing process."

He said, "If you change your mind, call me." The last thing I said to Hugh was "I wouldn't sit by the phone." That was it. I felt that way. It was unfair to the Arkansas people. You look at what happened to Glen Mason when he was looking to go back to Ohio State from Minnesota. He made the comment, "That's the job I want." Then he didn't get it, and he never could repair the situation at Minnesota.

> **"When I was coaching at South Carolina, the games against Ohio State were very special."**

I learned so many things during my one and a half years at Ohio State with Woody. Two things stand out—football is a game of fundamentals. It's about blocking, it's about tackling. The other thing is that the coach's obligation is not to be popular, not to be well liked by the players. Your obligation is to make your players the best they can possibly be. That means you're going to have to have standards. You're going to have to have demands. You can't compromise. These are the things you have to believe. Those were the things I learned from him.

Woody ran an honest program, never cheated, and couldn't stand people he felt did cheat. He felt that if you ever bought an athlete, you couldn't coach him, you could not control him and you couldn't discipline him. The main thing was standards, and, whatever you do, don't get caught up in the X's and O's. It's about blocking, tackling and execution.

Late in my career, when I was coaching at South Carolina, the games against Ohio State—in bowl games at the end of the 2000 and 2001 seasons—were very special. The games I coached against Ohio State while I was at Notre Dame—1995 and '96—were special too, but I didn't get to enjoy them as much.

The 1995 OSU-ND game, I was coming off of spinal surgery and just coming off the neck brace. We were ahead by three points, and Ohio State punted. Their guy ran into our kid when he was trying to catch the ball, and we fumble it, and they recover it. They had a great football team, had a great tailback, had all the receivers, and they had Shawn Springs, Mike Vrabel—they were a great team. But, we had a chance to win it.

Then, the next year we were undefeated. We had just beaten Texas the week before, so we were on a real high. We had something happen on our team off the field that I wasn't aware of until after the game, but getting ready for that game, I was so excited. We were playing OSU at home. There was just something missing on our team. I didn't know what it was and didn't find out until about 10 days after the game. That was a little disappointing, because we ran a punt back to make it a two-point game, or something like that. We got called for a clip on it.

At South Carolina, it was really special. I had been out of coaching for a while, and to have South Carolina be able to play against Ohio State was really very meaningful to the people at South Carolina.

Any time you went against Ohio State, to be in that stadium, what goes through your mind are all the games you've played there—beating Purdue, beating Michigan. We went undefeated that year (1968). It's not as much about the great memories as it is having great respect for Ohio State. It was just a pleasure and a privilege and a blessing to be a good coach for Woody. Woody turned out a lot of head coaches. He has never turned out a head coach that failed to win. Did you know that? Whether you go back to Doyt Perry, Bill Hess, Gene Slaughter, Bill Mallory, Earle Bruce, Lou Holtz, Bo Schembechler, Rudy Hubbard, George Chaump, Dave McClain—everybody he ever turned out won.

Woody's stormy side was more of a media fixation than anything else. Woody was very, very strong-willed. He was a captain of a ship in the Navy. I tell you what—I defy you to go find anybody who ever did anything with their life that played for him that didn't have distaste for certain things he did while you were there. And yet, at the same time, you love him, and you'd do anything for him.

Everybody who ever played for him loved him after they were done, because they understood one thing. He genuinely cared about his players. He didn't care about the media. He didn't care about anything else. He cared about them graduating. He cared about them living the right way. You didn't read many scandals about Woody Hayes' players doing this and doing that. He was tough on them, but he made them better. Every single one of them absolutely respected him.

There is a side of Woody Hayes a lot of people never saw. Woody Hayes never went through East Liverpool, Ohio, without stopping and calling my mother to see how she was doing. He'd go to Vietnam, and he'd take down all the phone numbers of different people and would come back and call every one of their families personally. There are so many great things he did.

"Woody Hayes never went through East Liverpool, Ohio, without stopping and calling my mother."

One of the football players, whose name I won't mention, had been a wingback for Ohio State. In the spring of '69, he was backing out of his driveway, and, unbeknownst to him, his son had come out. He ran over his 3-year-old son and killed him. Woody Hayes left practice . . . did not come back for a couple of days. He stayed with him 'til he felt he was OK.

There are so many things. He was smart. He was well read. I have the utmost respect for him. People who have played for him, coached for him, feel the same way I do. I'll defend him to the nth degree. He had the greatest influence on my life of anybody professionally. Even though I was only with him a year and a half, I tell you this—it was a tumultuous year and a half. But it was a year and a half I wouldn't trade for the world.

In 1996, OSU beat Pitt 72-0. Pitt was lucky to score 0

THE WRITE STUFF

BOB GREENE

Bob Greene's career as a New York Times *bestselling author and an award-winning journalist has often pulled him away from sports. His love for Ohio State football keeps bringing him back. Growing up near Columbus in Bexley, Ohio, Greene developed an admiration for Woody Hayes and what he stood for, something that only grew stronger as their paths intermittently crossed in the years that followed.*

A lot of people assume I did go to Ohio State, because I'm sort of associated with Columbus and I talk and write about Ohio State a lot. The only degree I have from there is an honorary degree. One of my buddies went to Ohio State, and so we were up there a lot.

My work on my latest book—*And You Know You Should be Glad: A True Story of Lifelong Friendship*—brings me back to that special time when I lived in Ohio and followed Ohio State football. It's about my best friend I had since I was 5 years old. He was diagnosed with cancer, and all the best friends came back together to see him through to the end. In so doing, we revisited our friendship.

Ohio State defined, especially as a kid, who we thought we were and were proud of being. We'd never heard the phrase "fly-over country." We sensed, even as kids, New York and Washington on one coast and Los Angeles and Hollywood on the other, were where the opinion makers were. We wouldn't have used that phrase as kids, but that's where the big shots were.

We just sensed, in the middle of Ohio, that nobody really paid attention to us . . . except, up there on that campus, there was Woody Hayes. He didn't have to go to the world—the world came to him. Every time there was a big game, we knew the sportswriters and the big television networks would fly in. It never even had to be explained to us that because of what Woody and that team were doing up there every

Saturday in the fall, the world paid attention to Columbus. The world paid attention to central Ohio. It was just about the only time we sensed that anyone really did pay attention to us—by us, I mean the city.

Certainly, when **JOHN GLENN*** went into space, the world paid attention to the middle of Ohio. But Woody did that just by being there. And we also sensed that Woody wasn't trying to go anywhere else. Woody didn't have any grand ambitions to go the pros, or to go to the University of Miami, Florida, UCLA, or USC. Woody was where he belonged, and it gave us a very centered feeling.

He would put out those paperbound books that he self-published, through a self-publishing company in Columbus. And he would go down to the Lazarus Department Store, and he would sit there and sign autographs. Woody just made us feel there's something big about the town . . . and Ohio State is it. I met Woody for the first time when he was signing books. He was just a gracious, nice man to kids.

There was something we would do after games, as a kid. We would run on the field. I'm sure you couldn't do it now, because of all the security, but if we were lucky enough to get tickets from our parents to go to an Ohio State game, we would run onto the field afterwards and try to get players to give us their chinstraps from their helmets. Sometimes, you'd encounter Woody on the way off the field. He was pretty gruff, but *you were that close to Woody Hayes*!

As I got older and started writing, I would meet him covering stories, and he was just gracious. When I was working summers at the old *Columbus Citizen-Journal,* Woody would call in, and you'd talk on the phone to Woody Hayes. It was like talking to the president of the United States—right in Columbus.

When I got older, it turned out that he read my writings. Because of that, we started talking as adults who knew each other. There were times I had dinner with him. I never could quite process that I was getting to know Woody Hayes. Obviously, "friend" is a sort of presumptuous term, and I would not want to use that, because we didn't spend enough time together, like you would talk about your lifelong

---

Former astronaut and Senator ***JOHN GLENN** was Ted Williams' squadron leader in Korea. Ted Williams was John Glenn's wing man.

friends. But as someone you were friendly with and someone who knew you and someone who would occasionally drop you a note . . . I just admired him tremendously, in good times and bad. He struck me as a guy who knew who he was and had a tremendous amount of self-knowledge, and he was a good, good man and an interesting man, someone that those of us who grew up there could be very proud of.

Woody was always listed in the Columbus telephone directory. Whenever I would write about him, he would acknowledge it to me when I would bring it up, because I, like you, thought it was pretty interesting. When I would bring it up, he'd say, "Yes, but if you don't have to, don't put it in the article. If you put it in the article, everyone will start calling me."

> **"Woody was always listed in the Columbus telephone directory."**

His reason for being in the directory, he told me, was "if you're going to be a member of this community, you've got to be like everyone else." Think about that—you're the coach of the Ohio State University football team, with all the emotion that engenders. You look in the phone book, there's "W. W. Hayes, 1711 Cardiff Road." Anyone could call him up, in the middle of the night, to berate him. He just thought that if you're the head coach of the Ohio State University, you are a member of that community, and it would be the wrong thing to do not to be available to everyone in town. And he was. Until the day he died.

He said they did get some of those calls in the middle of the night, and nasty calls, and that he and Mrs. Hayes would politely pick it up. But he never got it unlisted, and, as far as I know, there wasn't one number for the public and then a real number for him. Anytime I was in town to call him, I would just call that number in the phone book. For all those years. There were some years, especially in the early years, when fans were trying to run him out of town. I cannot think of a public figure in this country who has a listed number like that. That would be like **MICHAEL JORDAN*** having a listed number in Chicago, or Alex Rodriquez in New York. It's unthinkable, and yet, Woody never stopped doing it.

> In 1994, the White Sox recalled ***MICHAEL JORDAN** from Double-A Birmingham to play against the Cubs in the Mayor's Trophy Game at Wrigley Field. Jordan singled and doubled against the Cubs.

I didn't consider going to Ohio State University, because I just figured I should probably get out of Columbus to see a little bit more of the world, and I had heard of the journalism department at Northwestern. Yet the greatest honor of my life is that I got an honorary degree at Ohio State and gave the commencement address in Ohio Stadium. It was supposed to be in 1997, but it got rained out so they asked me again in 1998. I stood in the stadium, and I talked about Woody.

> **"When they fired Woody, they fired me. I'm not going back to that stadium."**

At the time Woody was fired, I said to my mom and dad, "When they fired Woody, they fired me. I'm not going back to that stadium." I'd gone there my whole life, when I was lucky enough to have a ticket as a kid, and then covering games. I just didn't want to go back there. But I did go back there twice—the commencement address that got rained out in '97 and the commencement address that didn't get rained out in '98. I'm not trying to make any big point about it. To me, I associate the place with Woody. I felt bad for what had happened to him, and I just didn't feel like going back. I was even invited back, at one point, by one of the university presidents to see a Michigan game in the university box, and I just said, "No, thanks." There were just too many memories. I know it probably sounds stupid to say it.

I do watch all the OSU games on television. I still root for them. But, it was just such an important part of my life being in that stadium with my parents and seeing Woody down there with the baseball cap and the short-sleeved shirt down on the field. I never went back to a game after that. But Woody did, didn't he? He went back to dot the "i."

Woody would talk about his stormy side, and he would say, "I know what people think of me. They think of me as a 'big, dumb football coach.'" He would put it in quotes, as he said it. He was aware of his shortcomings, and he was aware of his failings. He paid a pretty dear price for it. Rather than dwell on it when I wrote about him, I tried to paint the humanity of who he was. He was a complicated guy. Whatever "bigger than life" means, Woody was bigger than life.

ESPN did a biography on Woody. One of his former players, it may have been Daryl Sanders, talked about it. He said, "Listen, he didn't make excuses. He was who he was." There were so many things about him.

It was hard to sum it up anecdotally, but you would constantly hear from families who had kids in one of the university hospitals. Woody would be there visiting a football player who was in for an injury, and he would see a kid, and he would come back and sit with him. He would do that all the time. After *The Woody Hayes Show* on television on weekends, Woody would make the players who appeared with him on the show go on down to Children's Hospital with him to visit kids. It was part of the deal. "You come on my show, we're going to go to Children's Hospital."

He was a decent guy, and he had a temper . . . and he lost it. I think he always deeply regretted it when he lost it in a public way, but then, he would lose it again. I remember when he came back—the first public appearance he made after the Clemson problem was at the Neil House in downtown Columbus. He spoke to one of the Columbus civic clubs, and I flew in to watch him. The first thing he said was "I've got a son who is a young lawyer in this town [he turned out to be a judge]—Steve Hayes—and he's probably a little embarrassed about his old man right now, but I think he'll get over it."

He wasn't just a football coach. He was a complicated human being. The people in Columbus understood that. Now that he's been gone for so long, they paint almost a caricature of him. I see it on the broadcasts of the football games sometimes—now they've got a guy who dresses as Woody, and they've got that band that dresses like him, too. He's become sort of like a lovable cartoon image of himself.

He was just such a studious person. The stories about him reading history, that wasn't just some sideline of his life. He was a voracious reader. He told me, as he got older, he had trouble falling asleep at night, and he would read himself to sleep reading books of history. He told me that when he would go to other campuses, either recruiting or for games, or just happened to be passing through a town, instead of going to a movie or going shopping, he would go on campus and ask the kids on campus, "Who's the best professor? Who's the most interesting professor?" And Woody would go sit in the back of their classroom and watch their classes.

That's like the "name in the phone book" thing. People just don't do that. These professors at some campus around the country would look out, and there would be Woody Hayes in the back of the room, because he'd heard this was a good class, and he went there to learn something.

In his later years, Woody was quite reflective. The last time I had dinner with him, we went to his favorite restaurant, the Jai Lai. It was a snowy night. I went up there, and Woody was waiting. I wanted to get there early, because I didn't want to keep him waiting, but Woody was there first, waiting by the host's desk. As I recall, even at that time, they had the portrait of him in his football-coaching clothes up there. The phrase was both for him and the restaurant, "In all the world, there's only one." The portrait was up and the slogan was there . . . and there was Woody sitting there. I said to him, "Coach, I got here 10 minutes early. I didn't want you to be sitting around waiting for me." He said, "Well, I didn't want to make you wait." Rather than making an "entrance," I recall that he was sitting in a wooden chair near the host's desk just hanging out.

Of course, everyone who came in knew it was Woody Hayes. He would sit and talk. He didn't want to dwell on his own self. He was more interested in talking about you and about the world. He was very, very pleased that he became such a beloved figure in his later years. He became head coach in 1951 and died in 1987, so for 36 years, he was the most famous man in Ohio. But he never acted like it.

He would be reflective. One visit, we just drove around Columbus. He had agreed to go to Westerville North High School to make a speech to the kids. We're driving around Columbus in his pickup truck. I was staying at the old Sheraton Columbus—I'm not sure what it was called at that time, may have still been the Sheraton. I said, "Coach, where should I meet you?" He said, "I'll just pick you up." So, I go outside, and there was Woody sitting at the curb with the engine running. We just drove around town. I think he was very glad he never left Columbus. I think he was very glad that he was so accepted back in the community.

From what I understand, the two great moments of his life, after he stopped being coach, were dotting the "i," and also when he was given an honorary degree from Ohio State. He stood there with tears in his eyes. I think the exact phrase was "Students, faculty and especially to parents who have worked so hard to put your children here, today is the greatest day in my life."

He gave this speech in St. John Arena instead of at the stadium. I was not at the ceremony where Woody spoke, but I've seen footage of it, and it was not in Ohio Stadium. I'm thinking it would have been nicer if they would have let him give it in the stadium.

At times, Woody would reflect back on the coaches that preceded him, but I can't even recite them from memory. It was called the "graveyard of coaches" before he got there. I know for a fact that in those first years, they tried to run him out of town, because, as I recall, no one wanted him—they wanted Paul Brown. They changed the words to "Carmen Ohio." They would sing during the games, "Oh come let's sing Ohio's praise, and say goodbye to Woody Hayes." They wanted to run him out of town.

> "They would sing during the games, 'Oh come let's sing Ohio's praise, and say goodbye to Woody Hayes.'"

Then, here comes Hopalong Cassady, and everything changed. Had Hopalong Cassady not come along, and had they not won that national championship, who knows? He never discussed that in later years when he became such a legend. But clearly, it stuck with him. His greeting from Columbus, Ohio, was "Get out!" Maybe Jim Tressel can identify with that also. Not the "get out" part, but Tressel was certainly no one's first choice among the community.

Tressel was like Woody—who's this guy? You have to remember, when Woody came to Columbus, it wasn't like he was a known quantity. He was like Tressel was when he came there. "Why are we hiring Woody Hayes? Why don't we get Paul Brown back here?" When Tressel came, it was "Why don't we get a big name?" So there's a pretty good parallel there. You win yourself a national championship, and the city changes.

THE BUCKEYES GAVE HIM GOOSEBUMPS

R. L. STINE

Children's book author R. L. Stine likes to tell people he grew up on a pig farm and that the only word he knew was "Oink"—until he was captured by little blue aliens, which inspired him to learn the word "Help." Actually, R. L. Stine has been putting words together for audiences since age 9, with the 1965 Ohio State grad's most notable works being the "Goosebumps" series, which will soon make a return with 12 new books. But before Robert Lawrence Stine sold his more than 300 million books worldwide, he spent his days at OSU lampooning the fanatic side of the Buckeyes, which he admittedly, in later years, became a part of.

I've always been a big Ohio State fan. I understand the whole Michigan thing—to a point. I grew up in Bexley and attended Bexley High School and then Ohio State. We were very poor. We lived three doors from the railroad in a tiny little house, five of us, right on the edge of all the mansions. In the next block, all the mansions started. The governor's mansion was about two blocks from us. It was weird growing up in Bexley.

I went to Ohio State, but I lived at home the whole time. I didn't have the money to live on campus. My mother was a housewife, and my dad was a blue-collar worker, working in a warehouse. He loaded and unloaded trucks. I was a big football fan. You really had no choice in Columbus. You HAD to be a football fan. When I was a kid in Columbus—this is true—there were eight AM radio stations. On Saturday afternoons, all eight of them would carry the Ohio State game. There was *nothing else* on the radio. They each had their own announcing teams doing the games, too. It was amazing. When I was in school, we used to go to the games, and they gave us the worst seats. The students were all up in C Deck, up in the top, as far away as you could be, exposed to the wind and the snow and everything . . . but we loved it—we just loved it.

I never did meet any of the players nor Woody. You have to understand that I was the editor of the humor magazine, the *Sundial,* which had been around for 100 years. James Thurber had been editor of the *Sundial*—Milton Caniff and a lot of people. That's all I did in college. I was editor of the humor magazine for three years out of the four I was there. We spent our time making fun of Woody Hayes. He was our big target.

We made fun of Ohio State. The administration hated us and would look for any excuse to shut us down. I was constantly being called into the dean's office—always. We called it "Ahia" State, with "A"s. We sold "Ahia" State sweatshirts. They said, "Ahia State, the Big Farm." We made money on the sale of those shirts. We sold a lot of them—to Ohio State kids. We had a pig on the front or something. Yes, that was my idea. It was good.

Woody never tried to chase us down, and he didn't slug us or anything. We wouldn't make fun of the football team, but we made fun of the fact that it was such a football school. I, of course, being in the English department, felt that *that* part of Ohio State was totally ignored and undervalued. Even as students, we all felt the school had no interest in us.

I started writing children's books—you want kids to read. So my passion for that just developed. The thing that's known in children's publishing is that girls read and boys don't. It's just true. I went on this quest to try to find something that boys would read—trying to get them reading. It took me a long time. I can show you flop after flop of book series, until we found the scary stuff that boys would read.

"Fear Street" was my first scary book series. It was for teenagers, and it came right before "Goosebumps." When we started writing "Fear Street," it was for girls. Then, the fan mail started coming in. I started getting all the mail from the kids—and half of it was from boys. I thought, "Oh my God, we've found something. Boys are reading this." We had found something boys like to read. Then, when we started "Goosebumps," it was the same story.

Lately, I've been doing a funny series for kids and have been having a great time with it—not scaring kids for a change. I've been scaring kids for 20 years, so it's been so much fun to write a funny series. It's called

"Rotten School," from HarperCollins. It's about a really rotten boarding school. This fifth-grade con man, this kid, is sort of a Sergeant Bilko for kids, who runs the place. I'm doing 16 of those. I'm just about finished with that series, and I've had a great time, but now I guess it's time to go back and be scary.

I haven't been back to Ohio State for a long time. For a while I was doing a lot of appearances in Columbus. I went back to all my elementary schools in Bexley, and I spoke. I went to three different elementary schools in Bexley for various reasons. That was fun to go back.

The first building I walked into, this old, old woman came running at me. *Running at me.* Threw her arms around me. She said, "Bobby, Bobby." It was my kindergarten teacher. She was like 150! She got too old to teach, and they made her a crossing guard. She was an unbelievable woman. She might still be around—Miss Barbara. That was kind of scary. I had to pull her off me. Our class picture was like an etching—we didn't even have photos back then. It was this black-and-white thing, our class photo. She said, "You never talked." I said, "Well, I talk now."

I still follow the team. Now I'm lucky—my son went to **WISCONSIN***, and now I have two teams. I try to watch the Wisconsin games and the Ohio State-Michigan games, and I'm a Giants fan and a Jets fan. So, I do a lot of football. When football season ends, I don't know what the hell to do on weekends. I sort of wander around lost.

I think some of the coaches who have come along since Woody would have been good for my *Sundial* magazine.

Coach Tressel has done a great job. They have great teams in recent years—they've been in the national championship twice, and they won it. The Maurice Clarett story—what a tragedy that is. I was very upset about that. I've been watching football for over 50 years, and he was the best college running back I ever saw. Better than O.J. He was unbelievable. To have one year of playing, and now he's in prison. It's horrifying.

Arnold Schwarzenegger graduated from the University of
***WISCONSIN** in 1979.

THE HORSESHOE CAN BE A ZOO, TOO

JACK HANNA

Jack Hanna is seen on television presenting animal after animal to the hosts of Good Morning America. *He introduces wild creatures to late-night television's wise guy, David Letterman. He shares bits of wildlife trivia with talk-show host Larry King. He can be seen as the target of the wildlife kingdom's lighter side on* TV's Bloopers and Practical Jokes, *and he can be seen sauntering around the Columbus Zoo grounds in his familiar khaki safari gear, greeting guests and checking out the animal collection. He has a serious side, too, and it's all about Ohio State football—from converting from his boyhood favorite, Tennessee, to forming a bond with current Buckeye coach Jim Tressel.*

The reason most people didn't realize I had a college football career—even though it was a bad one—is, well, I played college football in Ohio at **MUSKINGUM*** in New Concord and I didn't even know who Woody Hayes was.

I mean, I was preoccupied with animals then, and always had been. I grew up on my dad's farm outside of Knoxville, Tennessee. I loved animals. I went to work on a dairy when I was about 12 years old, cleaning cages. I did that for four years. My dad was also a veterinarian. That's where I fell in love with all the animals. I told myself when I was 16, "Someday, I'm going to be a zookeeper." I never wavered from that dream.

Jon Gruden, the youngest coach to win a Super Bowl, was a quarterback at ***MUSKINGUM** before transferring to the University of Dayton . . . Gruden was a ballboy for the undefeated 1976 Indiana basketball team.

My other passion, though, was football. I was also a big Tennessee Volunteer fan. Coach Phillip Fulmer at Tennessee is a very good friend of mine. So you can see why it was hard for me when I first got here to accept Ohio State, in 1978. But then I went to my first Ohio State game in November of 1978, and saw them play Michigan. And the next game was the Gator Bowl game that ended Coach Woody Hayes' career.

"Man alive. This is just like Tennessee, except it's all scarlet and gray and not big orange."

I didn't think it was crazy. I said, "Man alive. This is just like Tennessee, except it's all scarlet and gray and not big orange." I'll never forget that as long as I ever live. That's all you could see. The fans in Tennessee were just like the ones up here, just gung-ho. From that point on, I became a huge Ohio State fan.

I'm sorry to say, though I got to go out to the bowl game in January of 2007, I don't get to many games because of the TV commitments and traveling all over the world. But boy, my first 10 years here, I'd go to three or four games a year. And it was really the highlight of my life, because the first seven years I was in Columbus, I never left the zoo—never, ever left the zoo for one day or night, ever, for seven years, except to sneak out to Ohio State games. So my big deal was to go to the games for a few hours.

And then I got to go on the field and do a halftime show sometime in the late '80s. They played all kinds of animal songs. I didn't really know what it meant then, but I didn't get to dot the "i" in Script Ohio. I wish I could have.

I've got to know all the coaches pretty well after Woody. Coach Jim Tressel is just a great guy, and he and I are good friends. I knew Earle Bruce. John Cooper was a friend, because he's from Tennessee. And Jimmy Heacock, the defensive coordinator for Coach Tressel, is a good friend.

A lot of people don't know this, but one of the things that brought us to Columbus in 1978 was that our youngest daughter, Julie, had leukemia. We went to Children's Hospital here, so they could treat her for the leukemia. So it wasn't just the zoo that brought us here. Let's just put it this way, if it hadn't been for St. Jude's and Children's Hospital, she wouldn't be here. And now, she works for me at the zoo.

Now, I continue to visit the children at the hospital. We have a lot of the special-risk kids around the country come here to meet me. I've got pictures of them all. I don't have pictures of a lot of celebrities on my wall, but I've got pictures of kids who aren't here anymore. I just got through helping Children's Hospital raise money for their hospice program.

That's one of the things that drew me to Jim Tressel. He believes in the same kinds of things. My son-in-law and I are involved with Young Life, the Christian organization at the high school. It's not just athletes, but for anybody in the high schools. Well, when he won the national championship in 2002, that year we asked Jim Tressel to speak. It happened to be the Tuesday night after he won the national championship. He had scheduled that thing six months in advance, not knowing what bowl the Buckeyes would go to.

To make a long story short, he wins the national championship. I called his secretary that Monday and said, "Golly, this is tremendous. Don't worry. I'll go ahead and take care of the meeting myself. Tell Coach Tressel thank you and everything." She said, "What are you talking about?" I said, "I wouldn't dare infringe on him." You can imagine the interviews and all he had to do. She said, "No. No. He's coming." I said, "What? Well, tell him he can just come and say hello and then leave right away."

He comes up there 15 minutes before the program, 5:45, I'll never forget it as long as I live. I waited at the front gate for him. He came by himself, shook my hand, walked in there, sat down. Had a pop and chips and stuff. He stays there an hour and a half. Eats dinner. Gets up and speaks after two other people spoke. That's the kind of person Jim Tressel is.

The reason I'm impressed with Jim Tressel is that if you talk to Jim Tressel just out on the zoo grounds or anywhere, it's not necessarily about football. Some coaches—all they can talk about is football, football, football. But Jim Tressel is a guy that impresses me. You wouldn't know Jim Tressel is a football coach. In other words, he's just a great person. He's a great human being. He's a great Christian. He's a guy I would love to be more like.

THE PERSON TO BE DURING A GOLD RUSH IS THE ONE SELLING THE SHOVELS

LES WEXNER

He didn't dwell on the bark. He looked beyond it. He enjoyed the victories, but knew there was something more. He couldn't separate the coach Woody Hayes from the man—nor did Les Wexner want to. Wexner's own hard work and a creative spark helped lift him from a local kid struggling to pay his way through Ohio State to the chairman and CEO of Limited Brands, Inc. (Limited Brands include Victoria's Secret, Bath and Body Works, Express, White Barn Candle, Henri Bendel, and the Limited.) But the 1959 graduate and current member of the OSU Board of Trustees was so influenced by Hayes' generosity, that it opened his mind and heart to philanthropy and reinvesting in the Columbus community. And now Jim Tressel comes along. And it's not just the wins in the spotlight that have Wexner cheering, but the ones behind closed doors as well.

Woody Hayes and Jim Tressel have similar values. I didn't know Woody as well, but I've read about him and his books, about how he always talked with players. It's almost like Woody reincarnated—different body, different personality, but virtually the same kind of values.

I know Maurice Clarett is on hard times, and Jim goes to visit him in prison. He and Jim correspond. Jim never calls himself a "coach." If you call him "Coach," he'll say, "I'd prefer that you call me Jim, or see me as a teacher. I don't see myself as a coach. I'm a teacher trying to help young men learn about life."

Tressel told me Maurice writes him a long letter every week. Now he's beginning to understand the things that coach was telling him. He didn't understand them at the time, but they stayed with him. I believe he's looking forward to helping him when he comes back to society. Jim Tressel's a very good guy, a very good guy. I'm a big fan of his.

I wasn't a "whoopee" Ohio State football fan. I got married later in life, 15 years ago. I asked my wife, Abby, "Do you want to go to a football game?" She said, "No. That's rah-rah stuff. I went to **COLUMBIA***, and football isn't important. That kind of rah-rah stuff isn't me." Then, for whatever reason, we went to a football game . . . she's turned into the most rabid fan.

My wife is a summa cum laude, Phi Beta Kappa—very smart, very capable. She's chairman of the Children's Hospital. She's chairman of the Columbus Foundation. *Now* she's like, "We have to go. We have to go to the National Championship Game. We have to go to Michigan. We have to go to all the home games."

When the athletic director's job was open, she said, "Maybe I should apply." I said, "You don't know anything about sports." She said, "Well, I understand organizations. One day, I could be an assistant AD."

My children are 13, 12, 11, and 9. The kids are just rabid fans. They know more about football and the players and where they're from and what they do than I've ever known. She does, too. She'll go to spring practice. She reminds me that she picked out Troy Smith in his first spring practice as a great football player. She *did*. I don't know how she did it, but she did.

I have long roots to Ohio State. I've chaired the first endowment campaign. I've been on the board, and the chairman of the board at the university. I'm a contributor, fund-raiser, done a lot of things. She and the children are probably the most rabid Ohio State fans—and it's true about football or basketball. The back half of this past season, they had to go to every game. We had to watch the NCAA Tournament. They're much more interested and engaged fans than I am.

The first game Abby went to, after she saw the marching band, she thought it was an interesting "orchestra" and wondered why they were playing those songs she had never heard. But, by the second game, it

America's first televised sporting event was a 1939 Princeton-*<u>COLUMBIA</u> baseball game. The star for Columbia, Sid Luckman, is better known as one of the all-time great quarterbacks.

"I had no money, and my parents had no money."

was like, "This is really great. We have to go. We can't miss it."

Since I worked on most Saturdays while attending OSU, I probably only went to about half the football games. I guess I was a pretty normal student fan, not fanatic. Football players, Woody Hayes were celebrities. Probably the closest physically I ever got to one was in college playing backyard basketball with Tom Matte. I did that just a few times. Of course, I couldn't beat him. My memories of Matte were that he was the first person I ever saw that was as thick as he was wide.

I met Jim Parker. I had a friend who was confined to a wheelchair, and I used to help him get around campus. Jim Parker and he coincidentally had classes in University Hall. Parker could just pick him and the wheelchair up like it was a sack of potatoes.

Eventually my dad and I had a typical father-son conflict. I had ideas about my dad's store. He didn't like my ideas. In hindsight, I think I practiced my own self-psychiatry. I just decided my ideas were good, and I wanted to prove to my dad that they weren't dumb ideas, so I opened a store to show him my ideas weren't dumb. I made more money in my first year than my father had ever made in his life. My dad thought I'd cooked the books. My mom stayed in the middle in all this. She was very supportive of her husband and very supportive of her son.

My parents had a typical mom-and-pop store. If somebody wanted a necklace or if they wanted jewelry or somebody wanted an umbrella or somebody wanted a wedding dress—it was like anything anybody wanted to buy, my dad and mom felt it was an opportunity and didn't want to disappoint a customer. It was really everything for everybody.

The influence I had at Ohio State was the era of specialization, at least my understanding of it. My friends weren't going to become just dentists, they were going to become orthodontists or whatever. If they were doctors, they were going to become dermatologists or cardiologists. Everyone was thinking about specialization.

My parents were generalists in a specialty store—as a women's store, kind of everything for every age of woman in virtually every size, because they saw it as all increments. The business I invented in my mind only sold preppy sportswear. And my dad told me, "You can't earn a living selling such a *limited* assortment." And The Limited was born.

I had no money, and my parents had no money. And I did not invent the idea of borrowing the money. My aunt said, "You've got to do something, and I've got some money. I'll loan you some money if you can figure out something to do to get yourself started in life."

She was a spinster. She had $5,000. She said, "I'll give you the money if you promise to keep it in the bank." I said, "Well, what am I going to do?" She said, "Well, banks loan money to people who have money, so maybe you can borrow $5,000 from the bank to get started." So, that's how it happened. My dad couldn't have loaned me $5,000.

I started with a negative net worth. If you have no money, and you borrow $5,000, you're in the negative numbers right away. The inventory commitment was leveraged, the fixtures were leased. I figured out that before the first store opened, in terms of rent, you annualize the rent and fixture leases and some other stuff, that I owed close to half a million dollars. If anybody knew the other people were loaning me the money . . . It was really bad. I got an ulcer. I kept having nightmares—"I'm going to be the youngest, biggest bankruptcy in the history of the world!"

The second year I opened a second store. The third year I opened another store. It went from no stores and negative net worth to six stores and substantial income.

I was influenced by **WOODY HAYES***. I'd heard him say "Pay forward," probably when I was in college, or I had read about him saying that. When I started the business, I felt very guilty, because I'd been so lucky. It was like, "If you're this lucky, what do you do?" Do you buy a new car? Do you buy a suit? I never knew what people did with income. We were always scraping.

I later met Woody socially, when he was still coaching. It might have been at a party I was invited to at Darby Dan's when he was coach. He used to have those parties before the Michigan game. I went to a couple of those, and I met Woody there.

As a young boy in Newcomerstown, Ohio, ***WOODY HAYES** was a batboy for a semi-pro baseball team managed by Cy Young.

After Woody retired from coaching, he spoke to leaders of the business on two or three occasions. He would come out and talk about leadership and "paying forward," responsibility, and doing your best—the kinds of things a coach would talk about.

Finally, now for the rest of the story. When Jim Tressel came here, we reestablished the idea of the Michigan party, only it's at our house. We're going to use it as a fund-raiser for the athletic department, and as a social thing for our friends. It's their guest list. What it's morphed into is all the captains from all the years organize their classes, so it's a reunion of players and people who support the university. We're going to do it for the basketball team next year and the football team.

"I'd have kissed Hop Cassady's butt if I'd known him in college."

I had a friend in college named Irwin Thal. Irwin was manager of the football team. He was rejected for medical school. Woody Hayes took him by the hand, and took him over to the dean and said, "This boy is going to be a doctor." The dean said, "Well, he only has a 3.0 and he can't get into medical school with a 3.0." Woody said, "Bull[bleep]. He's going to be a doctor." He literally forced Irwin into medicine. Irwin is now retired, as a distinguished physician from Toledo.

My orthopedic surgeon is a guy named Bombach. Dr. Jaren D. Bombach played on the national championship team, and he told the same story about Woody shepherding people through life, through college. Teammates would go back to Woody for advice or help over the years. At one of these fund-raisers we had for the football team's Michigan party recently, Hop Cassady was there. I'd have kissed Hop Cassady's butt if I'd known him in college.

I said something like "I'm so happy to meet you after all these years." He said, "It's nice of you to do this for the football team. Nice of you to invite me. Woody would be happy to know that you're doing this." Hop and other athletes went through hard times, and they'd always go back to Woody, and he'd help them find a job or give them life's advice.

To parallel that to Tressel, two years ago he called me up and said, "I'd like to invite you to come to practice." I said, "Oh, I don't want to bother you, Jim." He said, "No, I want you to come and bring your kids." I said, "OK, thank you very much." I'd only been to one practice, maybe when I was in college. They were open, and I was curious to see what it was like. So, now, as a grown-up, I was curious again to see what practice was like.

They were doing all the things football players do. He blows the whistle and says, "Huddle up." I was about 30 yards away. He said, "Les, would you come over here? This is Les Wexner. He's a trustee of the university. He's a very good friend. I asked him to come." He said nice things about me. He said, "The reason I asked Les to come is I want him to talk to you about leadership and ethics." These guys were all so . . . I felt like a mouse! It was a thrill.

Tressel's wife, Ellen, is lovely. They just did a fund-raiser for the Coalition Against Family Violence, and he and his wife were the host and hostess. The community does a fund-raiser for the James Hospital every year, and he's always involved and gives money. In some ways, I think coaches, because of their nature in towns like Columbus, have a place in the community, so that they are asked to participate, which he does, when asked. But he also volunteers, because he's a part of the community. He's a coach . . . and he's a citizen. In my judgment, he displays excellent citizenship.

In the ways you give back, it is selfish because you get to see things, and people sometimes say nice things about you in the here and now. I think—and we preach that in the business—that everybody in their own way can help to make the world a better place. If it's a dollar a month, if it's reading to a kid once a month or an hour a week, you can at least try. When I was a kid, I was more on the beneficiary side than the benefactor, so I know how difficult it is when you're a college student to give five bucks to United Way. It seems like a fortune, but I think things like that, you're lucky if you can see them, and you're luckier if you can do them. I feel very badly for people who don't see life that way.

Can you read this?
Miami Hurricanes can't.

WIT HAPPENS

RICHARD LEWIS

From the man who brought you the date from hell, the life from hell, the mother-in-law from hell, comes the college experience from . . . heaven? Comedian/actor and author of the book The Other Great Depression *Richard Lewis, now 60, had surprisingly few neurotic experiences during his days as a student at Ohio State. The one notable one involved a grocery-shopping experience and a coaching icon.*

I was born in Brooklyn, raised in Jersey, but there's a Columbus/ Ohio State aspect in my body that is always fighting to take over. I'm proud of it. I wear it like a badge of honor. It's just part of our DNA after the first Michigan game. I plan my concerts around that game. I will not let them get in the way. That's just where it's at.

I'm not any different than the majority of people who have graduated or gone to the school. There's just something about it. It is the greatest rivalry in college sports. There is no doubt about it. There are some great ones, but this is it. It's something very special, and people at Ohio State should never take it for granted and should realize how lucky they are

"No. No. No. We went to Ohio State." And then they put handcuffs on me. People are so energetic when it comes to saying "Go Bucks." I've seen people do that at funerals. "Go Bucks!" "Can we bury the dead first before we discuss the game?" And, then I'll say, "Father, what's the point spread?" It's just overwhelming. It consumes our body and our spirit. Once a Buckeye, always a Buckeye.

When I was growing up in Englewood, New Jersey, I had a couple of friends in high school, one year ahead of me, who had gone there. Mickey Appleman, who became a very famous, world-class poker player, was a soccer player at Ohio State. They introduced me to him. They were in the AEPi fraternity. One thing led to another. My parents and I visited the campus. Once I walked on the Oval, I went, "Whoa. This is it." The other thing which was important was they let me in. That was crucial. Getting in—the Oval aside.

Back then, in the late '60s, it was just an astonishing time. Unfortunately and sadly, even ironic, the Vietnam War was going on. And it was much like it's going down now in Iraq in terms of people being really disturbed by a lot of it.

I was there during an amazing time politically—a torturous time politically, but certainly amazing to be a youngster trying to figure things out. Also, being a huge music freak, it was the two or three or four years that developed what now has become classic rock to this day. Every day it seemed like, "Oh wow, the new Beatles album's out. And the new **JANIS JOPLIN*** album's out." To people who loved rock and roll, certainly many college students, it was that genre of music. There's nothing like it, and there has never been anything to match it. It was really quite a great time to be in college.

Bruce Vilanch, the comedy writer, also grew up in Jersey and went to Ohio State. He went to another high school, but my father catered his bar mitzvah. Sadly, my father was booked during my weekend!

My father died about a year after I got out of college, which was really tragic. I'm not suggesting that led to my ultimate alcoholism, but it certainly pushed me in that direction. I can say I'm 13 years in recovery, which, of course, made the 2000 gaffe in the Ohio State men's basketball media guide pretty painful to me. For whatever the reason, the media guide jokingly said I was a drunk when, of course, I had already had six years of sobriety, was really a tough thing for me to deal with.

Under famous alumni, it said, "Richard Lewis: actor, writer, comedian, drunk." I took the high road—I wasn't going to throw away all the work I had done for Ohio State over one person's gaffe. It was a very disturbing time for me. It was in every wire service. My picture was everywhere—after six years of sobriety, having people think that

Coach Jimmy Johnson and ***JANIS JOPLIN** were high school classmates at Thomas Jefferson High School in Port Arthur, Texas. Jimmy Johnson didn't know she sang. They hated each other. She called him "Scarhead" and he called her "Beat Weeds."

maybe I had fallen off the wagon, which is no big deal, it's a disease. But it's a big deal for someone who has already worked hard at being sober and won awards for doing service in the recovery field. It's pathetic how much I fight and struggle. Certainly in the business I'm in, you don't want people thinking that you're lying.

It was a libelous situation. But I decided to go, "You know what. I know the truth," and the truth won out. The president and the athletic director at the time were more than sympathetic and incredulous that it happened. In fact, the president was going to fly out to my house in Hollywood and apologize in person. But I said, "No. Run the university. There's bigger fish to fry. I'll deal with this some way."

"In fact, the president was going to fly out to my house in Hollywood and apologize in person."

It was such a crushing blow to me, not what the person did, as much as whatever his motives were. I have no idea. He might even have written me a letter to apologize, but the damage had been done. I was in every paper and it was on radio shows and sports shows. Some people like to jump on you. It was a tough time for me for many months. It's one thing if some jerkoff in show business and jerky guy says something, but when it comes from your own university, from someone who worked at the university, it was just a blatant mistruth—if that's even a word.

You have to know how to do what's right for you in your life. I don't preach about this, by the way. Most of my friends do drink, and those who have problems—if I can help, I help. The truth is most of them don't, but, in this case, this was like a great example of why you have to just feel comfortable in your own skin.

By the way, when I went through that horrific time with that situation, Rex Kern wrote me one of the most beautiful letters I ever received. This from a guy who went undefeated, won the national championship—I met him a few times. He said, "Richard, I'm in your corner. This should not have happened."

He was implying that he knew that I was a sober graduate and alumnus, and that I was doing the right thing for me, and this thing shouldn't have happened. To get a letter like that was sort of surreal. It's not like we're bosom buddies, but here I was sitting in the stands, his age, watching him lead the team to an undefeated season. And decades later, going through this hell—really, because it was hell—he reaches out to me.

I have been doing comedy for 37 years and have continued to do all the shows that the college students watch, and I have never stopped. I'm still with Bill Maher and Conan O'Brien. I'm very proud of being a graduate of Ohio State. Also, wherever I go, all over the country, I am an ambassador of sorts, only in that I talk about Ohio State everywhere in front of millions of people in the print media and on radio and on television—whenever the opportunity presents itself.

When I was at OSU, I didn't miss one game—from my freshman year through my senior year. In fact, I stayed six months after I graduated, because I was frightened to come back to Jersey and get a job. I remember calling my father after I finished my business courses and saying, "I think I'll stay on for another two years." It was a very brief conversation. "Get a job!" Click. My days were numbered on High Street. He was right. I was just petrified.

I just turned 60, and it's frightening to me. I speak with my friends at Ohio State—my best friends still live in Columbus. It feels like yesterday. I was in a fraternity for a year, and then I left. It wasn't for me. There was some kind of reunion, and I'm on the phone with these guys. It was just like yesterday. I'm on the phone saying, "We're gonna kick the ZBTs' a--." It's the greatest time when I go back there, and I tell college students, "Just don't squander it. It's a wonderful four years." I tried to stretch it out. During the last few quarters, I really wanted to stay there as long as possible. I knew what the consequences were—reality.

I hardly missed a game since I graduated in terms of watching them. I had tremendous ties with the athletic department. Archie Griffin I consider a friend. There's athletic director Gene Smith, and we've been in touch. Before the tragic Florida bowl game, I did *CBS Sports Spectacular* to promote Ohio State, and I did one other network show. I was on the pre-BCS game show. I was the Ohio State representative. The Gators didn't have anybody with the guts to go up against me. They would have had the last laugh, unfortunately. It was just a terrible game for us. We were flat. It wasn't our team.

A lot of times I'll have an e-mail already written to Gene and to Archie—written, thinking we're going to win, but you never know. You just want to pop that e-mail out. Then, all of a sudden, the last two minutes, the other team wins, and it'll be a nightmare. I have this obsession—I have a lot of these obsessions, compulsive things. As soon as the game is over, I punch "send." They must think I'm a nutcase. Within one second of the victory, I go, "Yeah. Go Bucks."

Archie really has been very sweet to me and very supportive. I adore the guy. You cannot ask for a better guy who is more well liked, and no one is going to win two Heismans anymore. They're turning pro at age 9 now. I think his record will stand with **JOE DIMAGGIO'S** * as one of those types that are really steroid-free.

With football, I close my eyes. I'm walking through the oval with a handful of buddies. We're sitting in those crummy end-zone seats as freshmen and couldn't care less; although, to this day, I have calluses on my behind from those seats. It was just surreal. In '66, the team wasn't that great. They had a couple of good players. Then, man, everything turned around.

To this day, one of the most frightening situations was at Big Bear, the old grocery store there on Lane Avenue. I was getting chopped meat. I made great burgers. I saw this nice package of chopped meat, and just as I went to grab it in the freezer, some guy, in a funny manner, slapped my hand and went, "That's mine."

I looked up, and it was "The Man." It was Woody. I shriveled to about an inch and a half. I became like one of the dwarfs in *Wizard of Oz*. My voice went up 20 octaves. I went, "Woody, you can have anything you want. I'll even come over and barbecue them for you." I panicked. Far be it from me to take Woody's burgers. I came home to about eight guys and everybody said, "Where's the meat?" I said, "Woody has it." And they said, "And, by the way, why are you an inch tall?" "I don't know. You've got to get me to a doctor. I shrunk." It was the most frightening mistake. The last person whose mouth you want to take food out of is Woody.

Woody Hayes is a guy that defined college football for decades and

To accentuate a wiggle in her walk, Marilyn Monroe would cut a quarter of an inch off one of her heels. . . . The combination on Monroe's jewelry box was 5-5-5, *<u>JOE DIMAGGIO'S</u> number.

decades and historically. It was just sad that that one moment, that one flustered moment where he wasn't thinking properly, had to happen. It was sad. I think down the line, it won't be revisionist history, it will be like, "All right. He really had a bad day."

It's obvious that these sports icons historically have trouble leaving. Perhaps he was a little overly tired with the responsibility and pressures of college football. I'm not excusing what he did, but, perhaps, maybe if he had retired a year or two earlier, this wouldn't have happened, and maybe he could have been more of an ambassador for our team. That said, Coach Tressel, the "new" Woody on campus—I have nothing but amazing vibes from this guy.

I felt it in 2002, when we won the championship against Miami. I was on the field. I was screaming and yelling. I knew, at that point, because I had gone to so many games, how not to get in the way of the coach, not to get in the way of the players—stay 20 yards away from the players. Roger Clemens from the **NEW YORK YANKEES*** sees me going up and down the sideline. He turned to some of the guys, some former football greats on the sideline, and said, "That Lewis is nuts." I remember, particularly, Eddie George saying, "Hey, man, we're Ohio State. Thank you." I turned to Clemens, who was standing there with one of his sons and went, "By the way, get the hell out of here. Get away from my team. You're from Texas. Get out of here. Who the hell invited you?"

With a twinkle in our eyes, we almost came to blows. If his son wasn't there, I might have thrown a good left hook, which I didn't throw, and then he would have killed me. But I would have gone down fighting. My last words would have been "Go Bucks!"

***YANKEE** Stadium is known as "the House that Ruth Built." The school that Babe Ruth attended in his youth, St. Mary's Industrial School for Boys in Baltimore—now called Cardinal Gibbons High School—was known as "the House that Built Ruth." . . . The cement used to build Yankee Stadium was purchased from Milan, Ohio native Thomas Edison who owned the huge Portland Cement Company.

I ran into a Michigan fan yesterday. Then, I backed up and ran into him again.

Chapter 2

A Hard Way to Make an Easy Living

Buenos Noches, Coaches

THANKS FOR THE DANCE, EARLE

EARLE BRUCE

Hall of Fame coach Earle Bruce has kept rein-venting himself in the two decades that have followed his near run at a national title and a string of 9-3 seasons. The 76-year-old former Buckeye head coach and player's latest ven-ture is a sports website—earlebruceonsports. com—launched in July of 2007. He really never laments these days how tough it was to coach at OSU after the legendary Woody Hayes. Besides, that wasn't the toughest challenge he faced in his football career. Play-ing for Woody, after being recruited by the mild-mannered Wes Fesler, was the real rude awakening.

My coaching career started so unexpectedly. Actually, I was still a student and I hadn't really given coaching any thought up until that point. In fact, I was pretty sure football was behind me.

It was 1951, my sophomore year at Ohio State. I injured my knee and was having a lot of trouble during fall practice. I had a new coach, Woody Hayes, who I was still trying to figure out. I hurt it on the third day of fall practice. The knee was slipping in and out of place, because it needed a cartilage operation. I was told that if I got operated on, it would probably be the end of my career.

I went up on Main Street, on Route 40 and thumbed home to Cumberland, Maryland. When I got home, my mother said, "Coach Harry Strobel [he was an assistant] called and said Coach Hayes wants you to come back and help coach football and get your degree and finish your education." I said, "Mom, you mean to tell me he called and asked me to come back?" Normally when you're hurt, in all other schools, they take your scholarship.

I said that I didn't think he would want me, because he could get someone else for the job. She said, "No, he wants you to come back."

So, I went back and became a student coach. Little did he realize at the time that I was going to be the guy who followed Coach Hayes. There's a little irony in that.

I never saw Coach Hayes coming. I thought I'd play my whole career for Wes Fesler. But there's no doubt about it—the **SNOW BOWL*** did Wes Fesler in. I was at that game. Ohio State vs. Michigan in Ohio Stadium. It was the fall of 1950. I was sitting on about the 45-yard line, about 25 rows up. Freshmen were ineligible in that day and age, so I needed a ticket. Actually, I needed more than one, or so I thought. I ended up having to go by myself, because no one else could get there.

I actually thought I needed seven tickets for that game to take my parents and everybody who was coming from Cumberland, Maryland I went in to see Dick Larkins, the athletic director. Here I am, a freshman, and thinking, "Jeemeny Christmas, how do I ask for seven tickets?" I got my nerve up and went in and said, "I need to have seven tickets." They were $7 apiece. He said, "You've got them, Earle." I got the seven tickets.

Then, when the game came about, Cumberland people couldn't get to Ohio Stadium from their hotel in Worthington. I wanted to see the game, so I took the car and rode down from Worthington. As it turned out, you didn't need a ticket when you went into the game—no one was taking tickets. In fact, they were trying to sell tickets—two for a nickel!

When I got to my seat, I sat down. In front of me, there was a little old lady who must have been at least 80 years old, sitting by herself, with a blanket over her head. How she got there to the game and up those 25 stairs is beyond me. I know one thing—she's got to be a good football fan. She wanted to see that game.

We go through the first half. It's a 3-2 football game with 46 seconds to go in the half. Ohio State has the ball, third and nine, on their 20-yard

Pullman, home of Washington State University, has a population of twenty-five thousand. Martin Stadium, the home stadium for the Washington State Cougars holds thirty-eight thousand . . . In the late 1950s, the Cougars had a home game during a ***BLIZZARD**. The paid attendance was 1. The Athletic Department gave that paying fan a lifetime pass to Washington State football games.

line. No one could tell through the snow exactly where they were, so maybe it was their 25-yard line. There was a substitution, everybody knew that when they put in this big blocking halfback for Walt Klevay, that they were going to punt. That was a signal. So, in comes the halfback.

This lady in front of me jumps up, throws her blanket back and the snow comes all over me. She's shouting at the top of her voice, "Don't you punt that ball, Fesler. Don't you dare punt that ball, Fesler." We had made the substitution. I jumped up and said, "I'm with you, lady. Don't punt that ball, Fesler. Don't punt that ball."

"The first time I ever saw the Ohio State marching band come out, I thought, 'Oh my God'."

He punted. Michigan blocked it for a touchdown, 9-3. The game ended that way, and Wes Fesler never coached another day at Ohio State. Why not punt? Well, they could run the clock out. No one was stopping the clock. That game should have ended 3-2 in Ohio State's favor. There's no doubt about it. But it didn't. It ended 9-3 Michigan. So Wes was fired like anybody else.

Getting to Ohio State in the first place was unconventional. When I was in high school in Cumberland, back then Ohio State had a group of people called Frontliners. They were recruiters, and they came about because Michigan beat Ohio State real bad back in 1940. They organized this group to get their program going.

The Frontliners were a big-time organization. One of them came up to me at a basketball game after the football season and asked me if I was interested in going to school. I said, "Yes." He handed me a card and asked me to fill it out. He asked me if my buddy Jim Ruehl was interested in going. He was an all-state and probably All-American high school football player. He was headed toward Maryland, but when we filled out those forms and we took our visit, we liked what we saw as far as the stadium and meeting the coaches and the people.

We started school, and I really loved Ohio State. The band came out for the first game. The first time I ever saw the Ohio State marching band come out, I thought, "Oh my God." That's when I really became a Buckeye, I guess, when I saw that band go down there, and the drum major threw the baton over the goal post and caught it.

Coach Wes Fesler was the guy, and he was really impressive on and off the field. He was probably the most gentlemanly coach I ever played for and probably one of the most talented. He was a three-time All-American at three different positions—center, halfback and punter—when he played. He used to come out and practice punting sometimes with the players, just kicking the ball.

He was a dandy. He could almost call his bounce. He'd say it would hit on the 4-yard line and bounce back to the 8, and it would. I couldn't believe it. He never swore. The toughest thing he ever said to me was he came over when I was playing safety one time in practice. He put his arm around me and said, "I think you can do better than that, Earle." He was a real soft-spoken coach who did his thing. He had a good staff, and they were good people.

The difference between Woody Hayes and Wes Fesler—Wes Fesler wouldn't say "s---" if he had a mouthful. But, if you know Woody, he used to jump on his hat and yell, "s---, s---, s---, s---, s---!" No one knew how to take Woody Hayes. None of the players did. They had never heard that. They never saw that. They never got that kind of coaching where he would stop and run an assistant coach off the field because his players weren't doing too well. It was different like day and night.

The only thing I would say about Woody, the one thing he was really good at—and I think that might have been Wes Fesler's downfall—was the academic side of it. Wes was an All-American and a great student and a very intelligent guy. He just expected you to do everything your-self. If you didn't, you fell by the wayside.

Woody, if he recruited you and you were a mediocre student, he was going to give you help and tutor you. He was going to do things to keep you in school, so you could get your education and play football. He had a different approach to education. His dad was a superintendent. He realized how important it was. He knew that some people didn't really know yet the value of education until probably years after they were in college. He would really do a job with people on the education role. He really was mean and ugly on the football field. Some of the kids, when he took over, couldn't take that.

When the job came open after Wes was fired, all the football players signed a petition to bring Paul Brown back. That was the message—bring Paul back. That was all the people wanted, because he won the national title back in '42. But, the athletic director, Dick Larkins, didn't want him. They did interview him, and they didn't take him. We didn't have a coach.

Some of the players were talking, and I said, "I know who we ought to get as the coach. We ought to get that little old lady who was in front of me. She was the only one in the stadium who knew we shouldn't be punting the ball." After it was over, when they blocked it, everybody knew we shouldn't have punted the ball. But she knew it beforehand. I marveled. I kept thinking about that, so I recommended they hire her. It so happens they hired Woody Hayes, and he could take all the heat they could possibly give him.

When Woody Hayes came in, we didn't know anything about him. Woody was a political choice. He had a guy on the board of trustees that he knew real well that had studied his career a little bit and been a fan. That's how Woody got the job. There's no doubt about it. He had a good record at Miami of Ohio, but he was also very impressive in an interview. He's an impressive guy when he gets one-on-one where he gets to give his message, because he's a salesperson deluxe.

Woody was pretty stable throughout his career. He worked hard, too hard. He had a good knowledge of the game. He was a great teacher of the game of football—blocking, tackling, the fundamentals and especially the offensive theory to keep the ball away from the defense. I mean, he'd get the ball and 17 plays later, he scored a touchdown. OSU kicked off and the opponents ran the ball three plays and punted. And 18 plays later, the opponents got the ball again. The opposition would have had the ball six times, they're in at halftime, they don't know what the hell to do because the score is 14-0. He was brutalizing. Ironically, in 1951, the one thing that was really evident was that he wasn't exactly a running coach. He had a passing attack. We really threw the ball. But that would change.

All of a sudden, he decided he'd better become a running coach. He changed his whole theory. No mistakes and keep the ball and score touchdowns and keep our defense on the bench by taking the ball and moving it three yards and a cloud of dust. It was very systematic, very good.

I used to love it when I was a high school coach, to come down and watch him. It was some kind of perfection to see the teaching and everything. But, the people wanted a wide-open offense. Some of them didn't care whether you lost or not, but the coach had to care, because he was more likely to keep his job if you win the national title than if you lose and look good on offense—throw the ball and do all that stuff that fans get excited about.

Besides coaching under Coach Hayes, the thing that prepared me the most for taking over for him in 1979 was my two years at Massillon, in 1964 and '65. When I coached at Massillon High, there was as much pressure as at Ohio State. It's a great high school job, where they love football in that town and they want to win. They want to win big all the time, not just win. They were used to winning big under Coach Paul Brown, so they thought if it was a 35-0 game, it was a good game. They'd stay till the last minute. I never saw fans who stayed for every play. They didn't leave at the end of the third quarter when you were ahead 30-0. They were looking for more.

It was a place where football was something. They loved their game of football, and they wanted their kids to get a good education and play football and win. One time, someone in the Booster Club came up to me and said, "Well, you know what happens when you lose your first football game in Massillon?" I said, "No, what happens when you lose your first football game?" They said, "Well, we bring the biggest garbage truck in the county up with a load of garbage, and we dump it on your front yard." I said, "What?"

He said, "We dump a load of garbage on it to tell you that you'd better not lose. We don't like to lose." And that had happened. Coaches, when they lost, they'd get their garbage. I said, "I'm gonna coach, but you're not going to get any garbage on my yard, because I wouldn't want to clean that crap up. We're gonna win them all." And we did that. We went undefeated. When I left, they said, "We're sorry you didn't stay long enough to get some garbage dumped on your yard." I said, "I want to tell you something. I could have been here four or five years, and you'd never get garbage on my front yard."

After leaving Ohio State, I coached at Northern Iowa and Colorado State. And I'm glad I continued to coach. Eventually I came back to Columbus. Massillon had taught me one thing very well. They always talked about it at the Booster Club and other places, "You're the coach now. When you're not the coach, we're gonna support the guy that is the coach, because that's the guy you should support. Well, John Cooper was the coach, so I supported him. I liked John, but I don't think I was as much part of that program as I am now with Jim Tressel, because Jim worked for me. That's a different relationship. He was a really good friend. I was really good friends with Jim Tressel's dad. We had something going there.

When I look back on my career, I don't know whether I might have done some things different. Maybe, but I don't know what they would have been. I think I'm a good teacher of the game of football. My overall record is unbelievable. When I go through my high school coaching career, I've got the best record still at some of the high schools. I've got the *best* record at Massillon, because I'm undefeated—the only undefeated coach they've ever had. I probably have the best record at Sandusky: 34-3-3, something like that. My record at places is good, so I feel good about my coaching career, and I feel good about Columbus, Ohio. I was a student here. I have great friends here.

> **"They can make 9-3 sound good or bad, whatever they want to do."**

The press was one of the problems, I guess, in the sense that they give you a different image sometimes than what it is. They can make 9-3 sound good or bad, whatever they want to do. The school president, Edward Jennings, wasn't my kind of guy. He was my president, but he was a Michigan guy.

I'll never forget one thing—we were recruiting a kid from Fremont, Ohio. He wants to be a lawyer, to go to law school. I take him over to meet the president. The president talks to him. We're not going to get the kid, I guess, because the president comes over and says, "You can't compete with the Michigan law school." I said, "What did you say? This is Ohio State. You're the president of *Ohio State*. What are you saying?"

I have a different feeling about Michigan guys. I don't give a s--- about them at all, who they are, whether they're our president or someone else. To hell with Michigan. Beat them!

SOMETIMES GOD JUST HANDS YOU ONE

TED GINN SR.

Ted Ginn's name is synonymous with football, but his dreams are aligned with the bigger picture. His vision is to open an academy in Cleveland for at-risk boys, where teachers think out of the box and Cleveland public school students continue to chip away at what was once the nation's worst dropout rate system-wide: 72 percent. His own son, former OSU standout receiver/return man Ted Ginn Jr., failed the first grade and was told by his fifth-grade teacher he was destined to be nothing more than a "burger flipper." When Junior struggled in middle school, the security guard and head football coach at Cleveland's Glenville High demanded that his son be tested. As it turned out, he had some special needs and all that was required was some tutoring and restructuring. He ended up graduating in the top 10 percent of his class and earned a perfect 4.0 in the final grading period of high school. So the octane flowing through the Glenville-to-Ohio-State pipeline may be rich in talent, but it's really all about what Ted Ginn Sr. stands for.

People talk about the Glenville High School pipeline to Ohio State, but they don't always know what that's about. I mean, the first kid I really was able to get colleges to look at was Pierre Woods—and I had to drive him around the country, because colleges wouldn't come here to Cleveland. And then, he ended up at Michigan. Right now we have Jemario O'Neal, Ray Small, Robert Rose, Curtis Terry, Bryant Browning and Jermale Hines all on the OSU team.

I didn't follow Ohio State football while I was in school. And I did play football right here at Glenville. I was a center and a linebacker. I was only 143 pounds, but I was tough. I'd get up on you. I took it personal, though, with Ohio State because, at the time, none of the Big 10 schools would come in here to recruit.

It started happening all over again when I was a coach. I did a camp tour, as I call it, 4,000 or 5,000 miles in the summer. I started with Pierre. People wouldn't come to me, so I go to them. I couldn't sit here and allow people not to come and check us out. I think it was because of the perception of the inner-city school that they didn't want to come check us out. It's the perception that if you looked at my life—at a kid who has gone through trauma like that—the percentage of him being successful is not very good. These people—and society—continue to have these perceptions of people and communities and different areas. We need to attack that and stop it.

Jim Tressel and I have the same core values. He teaches these same things I try to teach. Ohio State is one of the largest universities in the country. Most kids in Ohio grow up wanting to go to Ohio State. It's a good fit for our kids, because of the values being taught there—about love and about passion and about being a great person. That's what changed my thinking about Ohio State—Coach Tressel.

To me coaching is a very simple business. It's not about X's and O's. It's about having the love, passion and understanding for children and wanting what's best for them, wanting them to do great things. I had someone do that for me when I was growing up, but it's needed now more than ever. It's not the '70s or the '80s. It's needed in sports. It's totally needed in education. This is the only opportunity you have to change someone's life and give them opportunity.

When Troy Smith got to Glenville, he was a very bitter kid. Personally, Troy was a kid who I thought had been lied to, used for his talent. He had some things he had to overcome in his family, but he had to be *taught* how to deal with that. I tried to work with him on that when he was here, and I still work with him on that every day.

When I told him the truth, I stuck with it. The truth that I told him, he didn't like it, but it was the truth. He finally bought into it because he had no other choice. I wasn't going to do it like everybody else was. Some people lie to you because they are looking for something. I wasn't looking for anything from him. That was the difference. I'm doing it because I love you. They're doing it because there's something they need from you.

A lot of times you have to break kids of their Pop Warner mentality in high school. Sometimes when they go to college, you have to break them of it all over again. Sometimes Troy didn't understand the total picture. That's why kids need adults, need mentors—lots of them. It's not all about talent, it's about everything else. It's about how you carry yourself and see things from a mature standpoint.

I'm sure my early years caused me to be the person I am today. I never wanted a kid to live like I had to live. Not that I missed any love—I was always around love. That's one thing I don't think I was short of with my grandparents and my mother.

But at the age of 19, your whole family is gone. That's rough. I always think about the core values my grandmother was teaching me. People in my neighborhood looked out for me as I was growing up. I had the core values I was taught by my coach, James Hubbard, and people like that. I wasn't a bad kid. People just embraced me. So many people in the neighborhood basically would look at you and say, "This boy's by himself." Whereas, today, if a kid is by himself, people say, "Man, I ain't got time to raise him."

As I grew up into my adult life, Mr. Hubbard brought me back to Glenville as an assistant coach. He was looking out for me so I wouldn't go astray after my momma had died. He said to me, "Come on over here and show that boy how to snap that ball."

He acted like he really needed my help. He never did tell me that what was really going on was that I needed *him*. And what he was doing was trying to save my life. I went along with him and had respect. Again, back then, he made me think I was helping him. I was tricked.

I don't do things the way everyone else does them. You've got to do what's best for the kids, not what the instruction manual tells you to do. I mean, I take kids to church. One time we had just won the regional championship game, and the next day I had several of the kids baptized. It's all about having that faith that you can get things done. Our kids need to know that. How do you live? You've got to have faith when you do something that it's going to work. God gives you that faith. That's what he teaches—teaches you love, teaches you passion, teaches you all that stuff. You've just got to follow it and believe in it.

My strong faith came from my grandmother. We didn't have a choice. People have got choices now. There were certain things I couldn't compromise. I couldn't compromise vacation bible school. You couldn't compromise going to revivals. You couldn't compromise going to Sunday school. You couldn't compromise any of that. Now they can compromise anything they want. Kids do what they want. Everybody can do what they want.

Another thing I've done that's not the way the school board would map it out is I've let kids stay at my house and have fed them, trying to keep them out of trouble. I try to think, "How did I get started?" When I saw the potential in the kids, I started doing it. I've been doing this at least 10 to 12 years and maybe longer than that. I looked and checked their home environment and their situation with their parents. Not that all the parents were bad, but maybe the parents didn't have the resources—not like I had them.

You sacrifice your home and your wife and your daughter and your personal space, but I thought it was all worth it. The key to it is that my wife bought into it and helped to sacrifice. The kids, my family, understood that we were fortunate to have a home, and we should help people. Ted Jr. liked having brothers.

Kids are so unaware, not knowing. It was just an opportunity for me to teach them. The only way you can teach them is to put them in your house. All the kids we brought in were pretty respectful. My wife played a role, my son played a role, my daughter played a role. They were thankful, but if they started being disrespectful, they wouldn't be in the home. If they didn't like it, they would leave. The ones who stayed were successful. The ones who left were not successful.

I turned our football program around, stressing the fact that they do have the opportunity and the hope to be successful. Academics are a part of it. Athletic teams are part of it. Mainly, I stress love, passion, understanding for the kids. A lot of kids don't know what love is. A lot of kids don't know what loyalty is.

Troy Smith sure didn't. But once he did, he had a chance to be special. Still, there were little things—like up until the 2005 season, he refused to really look at film and study it and take it seriously. I remember exactly when he changed—after Ohio State lost to Penn State that season. I had been telling him all along, but then I really bore down on him.

I told him, "You probably need to go in and ask for a transfer. He then asked me why. I said, "Because you're going to be a great college football player, but I think you need to go to Nebraska." And he said, "Why?" I told him that he needed to be in the wishbone. But then I also told him I couldn't think of any quarterbacks from **NEBRASKA*** that ended up in the NFL. That got him thinking.

I told him you have to use your feet and your arm *and* your brain. You have to learn your craft if you want

> "Because you're going to be a great college football player, but I think you need to go to Nebraska."

people to see you as a quarterback and not as an athlete. Things happen in a split second. You have to be able to make decisions. I know Tress had been talking to him about this for a long time. I had too. But it finally got through to him. That's the thing, you never give up on young people.

You have to get kids to trust you. You have to get them to believe in you and have a vision and build a foundation, because the average kid, they don't have a great foundation. They don't have a vision. They don't have a purpose. So you give them a purpose. Kids are looking for that structure. They're looking for that love and passion. I just wish I had more help. But I know the Lord isn't going to give me any more than I can handle.

Troy had a lot to overcome in his life. The ones you lose, and there's not a lot of them, are the ones where the structure of their life or the structure at home isn't right or there's some kind of shortcoming somewhere that they can't get past. And that's what puts them at risk.

Even kids in private schools, even kids with 3.5 GPAs, even kids with money become at risk, because they get in situations where nobody's willing to push them. It starts with our education system. Education isn't a part of life. It *is* life. People say someday we're going to have to do things different, because this is coming, that's coming. Well guess what? It's here. Now is the time to give our kids what they need. Every last one of them.

Academic All-American teams have been picked every year since 1952. *NEBRASKA leads all colleges by a wide margin in number of players selected.

NAME THE INDIANA COACH . . . WIN VALUABLE PRIZES

BILL MALLORY

Bill Mallory's first exposure to Ohio State football was at a game in which the Buckeye fans booed their coach for losing to Indiana. Even the family friends who provided the young Sandusky resident with his ticket and his ride that day derided an unproven Woody Hayes. Years later, Mallory would have his own complaints, but far more admiration, for the man who launched his head coaching career. And 36 years after that first IU upset, Mallory was on the opposing sideline when the Hoosiers finally won again. That game helped bring to an end the Earle Bruce era at OSU and had Mallory in the mix, along with John Cooper, to take over as the next head coach. But it wasn't, as Bruce called it, "the darkest day in OSU history." Bruce, Mallory and Hayes had all lived through the dark days—many of them—together as they forged a Buckeye renaissance.

For my wife and me, going to Ohio State was a dream come true. There was never any question in my mind about coming to Ohio State as an assistant coach. I had always hoped that someday I could come to Ohio State and work for Woody Hayes

I got there in January of '66. A few years later, we won the Rose Bowl and beat Southern Cal and we were national champs. But when I came in, the program was struggling. Earle Bruce was hired on when I was. A year or so later, Woody hired **LOU HOLTZ***. We pulled together and went to work and got the program back going again like it had been.

> In 1986, Skip Holtz played in 11 Notre Dame games as a member of the special teams. He carried the ball one time for one yard . . .
> ***LOU HOLTZ**, Jr. co-wrote the movie "The Cable Guy" with Jim Carrey.

When I got to Columbus, I was surprised at the shape the program was in. I'd been away from Ohio, at Yale for a year. I worked for a gentleman at Bowling Green before that by the name of Doyt Perry. There were three people that Woody just had such great respect for—Doyt Perry, Bill Hess, who went to Ohio University and had great success, and then later, of course, Bo Schembechler. Not that he didn't have great respect for others, but those three were particularly close to Woody.

When I came, after being gone a year—of course, you always look at Ohio State as one of the top teams, not only in the Big 10, but in the country—I was taken aback when I came in and saw that the talent level was down. We weren't as good as we should have been

By the time I came in '66, Woody was getting some heat. He'd indicated that things weren't good. We had a losing season that first year I was there. He made the statement, "I don't know that I'll be around," because back then they just had yearly contracts. He said, "If any of you want to look around for something else, you go ahead and do so." At that point, that really pulled us together, because Woody was focused. He was such a great leader. He was determined he was going to take that program and get it back on its feet.

It started with the duty of being the "weather man." The first year in, you get the weather detail. I couldn't wait for new coaches to come in, because it passed to Lou Holtz. But that first year, I was in charge of weather. Woody had had a good running back out of Akron. He got hurt, twisted an ankle on a muddy field. And ever since then, the tradition of having an assistant coach being the weather man raged on. I had to stand up and give a weather report. I'd usually call the airport and get their report of what the weather was going to be. If the weather wasn't like what I said, I'd just get my rump chewed good. I got down on the weather bureau, because I didn't think they were very accurate. They're a lot better today than they were back then. I got my butt chewed a few times there when I'd say it was going to be nice, and it wasn't.

We had a fellow named Ralph Guarasci, who took care of our grounds. He was a good guy, but he was stubborn. I'd get with Ralph and say, "It's going to rain, Ralph, so I want to get that field covered." He'd say, "I ain't gonna cover it. It'll kill the grass." I'd say, "Well, I'd rather have the grass killed than me." I'd have a devil of a time getting him to cover that field. We're getting ready to go play Minnesota, and I get the weather report. We're going to get rain. I got hold of Ralph and said, "We're expecting rain, 90 percent chance of rain this weekend. Make sure you cover that field, so that we don't have any problems." We weren't having a very good season anyway. I wasn't sure he was going to do it, but I sure stressed it strongly that he should do it.

On Sunday, Tiger Ellison, one of our assistants, would go to church. The rest of us had to be in the office at 8 o'clock, but Woody would let Tiger go to church. Tiger would get in about 10 o'clock, and the rest of us were already there, and we'd be there all day. Into the evening, about midnight, Lou McCullough said, "Let's go. We're done." We'd take our shoes off and tiptoe down the hallway so Woody wouldn't hear us. Otherwise, he'd be yelling at us to stay around. By midnight, we figured we had all our work done . . . but the offensive staff was still in there. We walked down to the parking lot. It was raining like you won't believe.

The coaches all take off to go home. I got to thinking, "I'm going to check the practice field to see whether Ralph covered it." I go out there. Sure enough, Ralph hasn't covered it. I thought, "Oh boy. I'd better go back and tell Woody." I went back and knocked on the offensive room door. He said, "Come in." I walked in and said, "Woody, we've got a problem. It's raining like heck out there, and Ralph didn't cover the field." He said, "Did you tell him?" I said, "Sure, I told him, but he just didn't do it."

Woody sat there momentarily. His offensive coaches were there—four haggard guys—and it's about 12:30 a.m. when I'm telling him this. He said, "We're going to cover it ourselves." I tell you right now, those poor coaches in there—their heads dropped right down on the table. He said, "Where's the defensive coaches?" I said, "They're all gone home." He said, "Get them and tell them to get out to the practice field."

We're all out there now, and it is raining like heck. We've got these great big canvases on cylinders, and Woody is trying to tell us how he wants it done. It's blowing and howling. We're getting the tarp off these big cylinders. The wind gets underneath, and it looks like a circus tent. We're all gathered around there. It blows up high, and Woody is out in the middle, and we can't see him, but we can hear him. He's yelling at us to get those cylinders on those tarps and try to get it back down.

It took forever. Finally, it was after 3 o'clock in the morning before we finally got that tarp laid. I'll never forget.

After we were done, you talk about a real sorry-looking group. I looked at Tiger. He'd been at church, so he was all dressed up with his coat on. I don't know what happened, but his coat and pants had shrunk—they must have been wool. He looked like he had knickers on when you looked at his pants. Larry Catuzzi was an immaculate dresser. He had on a cashmere sweater which now looked like a miniskirt, because it was hanging clear down to his knees. Lou McCullough, who I had called and gotten out of bed, came out in hip boots and pajamas and wearing a raincoat. It's too bad we didn't take a picture, because that was one sorry-looking bunch.

Finally, when we got it all done, it stopped raining. I'll never forget Hugh Hindman, when I was walking out. Now this was my first year there. I'm walking back to the car and Hugh turns to me and says, "Welcome to the big time!"

> **"He had on a cashmere sweater which now looked like a miniskirt, because it was hanging clear down to his knees."**

The recruiting had leveled off a little bit there for Woody. We, as a staff, without question, were able to pull together and come up with some good-quality players. My second year was John Brockington, Rex Kern, Jim Stillwagon and that group. That was a very talented group of young men. We were very fortunate to come up with that class. It really blended in well. When those guys were sophomores, we had a good chemistry. We got good leadership out of the seniors, and got some good important play out of the juniors. Then those sophomores really rounded the team out to make it a very fine football team.

I give a lot of credit to Tiger Ellison, who was our freshman coach. He'd been a great coach at Middletown High School and had such great success there. What had happened is that Woody was getting some players, but he wasn't keeping them. He was losing them and maybe they weren't getting the kind of direction they needed. He'd hired Tiger, who had been there a year or two before I got there. He was perfect for that. He was a parent-type coach who really did a great job with those players, getting them adjusted. Back then, freshmen were ineligible.

Woody ran a complete program. It was just a program that was geared to win. He did a great job in developing his players as total people. Education was very strong with Woody. There was no one at that time who did a better job. We were one of the first to have an academic support person. He was strong on tutoring. He felt that was part of teaching. It was not a spoon-feeding operation, but it was a situation where you worked with your players, not just with football, but with the academics. He was very, very strong about the academic side of it.

Woody's father had been a teacher, administrator, etc. He was very academic-minded. I had minored in history, and I used to love to hear him talk about World War II, for example. He would really get in and talk about that in depth, because he had served in that war. He went abroad to spend time in the summer with the soldiers who were fighting in the war. He'd come back and write letters to their parents.

When I got the head job at Miami of Ohio, he called me in. He didn't talk to me about X's and O's. He said, "I just want to talk to you as you are now pursuing your head coaching career. Remember, what is first and foremost is that you are doing a good job with these young men during their college life to prepare them for their future. When they come out, they can make something of their lives and amount to something. You gear your program in that regard as far as the academic side of it, taking a great interest in the young men."

He always said discipline was 99 percent participation. He was a strong believer in communication with your players. I always took on the philosophy that coaching was teaching and parenting. A lot of that came from Woody. He thought you needed to be always there to be with and support them and give them good direction off the field as well as on the field. That's something I really took with me as I went on. He said that if you run your program that way—the development of the person as a total individual—then the winning will take care of itself. He wanted a person to know how to act and conduct himself. He wanted them to be polite and know etiquette. He wanted that person to have polish and be well rounded and be that total individual.

Lyle Clark was a great defensive line coach whose place I took. He approached me and said, "You know, Bill, when you get a chance, I'd like to have you stop out and see me at the house. I'd like to talk to you about Woody." He said, "I want to paint a picture of Woody, so you'll have a good understanding of him because some of the young bucks like you have come in here and some have gotten discouraged and got out of coaching. He's not the easiest guy to work for. He's very demanding." He said, "Ninety percent of Woody is as good as you'll find anywhere." And it was. Woody had a big heart. He'd go over to that hospital and walk through there when he had time and see people over there. He was always quick to help people in need. There were a lot of things that people didn't know that Woody did. He was big-hearted in so many ways that way. But then he said, "That other 10 percent—you might call it the dark side, or however you want to term it. He can be just a pure-bred a------. Many times that overshadows the 90 percent. He can be a complete a--. When he gets into that mood, just step aside and stay out of his way."

And, that was about it. When Woody blew his top, he blew. I don't know that that ever bothered me. He ripped my butt a few times, and that was good for me. He p----- me off. I tell you I could have driven my head through a wall. That was the way he reached you sometimes. And he could fire you up and get your attention. There wasn't ever going to be any complacency—I guarantee you. He kept you on your toes, and he was demanding, and he was that way with his players. He was very aggressive. That's what you read about. Sometimes, that 10 percent overshadowed a lot of the 90 percent that he did—just like what happened with the **CLEMSON*** situation . . .

My first year there, we had a group of prospects coming in. Lou McCullough made the comment to Woody, "Now, I want you to behave yourself." Woody would get in a player's face if he didn't like something. He might even give them a little rap. Lou said, "Woody, don't blow up, because you'll scare these kids. We can't have that happen." We were on opposite fields—the defense and the offense. Woody stayed with the offense most all the time. When he came down to the defense, we knew there was a problem. We would say, "Here he comes."

Sometimes he would drop to his knees and pound his hat on the

When ***CLEMSON** University plays in a bowl game, most of their fans pay their hotel and restaurant tabs with $2 bills to show their economic impact . . . and increase their chances of a future invitation.

ground. And here on this day with these prospects visiting, he got ticked off, and he dropped to his knees. I think he was going to start pounding the ground. He got down there, and he realized then what was going on and that those prospects were there. So he was there for a little bit, and he turned to the other coaches and said, "You know. It's amazing what you can see down here. You could really do a good job of coaching down here on your knees." So he made the rest of the staff get down on their knees for an *hour*. Some of the older coaches were there with him and one of them said, "Boy, I had to call and get somebody to help me up. We were down there for one hour, and all I saw were buttholes."

My first exposure to Woody was in 1951. I was a high school student in Sandusky, We had some friends invite me to go see Ohio State play. I couldn't get in the car quick enough. I had never been there to see a game. I went with them, not even knowing who they were going to play. I just was thrilled to have the opportunity to go. That was Woody's first year. Who do they play? Indiana . . . and Indiana beat them.

We would often hear that comment made about "We'll never, ever lose again to Indiana." I never dreamed that someday I would be the head coach at Indiana. When Indiana beat Ohio State in '87, 36 years later, Indiana had not beaten Ohio State since 1951. I shared that story with the players when we got in there on Friday. We always came down to the field and walked around. I pointed out where I had sat in 1951. I said, "Tomorrow we're going to make history. It's been 36 years since we've beaten Ohio State, so tomorrow we're going to make history." We had worked hard on that game. We'd come so close to beating them the year before. Earle Bruce was there then as the head coach, and we lost to them by just a marginal point.

I wasn't into moral victories. We put time and preparation in, and we were ready. To go in and beat Ohio State there in Columbus is not an easy matter. I'll never forget that we were tied 10-10 at halftime and then we came back and won 31-10. The kids were really bearing down that second half and came through with a good victory.

Earle Bruce called it the "darkest day in Ohio State history." I'm not sure what I thought about his remarks. We had lived through some dark days together in that first year under Woody. I was so pleased and proud of our players and staff for what we'd accomplished.

CAMPUS TOUR OF DUTY

BOB SEVEL

Among Bob Sevel has served as "the time-out guy" for Cleveland Browns football games and worked a dozen Super Bowls. But his most memorable time-out happened off the football field and on the campus of Ohio State, when the former OSU student and tour guide was taking a group of kids around and an unexpected attraction popped up.

It was the summer of 1983. It was a hot summer afternoon. A bunch of underprivileged children—campers—from Newark, Ohio, showed up. They met me, and I hopped on their van and gave a campus tour. With kids, you're trying to show them what kids like—Ohio Stadium, the campus. One of the things I'd always show them, and one of our famous buildings, is the Orton Hall Bell Tower. They like it because of the gargoyles and the bells and everything.

As we pulled up, off of Neil Avenue, I saw Woody Hayes. He's unmistakable. If you went to Ohio State, and you've seen him, you know it's him. I looked. I thought I was the only one who noticed him, but apparently not. I asked them to pull the van up. They pulled it up as close as they could to the entrance walkway to the Faculty Club next to the Orton Hall. I popped out of the van and said, "Hold on right here. Put your flashers on."

Now this is about five years after he had left coaching. I approached Coach Hayes from behind and said, "Excuse me, Coach." He turned around to shake my hand, and he had a cane with him. I said, "I'm sorry to bother you, Coach." He said, "That's OK, how are you?" He was in a hurry. I said, "I hate to bother you. I'm a campus tour guide. We have a bunch of underprivileged campers on the van."

Before I could say any more, he spun around, lifted the cane off the ground like he didn't need it and marched over to the van. In the meantime, all the children, the driver and the chaperone all come

"They knew this was Woody Hayes. I was surprised the kids knew that."

out of the van. They knew this was Woody Hayes. I was surprised the kids knew that. Again, 1983, it had been five years since he'd coached.

He walked over and eyeballed them. He looked around, stuck his neck out—he could be pretty animated, if you recall. He said, "Where are you all from?" I already told him, but he wanted to ask them. They all said, "*Nerk,* Ohio." He said, "One of our finest linemen ..." and he goes on to name off these great people from Newark, Ohio, who had played for him. Then he gave them a life lesson.

He said, "Kids, it's very important to be on time. I'm going to be late for a lunch appointment. I don't want to be late, but I'm very excited to meet you." He's telling the kids this. This is how Jim Tressel is, too. It's like it was *his* privilege to meet *them.*

He said, "I've got one question for you. Who are we going to beat this year?" It was like out of *Rudy* or **ROCKNE*** or some Notre Dame movie, I know. They said, "Michigan." I was so shocked by their response, at that age, on our campus, though I know they're Ohioans and only 35 miles away. They all knew what was important.

He shook all their hands. He thanked them. Said, "Go Bucks," spun around, still not using his cane, and marched right down this very nice brick walkway, up the stairs and into the Faculty Club. Nobody said anything until he disappeared. Then one of the guys said, "That was awesome!" All the kids went, "Yeah!"

It was probably five or seven minutes' worth, but Woody went from this crippled old man struggling up toward the steps of the Faculty Club to the spry young man who came over to give these kids a pep talk, as if they needed one. I think when I said "underprivileged" and "kids," that spun him around. I didn't say "Ohio State fans." I didn't say anybody had a camera, wanted an autograph. I didn't say we were 10TV of Columbus. Not anything like that.

When Knute ***ROCKNE** and seven others were killed in a 1931 plane crash, it was the largest disaster in U.S. aviation history up until that time.

It was very much a private moment in time with Coach Hayes. It was spontaneous. It was genuine. Those kids—I hope they don't forget it. I just wonder if they think about that. I had met him other times. It was not the first time I've encountered him. But to see him in action, focused on the kids, was an awesome, awesome life experience.

I've met Michael Jordan. I've met every famous athlete. I've met every Ohio State coach in my time. I'm not bragging. I don't know of anybody who had a presence quite like Woody Hayes. You knew he was a walking legend. He was, and somehow or other he still is 20 years after his death.

It's not because of the X's and O's. It's because Woody really cared about people, and he touched people. Again, I think Coach Tressel is doing the same thing. He knows what he represents. He knows that more people know who he is than they do our governor. Coach Bear Bryant was often quoted, "It's tough to rally around a math class."

FOOTBALL IN OHIO* involves all generations and both genders, all backgrounds. Of all the things considered, it's something that binds people most, especially Ohio State football. It binds the whole state. Miami's really good, and Bowling Green and Kent State have great programs, but I think all those people consider themselves Buckeyes, too. I think Ohio U people are the only ones who are sour on that idea. Everywhere Ohio University grads go, people say, "Oh, you're the Buckeyes." "No, we're not the Buckeyes. We were founded in 1804, 64 years before Ohio State." That's the chip on their shoulder. . . .

We have an annual Football Appreciation banquet in Cleveland. It started with Woody Hayes years ago to celebrate the football team after the Michigan game. It's always the Tuesday after the Michigan game. It was Coach Tressel's first time up as head coach.

We're setting up for this banquet, expecting 600 people, and there are a lot of things to do last minute. It's not your home or something. You get in there and have a lot of volunteers. As we were setting up, an hour before the banquet started, Coach Tressel arrived by himself.

NFL ***FOOTBALLS** are made in Ada, ***OHIO**. Each team uses one thousand per year. The balls are made from cowhide, not pigskin. The balls used by kickers are different and are marked with a "K".

Usually they come with players and coaches *and come in late*. It's just always a scramble. We all greeted him, "Oh, gosh, great season, Coach, great win over Michigan, thanks so much." Took a couple of pictures. Some people had some items signed. We had memorabilia we were auctioning off. That took 10-15 minutes. He said, "Is there anything I can do?" He could see we were scrambling. One of the women in the club was a bossy lady. She said, "Coach, if you could, put these banquet glasses on the table."

He takes off his sport coat, and he's out there putting banquet glasses on the table. There are other people in our club. They should be there, but they can't all be there right at 5:00. They're working. We all understand that. Here's a guy who just beat Michigan, finished his first year as coach at Ohio State. He's a Clevelander. He gets it. He knows. He's helping us set up a banquet for him and his players. He doesn't have to do that. I want to say *he shouldn't do that*. But he's not above or beyond that, and it's not just the impression he gives, he really feels that way, like "if you need me, I'm here—I can help. I want to help." He's about helping others.

I remember looking at one of the old-timers in the club, and I said, "This is where the legend begins. This is the type of thing we're going to remember, what kind of person this guy is." It doesn't mean he's gonna win a lot of football games and all, but you know he's a good guy and you know he cares and you know he's not above doing that. Most guys would just stand there. But he's not self-important. He's a Clevelander. His parents raised him right. He cares.

He just happens to be the most high-profile person in our state, I would think, on a national basis. I know we've got governors, and I know we've got famous singers and all these other people, and pro athletes, but I'd say he's the one. But he gets it. He acts like we would all like to think we could act in that position.

I would say No. 1, his faith is where he gets his strength. He wears a "What would Jesus do?" red wristband under his watch. It's very subtle, but it's there. You can look in the photos and find it. So faith is a big part of who he is. He knows there's more than just football, but he's focused on it.

DOWN AT THE CORNER OF WHAT AND IF

JOHN COOPER JR.

He has not been to an Ohio State football game since his father was fired from his head coaching position following the 2000 season, but 45-year-old John Cooper Jr.—a sales rep for Continental Office Furniture in Columbus—has plenty of warm memories from the Cooper era at Ohio State, including how his dad handled the tough times.

I don't go to any of the Ohio State games now. I watch them on TV, and I'll go down to tailgate, but I haven't been in to a game since my dad left OSU. I don't follow them real close—just kind of a casual fan now.

I was born in **IOWA*** in '62 right after Dad got finished playing at Iowa State. I claim that I grew up in Tulsa—that was the longest we were at one place before here. I went to high school and college in Tulsa. I followed Mom and Dad around, so I've moved around to all the places where Dad worked. I was just a kid, so I didn't really have much choice until we came here. Then, I *did* have a choice, but I decided I wanted to come with them.

When I was in Tulsa, one of the real good high schools was Memorial. We won state my senior year in football in the big-school division. It's the only time my school's ever done that so it was a lot of fun. After playing football in high school, I ended up playing for Dad at Tulsa. I don't have many good stories about playing for my dad, only because I was a defensive back. Pop pretty much stayed on the offensive side

> In 1939, the Heisman Trophy winner was Nile Kinnick of ***IOWA**. He is the only Heisman Trophy winner to have his university's football stadium named after him. In 1934, Nile Kinnick was Bob Feller's catcher on an American Legion baseball team.

most of the time. In college, most of your contact is with your position coach, so I really didn't have a whole lot of interaction with Dad on the practice field.

When Dad moved to Arizona State, I had played at Tulsa four years, but I had redshirted a year, so I did have a year left. I had been football-crazy from the time I was a little kid. Quite honestly, I was a little tired of it at that point. I just decided I'd had enough, and I went ahead and went with Dad when he moved to Arizona State. I had 12 hours left and I took my hours from ASU, but my degree is from Tulsa. I transferred them back.

I was 25 when we went to Ohio State. I was in sales in Arizona. Then, when I came here to Columbus, I stayed in sales and started being a commercial real estate broker. I knew a little bit about Ohio State football but not the full extent of how deep it goes. Dad was an assistant in the mid-'70s at Kentucky. He'd tell me stories about Woody Hayes and about Coach Hayes putting a little rip in his hat in the locker room and then going out to the practice field and tearing his hat in two, and throwing his watch down, and some of those famous tirade he used to do. I had heard a lot about Coach Hayes from my dad back then. I knew of Ohio State but I didn't know how deep scarlet-and-gray blood runs here, and I sure learned in a hurry.

I sporadically went to the practice sessions, although not as much as you might think. I went to every game. Part of Dad's contract was that he could bring my mother and my sister, Cindy, and me to every game. We went to every game with him, and I held his headphone cord. I was the cord carrier for 12 years. It was great. I loved it. It's the greatest job in the world.

It was cool, because I got to be three feet away from Dad all the time, during every game, every second. I got to experience a lot of cool things there with him—winning the **ROSE BOWL*** was one of the highlights of

The ***ROSE BOWL** Parade originally had nothing to do with the Rose Bowl football game. It was a celebration in Pasadena for the ripening of the oranges. . . . The 1942 Rose Bowl game between Oregon State and Duke was played in Durham, North Carolina because of fears that the Rose Bowl in Pasadena could be attacked like Pearl Harbor was three weeks earlier.

my life. I got to be right in the middle of all the action. I knew everything that was going on. I was his shadow. I'd follow him to the postgame press conference and listen to what he said.

After losses, it still was fun. I was always amazed how Dad could remember. He would remember in great detail everything that had unfolded. He could recite each drive and almost every play of every drive. I was always impressed by the way he would answer tough questions. He was always good about coming up with reasons why he did what he did, and a lot of times it would even surprise me what he said, because it would be something I didn't hear him say and wouldn't have considered myself. But he knew what he was doing.

My dad was always the same—as the coach, and as a dad. The first thing I think about is that we had several years that were real tough. My dad was under a lot of pressure many times, a bunch of times. In fact, I know there were four or five different games that were must-win games. If we didn't win, Dad was going to get fired. One of those, unfortunately, was the last one, but I think there were four or five of those that he weathered throughout his career.

No matter what happened, he was always the same person at home. He would come home and be loving to my sister and my mom and me. You would never be able to tell the amount of pressure he was under, because he would keep it inside. My dad has so much strength. I don't know how he did it. Little things that happen to me at work—I know I can't get them out of my head. Probably somebody could recognize that I'm stressed, but, man, I sure couldn't see it in my dad.

He gets all this from his upbringing. Dad was brought up real poor, eight or 10 miles outside of Knoxville, Tennessee, in a town called Powell. He had five brothers and sisters and they lived in a three-room shack, where they didn't have running water. The house ended up burning down, and we've got very few pictures of it. It had a cistern where they collected rainwater off the roof to run into a large concrete bowl. They had an outhouse. So they were from a real poor beginning. Dad was always trying to better himself, trying to be frugal and do the right thing. I've got to point back to that as the source of his strength—that journey he had to make to end up being a success himself.

When Dad was a boy in Tennessee, he used to sneak into the Tennessee football games. That's when Coach Neyland was the coach there.

In fact, he would sneak into some of the games, and he also would sell concessions at games. He would look at football as a way out of rural Tennessee and as a way that a humble guy could be a success.

When we first moved here, Dad did some commercials for a local grocery store chain, Big Bear. He included my mom and my sister and me as part of the commercials. He told Big Bear he wanted them to include us. That initial part was fun. I got a kick out of it at first, but as time went by and as we were here longer, I wished that I was more anonymous. I felt uncomfortable when I got attention because of who my dad was. I thought to myself, "I haven't done anything. I'm just a kid. It just so happens that my dad's a coach, but I haven't done anything myself." I just felt uncomfortable if I got any kind of attention because of who Dad was.

When people would criticize my dad, it was pretty tough—even when holding the cord on the sideline at the games, as I walked off the field with my dad, a couple of steps behind him. There are people who leave their seat and go position themselves down by the locker room so they can yell at a player or the coach. If they're disappointed about something, there are people who want to make you feel as disappointed as they are. People would yell the nastiest things you could think of. It was really tough not to lash back out at them. I learned pretty early on that was something I couldn't do and something that would be a bad situation for me, so I had to maintain my cool. It was very difficult at times. I've really heard some ugly things.

At times, we got some "For Sale" signs in the yard. It wasn't too bad. Some people did take some trees one time, but I'm not necessarily sure it was anger over a loss. That might have been just general vandalism. There wasn't ever anything that was too bad. We got some hate mail, but it was never anything that was threatening. It was just telling Dad how crappy he was, etc.

I think my dad is very content and very happy now with life after coaching. My sister has a 6-year-old daughter and a 4-year-old daughter, and they live right next door to Mom and Dad. Mom and Dad are very active in raising the granddaughters, and he just loves it. Of course, after he hasn't been coaching, he's played a heck of a lot more golf. He's getting pretty good. He's a real good athlete.

He helps the Cincinnati Bengals out, particularly prior to the NFL

Draft. He helps them evaluate college players. In fact, I rode with him a couple of years ago to South Bend, Indiana, to watch the Notre Dame guys work out on their pro day. He'll go to Notre Dame, and he'll go to Tennessee, and he'll go to Ohio and Pittsburgh and West Virginia, Kent or Akron—he'll go around to some of those schools and watch the pro days and help them evaluate draftees.

When I was a little boy, Dad had a wooden box where he would put stuff that he carried in his pocket—fingernail clippers, wallet, hair comb, whatever. In that box was a buckeye. I remember, as a little boy, asking him, "What's this little thing?" He said, "That's a buckeye. Put that in your pocket, and it brings you good luck." Dad always had that buckeye in that box. This was back in the mid-'70s, long before Ohio State was on the radar. His dad had told him that buckeyes were good luck.

And then, how ironic that later on my dad ended up being coach of the Buckeyes. He would carry a buckeye in his pocket, even back in the day. I used to carry one, too. I had one I put in my pocket every game day. I had a special one I had picked out that I would use, and I put that one in my pocket all the time. I still have it, but I just don't carry it like I used to.

> "I remember, as a little boy, asking him, "What's this little thing?" He said, "That's a buckeye. Put that in your pocket, and it brings you good luck."

Dad tells a story that, when he was a coach, he received a call. There was a person who had donated large sums of money to the athletic program. He was in the hospital, and this was in the middle of the week during the season. This man was going to undergo surgery the next day. He was in really bad shape—on his deathbed—and they wanted to know if Dad could go see him. Dad went to the hospital, and he's in the room there. The man was lying in the bed. Dad said he pulled out his lucky buckeye and said, "Here Mr. So-and-so, I want you to have my buckeye." The man's wife was there in the room. She said, "Oh, no, no, Coach, you better keep that. You'll need that Saturday."

A COACH IS A TEACHER
WITH A DEATH WISH

RUDY HUBBARD

He walked away from coaching in 1985, not sure if coaching was actually walking away from him. But former OSU running back and assistant coach Rudy Hubbard braved bigotry, closed minds and sometimes even the threat of the wrath of Woody Hayes to deliver two-time Heisman Trophy winner Archie Griffin to Ohio State.

When I look back at the career of Archie Griffin, I see class and greatness, but I also know how close it came to never happening, at least not at Ohio State. Archie was playing at Eastmoor High School in Columbus. I saw some film from his junior year. I had done my student teaching at Eastmoor when I was coming out of college, so I got to know Coach Bob Stewart and some of the other coaches there. That's how it all started.

Initially, I really didn't have a recruiting area like all the other OSU assistant coaches had. And when I got one, mine was not a really good fertile area. I ended up with southern Ohio—Gallipolis and all that. Those are areas that Ohio State traditionally had not been recruiting that heavily in. It didn't matter to me. I didn't think of it that way in the beginning. I just wanted to have an area like everybody else. This was in the late 1960s and early '70s. I couldn't find a place to stay the first couple of times I went down there, but I didn't think anything about it. Everybody kept telling me they didn't have any vacancies. Finally, I saw a black fellow walking down the street, and I asked him where I could find a hotel room. He said, "Well, it won't be in any of those places you've been trying. You'd better go down to this place in the black neighborhood." I could not believe it in Ohio.

I was really, really upset. I ended up staying in that little place, but it was filthy. Woody Hayes hit the ceiling when I went back and told him.

He knew how upset I was. He told me, "You won't have to go back there. We just won't recruit the area." So, I ended up with Maryland, Washington, D.C.—and we hadn't been recruiting those areas either—and some of the local areas, which would be the Columbus area.

I ended up recruiting Archie for Ohio State. I started getting a lot of local people involved—people who wanted to see Archie stay there. This was way before we knew he was going to be as good as he was. A lot of the people I got involved always wanted to have some kind of relationship with Ohio State but hadn't been able to. Some of them had actually graduated from Ohio State, so it was that kind of thing. In the process of recruiting Archie, we were able to generate some friendships that still last.

Archie's whole family was class. He had a couple of older brothers who had played. Then he had an awesome mother and dad. His dad was a hard worker. His mom was a dedicated housewife. They were just classy people. Archie was pretty much ready to go to Northwestern. He had a relationship up there with one of the guys who had traditionally done a good job for **NORTHWESTERN*** recruiting. He was a black fellow I knew about. He wasn't a paid coach, but he helped Northwestern recruit. They let him have almost like a coach's responsibility when it came to recruiting some of the black players.

Archie was a class guy. He wanted to be considered "not just a jock." That was what we had going against us. He felt like Ohio State in some territories was being considered a football factory, and he didn't want any part of that. He wanted to get a good education, and that was first and foremost what he felt like Northwestern would provide. Obviously, they had done a great job on him. We were able to get all that turned around. A lot of people pitched in and helped out. Everything was above board. We tried to get people who knew the family to let them know that we wanted him to stay home. We hadn't done a good job of recruiting local talent.

That was one of the things Woody always watched out for. He always

Former ***NORTHWESTERN** running back and TV color analyst, Mike Adamle, was the last NFL running back who wore a number lower than "20" . . . his number was "1". . . . His father, Tony Adamle, starred at OSU and played six years for the Browns.

felt like if you got somebody local and they didn't play, the pressure would be real great on both Ohio State and the player.

"That was it. Archie ended up with more than 200 yards that game . . ."

Early in Archie's career, we were going through a period there where we had come off of a Jim Otis and John Brockington and Leo Hayden-type players. We were just loaded with talent. We were coming out of that. Those guys came in and as sophomores in 1968 helped win a national championship, and now they were gone. We were going through a period there where we had a guy named Morris Bradshaw, and Elmer Lippert and Archie Griffin—those were the top tailbacks. Morris Bradshaw was a rangy guy, not real tough, but real fast. Elmer Lippert was a tough guy, but not real fast, a good ball player. Cornelius Greene was the quarterback. I had recruited him, too. These were all the same year—Archie, Cornelius, Woody Roach. I got Cornelius and Woody Roach from Washington, D.C.

The first game we played in 1972, Archie's freshman year, he got in the game right at the tail end. He ran hard but fumbled the ball and then the game ended. He got maybe two or three carries against Iowa. So that wasn't good, because Woody hated fumbles. We go into the next game against the University of North Carolina. They were tough that year. We started Morris Bradshaw. Elmer Lippert was listed as No. 2 on the depth chart. Archie was No. 3. How we got to that, I don't know. I didn't think that was the way it should have been. What happened was I was coaching the running backs, but Woody, before he hired me, coached the running backs. He had a hard time giving that up, so he made decisions a lot.

We're right in the ballgame, but we couldn't move the football. I kept telling our offensive coordinator in the press box that we were going to lose the ballgame unless we went right to Archie Griffin. So he told Coach Hayes that I said to put Archie Griffin in the ballgame. That was it. Archie ended up with more than 200 yards that game . . . and the rest was history.

I caught it now. Mr. Lippert met me after the ballgame. He wanted to tell me a few things . . . and he did. So I had to listen to that. And I did. But he was right. We had his son listed as No. 2 on the depth chart, and we went right by him. It wasn't fair, but we won the ballgame. From then on, Archie just took over—he just exploded

When I was a player, there were still things that were disturbing. Whenever we would come back to start camp every year, you had to run a six-minute mile. You can go from high school to high school all across the state of Ohio and many other states and you can count on both hands how many black kids ran miles. You just didn't see that. So to put that kind of test on us, I thought, was racist. But I didn't say "racist" at the time.

We would come back, and we would all do so poorly. Woody would be standing there at the finish line. He would start counting, 5:55, and he would get really, really slow. If he got to 5:59, it looked like it would be about two minutes he'd be on 5:59. He'd be trying to hope we'd make it. We used to laugh about that thing, because none of us would make it, and he was doing all he could. We would all be in a bunch struggling.

Some of the white guys did have a problem with it, but a lot of them didn't. When it came to the first day of practice, most of the black guys were not starting. We were put on the depth chart based on how we fared with that six-minute mile. Then, two or three days after that, the depth chart would change. I just thought that was all crazy, because you didn't have nowhere close to a mile to run while you were playing.

I grew up in a home where my dad was my idol, and I didn't need Woody for that. Woody was a great guy. I trusted him, and I believed in him as a coach. But he had a temper. My dad never hit me. But I've seen Woody swing at guys. One time, he swung at me, and it was really on. We had some issues with that. I'd always sworn that if a man other than my dad swung at me, it was going to be "all she wrote." We had to deal with that. Woody and I dealt with that.

All in all when I left, I was upset, and I let him know that. I said it publicly. He ended up being the speaker at an appreciation banquet at my hometown once I had left. I hadn't graduated—the season was just over. I let Woody have it at the banquet. Woody was a funny guy. He acted like he didn't even hear it. I was amazed. I really didn't care. I didn't think I would ever see him again. I knew I had to go back to school, but I didn't have to go back to practice.

I had seen other guys go back and finish school and not have anything else to do with Woody. I didn't anticipate any kind of relationship. I let him have it, man, but he acted like he didn't even hear it. He's a dedicated guy to whoever plays for him or coaches for him. It was tough to hurt him.

It was about a week after that, I got a call from him. He said he wanted to talk to me in his office. I'm thinking he's going to be upset, and we're going to have it out. I was scared of him, too. I didn't know what was going to go on. I went to see what he wanted, and he offered me the job. It just blew me away. And he offers me a job as an assistant coach at Ohio State.

I was the first black assistant in any sport at Ohio State, certainly in football. No question. I was one of the first in the Big 10 in football. And, I was reminded of it a lot, and not always in a nice way. As a matter of fact, I was told not to take the job. Somebody from St. Petersburg, Florida, wrote me a letter. I still have the letter. I had given it to my mother, and she pulled it out two or three years ago. Everything was typed, and they had their last name and first initial—there were four people on it. I didn't research it to see who these people could have been. At the time, my response and my dad's was that he brought a pistol down there for me. That was the way we handled stuff. I wasn't about to let anybody do something to me.

A lot of times, he didn't want to go home, and we'd be riding around. Just being around Woody, you picked up stuff about life that nobody else would be giving—things he had thought through. I don't know where he got it all, but he was a very wise man. A lot that he talked to the team and the coaches about, and things I picked up from him, I'm still using. It wasn't something he was just pulling out of a hat somewhere. It was good stuff. A lot of times when things get tough for me, I can remember some of the things he would say, and that puts me right back where I need to be.

He told me that the only security you ever really have in life is in your own ability to succeed. I say that to myself all the time. In other words, you've got to work at it, man. You've got to put something in. I could say stuff like that for at least a half hour. I'm using it on a regular basis. I don't think there are a whole lot of people I've been around that could have given me that much information that would be as helpful over all the years.

TAKE THIS JOB AND LOVE IT

BILL CONLEY

*He has drifted into the media now—doing radio, television, Internet chats, public speaking. And Bill Conley has even written a book (*Buckeye Bumper Crops*). He thinks the coaching bug might be out of him finally, but in some moments he's not so sure. What is definitive is that the former walk-on under Coach Woody Hayes made an indelible imprint on three different coaching regimes—Bruce, Cooper, Tressel—as an assistant coach and one of the nation's top recruiters.*

For being involved in recruiting for so much of my coaching career, it's interesting that I wasn't really involved with it as a player. I just loved the game of football. When I was in high school, I went to a game at Ohio State with my high school coach. After that game, I knew I wanted to play there. So I walked on. After my second year, I got put on scholarship.

At that time, a lot of freshmen would walk on. We'd start off with well over 100 guys. By the time it was all said and done, four of us actually made it through all four years. Of course, it was quite an experience. We won the national championship my freshman year in 1968. During that time period—1968-71—we won three Big 10 championships or co-championships. So, it was a good time.

There were a lot more scholarship players at that time. The coaches had to find some way to whittle the walk-on numbers down. That was before the test scores were really qualifiers to get into school. They decided to pick an arbitrary ACT score. If you were below it, you were gone. If you were above, you were OK. I was above it. It's one of those things. It's a tough job, because you're paying your own way, and you're trying to go to school, and you're playing football, but you're not getting any financial aid. You have to get student loans. It's just tough. You just hung with it.

As I got into coaching, I didn't start out with a plan to get so much into recruiting. I was a head coach at four different high schools in Ohio. In the '80s, when I went to Ohio State as linebackers coach, that was the first time, really, I'd recruited. When Earle Bruce got fired after the 1987 season, I went back to high school for a few years.

In '91, I came back to Ohio State as recruiting coordinator under John Cooper. The thing that was unique in my situation was that I had been a high school coach in the state and knew all the coaches pretty much in the state of Ohio. At that time, John Cooper had been at Ohio State for a few years, and, really, the relations weren't going great, because John, as good a guy as he was and as good a coach as he was, it was tough for him. He was a guy from Tennessee coming into the state of Ohio and didn't know a lot about the traditions of Ohio high school football.

Eddie George is the recruit I have the most pride in. He was a guy nobody had been recruiting except the University of Louisville. He was at Fork Union (Virginia) Military Academy. We had a student trainer, Danny Osman, who had gone to that school. He stopped by on the practice field one day when I was out there with my defensive ends. He said, "Coach, are you recruiting my buddy from Fork Union?" I said, "Who's your buddy?" He said, "His name is Eddie George." I said, "No, I've never heard of a George."

This was Eddie's last year in school, his senior year, and I'm talking about September now. It's not like the year before or the spring before his senior year when some kids fall through the cracks. I asked what position he played, and he said, "He's a running back." I thought, as recruiting coordinator for Ohio State, I knew who all the great running backs were. And I'd never heard of him.

I said, "Danny, come in tomorrow and give me the coach's name and number, and I'll call him," thinking the kid won't show up again—this is probably just a buddy of his that he's trying to get a scholarship for.

I called the coach at Fork Union and asked for a film. I asked who was recruiting him, and he said, "Just Louisville." I thought, "The kid can't be very good." I got the film, and about 10 days later, I looked at it. To be honest with you, I was going to watch six plays and turn it off and send it back with a nice letter for the coach. I just thought, if nobody was recruiting him, he can't be good enough. I watched the film and thought, "He's a big son of a gun for a tailback." He's running over people and running for touchdowns. I went, "Holy smoke! Who is this guy?" I called the coach back and got another film.

Bottom line, we started recruiting him, and as soon as we started recruiting him, then Notre Dame, Michigan, Penn State and everybody else started recruiting him. He visited Louisville the first week of December. He visited Ohio State the second week of December and committed to us on the visit.

He came to Ohio State with 15 tailbacks starting off. We had a bunch of good guys in front of him—Robert Smith, Butler By'not'e, Raymont Harris, Joe Montgomery. He was the 15th tailback and worked his way up. The great story is against Illinois, one of the few early starts he had, he fumbled twice inside the 5-yard line, and we lost that game. His senior year, he comes back and gets the same Illinois team in our stadium and rushes for over 300 yards and sets a school record. Then a couple of weeks later, he wins the Heisman Trophy.

"The recruiting of Andy Katzenmoyer was interesting . . ."

When he came in, Eddie was about 6-foot-3, about 210-215 pounds. By the time he played his senior year, he was around 232. He ran a 4.47 in the 40-yard dash at the pro combine. He was pretty impressive. He was a self-made guy. He worked out twice a day, with just a great work ethic, and was a good student—majored in landscape architectural design, which is a really tough major. He was just an unbelievable kid.

The recruiting of Andy Katzenmoyer was interesting, because of his ending up with the uniform No. 45, which, of course, was Archie Griffin's number. We hadn't retired numbers at Ohio State. We had so many great players so we had never done it. What happened with Andy Katzenmoyer was that in the process of recruiting, Coach Cooper told him he could have No. 45. Then John called Archie and wanted to make sure it was OK. Archie said, "If it helps get the kid, the No. 1 linebacker in the country, then go right ahead." That's what happened. Since then, of course, those numbers have been retired.

The thing about Andy Katzenmoyer was he was a very dedicated athlete. And he was a good student. People think he wasn't a very good student, but Andy was a very good student. He was quiet. He never said a lot. People took that as maybe he wasn't the brightest bulb in the lamp, which was completely not true. He was a smart, intelligent kid. He had some aspirations of going pro early, obviously. His academics slid a little bit, but not of any big significance. It was just one of those things that was really blown out of proportion—completely blown out of proportion.

As I go back through the coaches I worked for and their recruiting styles, Earle Bruce was really great at selling the Ohio State tradition. He had played for and graduated at Ohio State. He knew all the traditions. He was great at selling that. He had a great relationship with the high school coaches. That was huge.

John Cooper, his greatest thing was that he was smart enough to know that we needed to completely revamp the recruiting process, because things had changed. The Internet had just gotten started. He really turned that over to me to organize—to putting together letters, to setting up recruiting weekends, to publicizing our camp, which became really important. Our camp grew to be one of the largest in the country. That was a huge part of our success with recruiting. We had a lot of those kids at our camp.

There's no magic to recruiting—it's establishing relationships. If you can establish a relationship, it becomes tough for that kid to tell you no. The more you get them on campus, the harder it is for them to go somewhere else. We really emphasize that. We emphasize unofficial visits more than before. John was really good at understanding that the recruiting processes were changing.

When Joe Paterno takes off his glasses, does his nose come off too?

WE INTERRUPT THIS FAMILY TO BRING YOU THE FOOTBALL SEASON

JIM HERBSTREIT

Jim Herbstreit never transitioned into TV, as his highly recognized son Kirk has done. But the first half of the rare father-son Buckeye captain double has the distinction of serving as an assistant coach under both Bo Schembechler and Woody Hayes. He also, in fact, was on the same staff with both of them. A consultant now in the mass appraisal industry and resident of Chagrin Falls, Ohio, Jim Herbstreit reflects on a couple of generations of OSU lore.

Some people might not realize I actually have three children—Terri, John and Kirk. And my daughter was probably the best athlete among them. She had a lot of shin-splint problems. In today's world, she would have been an outstanding track athlete and soccer player. But the girls in high school just weren't organized very well back then.

Kirk, who is eight years younger than Terri and the child most people know, was a super, super athlete from the time he was old enough to move. My son Johnwas in the middle—four years older than Kirk, four years younger than Terri.

Having been a captain at Ohio State, I was determined not to hang a lot of pictures and plaques. I didn't want them to feel the need to match their father. I didn't push them. Kirk just came upon it naturally. He had a lot of natural ability in two sports, baseball and football. He just moved along and I just worked with him.

My other son played sports and had some quickness and speed but was smaller, like I was, and really took an interest in other things. I'd say they

"Dad, let's stop this. I don't want to go up to Michigan this weekend and go through the motions."

were all three athletic. Only Kirk really got into organized sports in a way that showed any real interest. I might have hindered the other two, because I was determined they would be interested in science, they would want to play the trumpet or play the piano or something.

When Kirk was in high school in Centerville, he had two pretty good years. When it got around to recruiting, the reality was that the real recruiting had been done when he was 5 years old. But he did go through it anyway. I didn't have to say a word. All I said to him was "This recruiting can get screwy."

Earle Bruce was the coach during Kirk's senior year in high school. But at the end of the season, his senior year, Earle was fired. Kirk was being recruited by Penn State and Michigan, and Southern Cal. He had four or five legitimate considerations, but he wanted to go to Ohio State. He was supposed to go to Michigan a couple of Saturdays before Christmas. Tennessee was doing a good job of recruiting him too, I thought.

He said, "Dad, let's stop this. I don't want to go up to Michigan this weekend and go through the motions. I know where I want to go." So I called the athletic director, Jim Jones. I said, "The kid knows where he wants to go." He said, "Well, give me a few days, because we're about to announce our new coach." Kirk actually had almost committed to Ohio State without the head coach being installed. Right after that, within the first day of John Cooper's reign, John called him and Kirk committed.

My own recruiting process was much different, in large part because I had to sell myself to Ohio State and not the other way around. I went to a small school in the Valley, just north of Cincinnati, in Reading. Reading and Lockland were little mill towns. I weighed 155 pounds so I was small, but in today's world I probably would weigh, say, 175. Our big people were 270, so it's comparable except for the huge difference in strength and mobility today. Kentucky recruited me. Purdue took one look, but I was pretty much a MAC recruit. I told Johnny Pont I was going to come to Miami of Ohio, but I told him there was only one thing that would keep me from it. I had a great love for Ohio State, and if I happened to get a shot at that, I probably would go there. My high school coach was an old Ohio Stater—a hurdler, back in 1926. He never had a kid in 30 years go to Columbus. He put the fire in me about Ohio State, but I didn't have any delusions about whether or not I was going to be recruited.

My senior year my high school team won the state baseball championship with pitcher Claude Osteen, who later went on to a great Major League career. But I also ran track, and the same weekend I had to run both the 100 and 200—it was the 220 then—in the state track meet. Both of those events were on the Ohio State campus in Columbus. My high school coach was working with Woody Hayes on films and told him to make sure he was in the stadium when I ran.

In those days, the baseball field was within jogging distance of the stadium. I was running back and forth between the stadiums. I finished fifth in the 100 in the state meet and third in the 200 behind Otis Paul Drayton, an Olympian who won a silver and a gold medal in the '64 Olympics. All that running back and forth impressed Woody. In fact, Woody was at the finish line of the 200. Then he invited me up the next week and made the scholarship offer. Even with my lack of weight, he offered me a scholarship. I hesitated about 15 seconds, just to not be too easy. It's been a great love of my life—the university and playing for Woody and having a kid come along and be a captain there too.

And yet when I first got to Ohio State, that first couple of weeks, it looked out of reach. I remember walking back to the dorm and thinking maybe I bit off more than I could chew. Then, when I got out on the field at our first scrimmage, I remember walking back and shoving my helmet up on my head and saying, "I can do this." I know I never mentioned my size to myself ever again.

I had a chance to play pro football after my college career, especially after getting two interceptions in the East-West Shrine Game. Money in those days was not a big enticement. So I went into coaching.

I was the first guy Woody ever selected directly out of college to coach a position. I was the defensive backfield coach in '61 and '62. Then I went with Bo Schembechler to Miami in '63 and '64. Then I got out of coaching. Bill Mallory asked me to come back when he got the job at Miami of Ohio after the 1968 season. I went back for another couple of seasons, and then I had a wife who was pretty ill. It seemed as if coaching was not going to be something that I was going to be able to do. I left coaching after a year with Mallory. I missed it, probably still even miss it a little bit now.

There was a huge difference going from being a player for Woody to being a coach for Woody. It was like going from a union worker to management. I used to get in trouble with Woody because I was so naive. Woody had an annual gathering at his house on Memorial Day. He thought this was a great thing to do. I didn't know it at the time, but the reason he had these was to keep the players out of trouble before finals. So at my very first staff meeting, he said, "I want to do a little something different this year." He asked for ideas.

Bo was sitting there and he said, "Why don't we take them to a park and let them bring their girlfriends?" That was lukewarm with Woody. Some guys didn't have an opinion. It got to me. I was sitting toward Woody at the end of the table. I said, "Well, why don't you just not have it? Woody, you have no idea how much those guys don't like coming."

God, did he get off on me. He had a fit. He said, "They'll be going home, and they'll have their girlfriends out and before you know it, we'll be in trouble. He won't be able to come back because she's pregnant, and they've got finals next week." Bo used to be the peacemaker. He said, "Take it easy."

I was just trying to be honest. The players hated that party. It takes a young guy time to know that there are rules that you haven't really seen sometimes and it takes you a little while to understand.

The experience of coaching those two years with Woody was really incredible, because I had Bo Schembechler in the room, and I had some older coaches on that staff. Of all those who had ever coached for Woody, his favorite was Schembechler.

You would probably think that there would be some bombastic stuff going on—having Woody as the head coach and Schembechler as his assistant coach. You read things, where Woody threw projectors . . . and that's a fact. Bo had a lot of influence during his time there. He came to Ohio State from being with Ara Parseghian at Northwestern. He came in when I was a sophomore on the team.

I had three years as a player with Bo, and I didn't see the inside of what was going on. So probably the most dynamic thing, when I look back on it, was the exchanges between Woody and Bo and between assistant coach Bill Gunlock and Woody, which were a lot more negative, because Gunlock was confrontational. Bo was much more crafty.

I'm not saying Bo was manipulative. He just knew how to work with him, because he understood Woody. Even after Woody's career came to the sad ending, the person who sought Woody out was Bo. Woody trusted Bo. Probably loved him like a son. He competed with him like an absolute b-----d. It was a really fascinating relationship. That relationship was probably the most meaningful of the time I spent there. Of course, when Bo left, it became something different.

This is how Bo worked Woody. Let's say Bo had an idea—a play, a formation, a scheme. He knew that it was too radical an idea to get it in right away . . . or even within that year. So he would go to Doyt Perry at Bowling Green, who was his bud. Bo said, "Put this sucker in." Then, when the idea worked, he would bring it to Woody as "Doyt's idea." And Woody respected Doyt a lot.

Sometimes Doyt would get to Woody first. And that's when it was really funny. He would tell Woody about how much success he'd had with it. Woody then came to Bo and said, "You know what Doyt's doing up at Bowling Green?" Bo said, "No kidding." Then Bo got it into his agenda for the next fall.

Woody was stubborn about some things, including staying on the sideline too long. He had told me, "The way I coach, when I get past 55, I probably need not to be coaching." Woody probably needed to hang it up a little sooner. Most of his friends would probably feel that way, too.

Another sticking point with Woody was Notre Dame. The Notre Dame games in the mid-'90s and the Fiesta Bowl a couple of years ago were a lot of fun and really interesting. When I was in school, Notre Damers would say, "Well, Woody's afraid to play us. Blah, blah. blah, blah. It's been 30 years. We knocked you off two in a row back in the '30s."

The truth of the matter was Woody did not want Notre Dame on his schedule because, in my group, if you took the first 15 out of 22 players on the depth chart, they were CYO, Catholic Youth Sports Organization, kids. So what he didn't need were a couple of losses back to back, or two out of three, or something to lose an edge in his recruiting. It was a factor with us. I know the old man didn't want to play Notre Dame. It was all about recruiting.

But make no mistake about it, Woody Hayes was a great coach.

Woody's greatness was in his ability to motivate and his ability to bring the greatness out in the people he had. He was not an innovator, in my opinion. There isn't anything special about three yards and a cloud of dust other than the fact that you commit yourself to it like that. When he did throw the ball, he usually threw for big numbers. He was not very innovative from a play-calling/playbook standpoint.

Now, he was innovative in technique. A couple of cardinal principles that were really ingrained in him were leverage to the open side of the field and respect for the open side versus the closed side.

In my mind, the finest college football coach ever in his ability to use his talents and use innovative ideas was Ara Parseghian. Ara was my hero. Bo built some of that in me, because he had so much respect for Ara. Ara was as good a football coach as there ever was.

Bo's greatness was very similar to Woody's—technique and the ability to motivate. Bo could be awfully damned tough on the field. He never got away from appreciating a good line coach.

Neither Woody nor Bo would really spend much time with the defense. I coordinated the defense for Bo at Miami. He was very respectful, even though I was a young coach. Once there was something going on in a scrimmage—something he just didn't like. Then and only then he'd get involved with it. He'd come down the sideline and get a little closer than you really wanted him to be, but not like Woody. Woody would take a clipboard . . .

I can't remember what game it was, but in the '60s, Earle Bruce was an assistant coach. Lou McCullough was on the staff coaching the defense. Frank Elwood was coaching the defensive backs. Earle had the misfortune of being down on the sideline. It was late in the game.

Woody liked a certain pass coverage in that situation—"Cover three." Lou liked "Cover four." You could darn near line those safeties up outside the stadium to be deep enough and safe enough for Woody. But the opponent would pick you apart in the sideline away from the help. They'd check into it. Our defensive coaches had a heck of a time camouflaging and working with that.

Well, we were up by about 10 points. Woody is saying, "Cover three." McCullough up in the booth is saying, "No. No. No. No. Cover four." So they go about five plays and Frank says to McCullough up in the booth,

"He's getting closer." Woody came down the field and Earle was down there and he said to Elwood, who was on the phone, "Hey, Woody's coming down the sideline. I've got to put cover three in there." But McCullough wouldn't do it.

Woody kept getting closer to Earle, and he's still saying "Cover three," and he couldn't get it in. Frank is watching him through the glass. Frank says, "When Woody got there, he took his clipboard, and he banged Earle right over the top of the head. He hit him! Honest to God, he hit him!" Finally, Earle got the "Cover three" in. That wasn't all that common, but Woody was crazy that way.

When Kirk was old enough, I would take him to the games and, normally once or twice a season, I would take him in the locker room. I'd always choose a game that Woody won. We'd wait downstairs. When Woody would come out of the press conference after the game, he'd sit down and talk to Kirk, put him up on his lap. If you're going to recruit, that's the time to do it. He was very good to both my sons and had both their names down. I wish I had a picture of Kirk sitting on Woody's lap. That would be a neat one.

> **"Woody would come out of the press conference after the game, he'd sit down and talk to Kirk, put him up on his lap."**

When Kirk was about 10, and John would have been 14, we watched the Clemson game, the Gator Bowl at the end of the 1978 season. It seemed like Art Schlichter threw five interceptions. Of course, the old man wasn't upset with the Clemson kid, he was upset with Art. Art was just a freshman, and he had a bad game. Woody couldn't handle interceptions. Passing was painful enough. Even fumbles were easier for Woody to take than interceptions. Art threw the ball away that night.

After the game, I turned the TV off and the boys were getting ready to go to bed. I said, "Boys, I tell you, I don't think the old man's going to get past this one." They said, "What do you mean?" I said, "Well, that's going over the line, and he may not be coaching anymore." They teared up. They loved Woody so much, Ohio State so much, the whole thing. Kirk, maybe even more than John, had tears welling up in his eyes. He said, "Well, Dad, we can still love him." That was neat. I put them to bed.

The reason Northwestern has two directions in their name is they don't know if they're coming or going.

Chapter 3

Put Me In Coach

Buckeye Heroes, Like Buckeye Memories, Never Grow Old

TO PLAY OSU, YA GOTTA BE GOOD
TO SCORE ON OSU, YA GOTTA BE LUCKY
TO BEAT OSU, YA GOTTA BE KIDDIN'

REX KERN

He was the son of a barber in Lancaster, Ohio, and the first person in his family ever to go to college. Rex Kern turned away a chance to play professional baseball with the **KANSAS CITY ATHLETICS*** *and pushed aside basketball scholarship offers from the likes of perennial powers UCLA and North Carolina. He ended up not only playing football for Woody Hayes, but standing up to him too—in a pivotal moment that helped lay the groundwork for the 1968 national championship.*

I've had seven back surgeries, a total hip replacement, a shoulder surgery, and numerous others. I'm not certain but most of these are football related. Yes, it has taken its toll, but I have so many wonderful memories of Ohio State.

One of my favorite stories occurred at the beginning of my sophomore season in 1968. Woody mentioned to me before the season, "Rex, there'll be times on the field that you're going to see things that our coaches upstairs and I won't see. You're going to have to go with your gut reaction." That gave me a great deal of confidence when Woody said, "Go with your gut."

During the very first game of my career at Ohio State, we're play-

The Oakland A's colors are green and gold because their late owner, Charles O. Finley, grew up in La Porte, Indiana and loved Notre Dame . . . when he bought the ***KANSAS CITY A'S**, he changed their uniforms to the Notre Dame colors. The Green Bay Packers also adopted Notre Dame colors because Curly Lambeau played at Notre Dame.

ing Southern Methodist in Ohio Stadium. Early in the game, we had third-and-long and Woody punted on third down. I believe he did this because we were such a young team and were backed up against our end zone. Since so many sophomores started that day, he was afraid we might make a mistake, and we certainly couldn't afford it at that time.

With about two to three minutes to go in the first half, we are near midfield and it's fourth-and-10. Woody sent the punt team onto the field to punt. My sense is we are just one play away from really breaking the game open. We're hitting on maybe six, seven cylinders instead of all eight. I huddle the guys up quickly. I could see in their eyes—or maybe I *wanted* to—"We're not going to punt now even though it is fourth down." Our defense is playing a great game. The SMU QB was Chuck Hixson. He held the NCAA passing record for years because of this game. (He threw 76 passes that day.) I had to take all this information in and in less than 10 seconds synthesize, analyze and compress it. I said to myself, "We're one play away."

> **"The SMU QB, Chuck Hixson, threw 76 pases that day."**

Woody wants to punt. I wave the punter off. I call our play. It's the worst play I could have called. It was "Robust fullback delay." Jim Otis would go across the middle. He was the only receiver out. Southern Methodist was in a "fire" game with their right cornerback blitzing.

Dagnabit, Otis gets hit at the line of scrimmage. One linebacker covers him. The second linebacker covers him. The defensive back is bearing down on me. I'm seven to eight yards deep in our backfield. The DB is unaccounted for and therefore unblocked. He hits me deep in our backfield, knocks me into the air where I do a 360 pirouette, land on my feet and spring 17 yards for the first down. The stadium erupted . . . and I was so relieved!!

Two plays later, I hit Dave Brungard over the middle for a touchdown. We went in leading at halftime and won 35-14. That was a new era of football that started that day in Ohio Stadium. I believe that set the stage for the "Super Sophs" and our great team of outstanding seniors and juniors as we went on to win the 1968 national championship. Our class went 27-2 during that stretch from 1968 to 1970!

Now this wasn't something I necessarily grew up thinking about. Early on, in my youthful years in Lancaster, Ohio, we didn't have peewee or Pop Warner football. I played baseball as a young kid and always dreamed of playing for the New York Yankees and being a catcher like Yogi Berra and playing on those great Yankee teams that had **MANTLE***, **MARIS***, Whitey Ford, Elston Howard, and so on.

I always wanted to go to Ohio State and play basketball. You see in 1960 when Lucas, Havlicek, Nowell, Siegfried, Joe Roberts, Bobby Knight and those guys won the national championship. I hung on everything the "Roundballers" did. In the fourth grade, one of my classmates pulled out a small picture of John Havlicek. I asked her where she got it. She said, "I just wrote the athletic department at Ohio State, and they sent me this picture." I thought that was the best thing in the world. I thought that was a million dollars. I envied her for having a picture of "Hondo."

Even though I started playing football in the seventh grade, I didn't really focus that much on football. My mother listened to every Ohio State football game on the radio and I was there to hear the play by play. But, still, I was an avid basketball Buckeye. Fred Taylor, Ohio State's legendary basketball coach, started to recruit me long before Woody.

In my early years I did not know that John Havlicek was a great high school quarterback, and was being recruited by Woody to play football and also recruited by Fred to play basketball at Ohio State. So, Woody lost out on Havlicek, and Fred said he'd lost out on me. I think Fred got a better deal than Woody did, but both John and I won national championships while we were at Ohio State. One in football and one in basketball!

> If Mickey ***MANTLE**'s strikeouts and walks were combined, he would have played the equivalent of seven years without hitting the ball.

> Roger ***MARIS** once held the national high school record for most kick returns for a touchdown in one game—five, at Bishop Shanley High School in Fargo, North Dakota. Maris received a full scholarship to play for Bud Wilkinson at the University of Oklahoma, but quit after two weeks.

UCLA and North Carolina and other outstanding basketball programs recruited me. Originally, I thought I would play both sports. My freshman year I did play both football and basketball—freshmen were ineligible for varsity competition in those days. I had my first back surgery prior to my sophomore year in 1968, when we won the football national championship.

We won the Big 10 championship and went to the Rose Bowl, and basketball season was already in full swing. By the time I got back to campus, I had not only had back surgery about six months prior, but, right before the Rose Bowl, I dislocated my left shoulder and wore a shoulder harness the entire Rose Bowl Game. On my return to campus I had shoulder surgery so basketball faded into the sunset.

Woody always had ESP. I had been talking to Marty Karow, Ohio State's baseball coach, at the end of my junior year at Ohio State and I walked into Woody's office and said, "Coach, could I talk to you a minute?" He said, "Rex, the answer is 'no,' but come on in and we'll talk about it." Woody said, "I know that we talked about maybe you being able to play baseball, as well, when you came to Ohio State but you're one of our captains and we need your leadership during spring practice. That's the reason I don't want you to play baseball." That was the end of the conversation.

So the thought of playing major league baseball went quietly into the sunset.

When I got to Ohio State, I thought our freshman football class was pretty darn good. Woody really built our class up. As I reflect back now, maybe Woody was just trying to make us feel like we were a special group . . . and he did make us feel that way! We had great athletes. Golly, it was amazing to see the talent we had on our freshman team.

It really started during the recruiting process. When I gave my word to Ohio State, Woody said, "OK, I want you to start calling these guys. If we can get this kid out of Cleveland, Larry Zelina, we will probably have the best class we've ever had at Ohio State. This guy is the most versatile athlete we've had since Vic Janowicz." So, with that kind of an introduction, we kept hearing about these great players. Then, when we came in as freshmen, we lined up against the varsity, and we didn't back down one bit, and we were very successful against our varsity.

Initially, I think the upperclassmen thought, "OK, here's a bunch of freshmen. We've heard it all before. We heard about these guys who were going to come in and take our jobs, and they're supposed to turn the world upside down." I haven't really asked that question to some of the upperclassmen, but our actions spoke louder than our words.

"We lined up against the varsity, and we didn't back down one bit"

At times our words were pretty darn loud. After a period of time, I think the varsity thought, "Hey, these guys can play and really help us."

They welcomed us. We worked so doggone hard in practice to do our very best to prepare them for their season and for their games. It was a maturation between the freshmen, "the Baby Bucks" as Tiger Ellison used to call us, blended with the wisdom and the knowledge of our upperclassmen. It was a wonderful combination especially toward the end of our freshman season. In fact we were coming together as a team, both the Varsity and freshman class for the 1968 season.

One of the reasons we had such great chemistry was how our upperclassmen embraced us. For example, Billy Long was the starting quarterback in 1966 and 1967 and an outstanding baseball player. Billy continued to play baseball during the spring of 1968 and this allowed Ron Maciejowski and me to take over the quarterbacking duties while Billy played baseball. During that spring practice we incorporated a whole new offense.

We went to the I-formation or Slot-I. It was more suited for our team's talents and skills. Because Billy was playing baseball, Mace and I had the unique opportunity to have the offense all to ourselves during spring practice. Mace and I were able to get a great handle on the offense. Come fall, it looked like there would be real fierce competition for the quarterback job. However, at the end of spring practice, I had this lingering—what I thought was a hamstring pull—problem which later turned out to be a ruptured disk. I had surgery at the end of June, 1968. I didn't know if I was ever going to play again because, in those days, one didn't really come back from back surgery.

In about 45 days, I worked myself into shape. When we stepped onto the practice field, I was No. 1 on the depth chart. Billy was very supportive. Billy couldn't have been better. I never felt any animosity from Billy about the situation or about he being a two-year starter and losing his job. He would give input and we would all, collectively, discuss our game plan. I didn't feel any conflict from Billy at the time.

The "scary" part of our season was going to the Rose Bowl, not because of the travel or the opponent, but because of where we stayed the night before our game. Woody was afraid there would be too much partying and celebration of the guests outside the football family, so Woody arranged for us to stay at one of the monasteries in the foothills of Los Angeles the night before we played Southern Cal for the "National Championship."

It was very stark. Basically we had a bed. We didn't have a roommate, which we normally did. We heard noises all night long. Jan White said "he was scared to death, because he heard coyotes howling all night long." It was so quiet you could feel the vibration and hear the sounds of the doors open and close. I don't think any of us had a quality night's sleep in the monastery. We would have probably had more quality sleep back at the hotel. But, that was one of Woody's idiosyncrasies. Plus we won!

Woody had many personalities, or multiple personalities or, let's say characteristics. One moment, he could explode and have a "megaton", we called it. If he really got upset, he would tear his hat off. He would tear his shirt off. He would throw his watch down and stomp on it. He'd grab a player. Punch a player. He would go into a rage.

We would just back off and get away from him, because you're afraid he might turn on you. He would just rant and rave, and that was his way of getting our attention and making us focus. Then, just like a light switch, he'd put his arm around you and say, "Well, Rex, how are you doing in your classes? I know that you had an English paper due this week. Have you gotten a report back? How did you do on that? How are your mom and dad and your brother doing?" He would just flip it off and on just like that.

Early on in our careers he would show us by example of how to "PAY FORWARD." Woody would say, "Come on let's go." Of course we went with him. What you really did not know was what he wanted you to do. We soon found out because he wanted us to go with him to Children's Hospital, University Hospital, or Riverside Hospital and just walk the floors and drop in to cheer somebody up who not well! He wanted no one to know about it. Especially the media!!!!!!!!!! It was his way of "PAYING FORWARD."

In one moment, he could be so upset he wouldn't talk to anybody, and the next moment, he would be giving a speech for an organization talking world politics, literature, and so on. When it came time for Woody to be paid he would say, "No, I don't need the money. Give it to Ohio State or our college of medicine at Ohio State or keep it for your own charity." That was Woody!

I was the first person in our family to go to college. There was a lot of trepidation, a lot of concern on my part about going to a large university and competing in the classroom. That was an ominous feeling to take. And yet education became such a big part of who I am and where it has taken me in my life!

Woody always believed in education. First of all, he wanted us all to graduate. Then, he wanted us all to go to law school. During Woody's first 25 years of coaching at Ohio State (which was the time period I ran the study) I found an outstanding statistic. The varsity football players, those who earned a Varsity "O", had a graduation rate of 87 percent during his first 25 years, when I did this study. Of those 87 percent, another 36 percent went on to graduate or professional school.

When Woody passed away, on the plane trip back to my home in California, I thought "What can we do as a group, as a team (The 1968 National Championship Team), to honor Woody the way he honored us?" I thought we should establish a scholarship in Woody and Anne Hayes' names. We would have the scholarship from our team. With the help of my teammates and especially Dave Foley, one of our captains, we embarked on another journey to pay tribute to a great coach, wife, and friends. Woody always talked about, "you don't pay back, you pay forward." Well, this was our way of "PAYING FORWARD". This scholarship enables Ohio State players who didn't get their degrees to come back and graduate. It helps players' families. It's what Woody Hayes was really all about.

To learn more about the Woody and Anne Hayes 1968 National Championship Athletic Scholarship Fund, visit http://giveto.osu.edu/index. asp.

THE WORLD WAS DIFFERENT WHEN HE PLAYED—FOR ONE THING, IT WAS FLAT

DICK SCHAFRATH

His dreams never included education. In fact, he intentionally tried to flunk out of Ohio State and was well on his way until his coach, Woody Hayes, made Schafrath move in with him. The standout lineman ended up helping the Buckeyes win a national title in 1957, and he was selected to the Pro Bowl six times during his 13-year run with the Cleveland Browns. Years later, when his résumé already included four terms as an Ohio state senator Dick Schafrath returned to Ohio State to make good on what had gnawed at him for decades. His autobiography, Heart of a Mule, *was published in 2006.*

I was 69 years old when I finally got my degree from Ohio State in August of 2006. When I graduated it was the greatest thing in the world. I had all my seven kids there and most of my 14 grandchildren. It was really one of the highlights of my life to be graduating and to have that group there with me. My degree is a bachelor of science in sports and leisure studies. It was just really special.

If only my parents could have seen it. My mom and dad came to the U.S. as German immigrants, and they never were able to go past the eighth grade, and nobody in the family ever did. When I had the opportunity to go to high school, it was something that stretched things. I really had no interest in going to college.

I was into playing football. I wanted to play baseball, because baseball didn't need the college education. I was scouted by the Cincinnati **REDS***,

*PETE ROSE is enshrined in the Summit County (Ohio) Boxing Hall of Fame.

and that's where I wanted to go . . . but Woody Hayes entered the picture and the picture scrambled. He came to our farm in Wooster, Ohio, and knew just what to do. He went straight to my parents. He knew how to sell parents, as you know.

Woody never talked to me there on the farm. He went to church with us as a family. He spent time cooking lunch with Mom. He toured the farm with Dad, and then kissed Mom on the cheek, and shook hands with Dad and said goodbye to all of us. And that was it. He never said anything to me. I came in a little later and said, "Boy, Mom, I'm not very impressed with Woody Hayes and Ohio State." She said, "I'll tell you what, son, you're going to Ohio State." Woody had sold her.

When I got to Ohio State, they really tried to orientate the freshmen into being good students, because in those days nobody played varsity ball. They were always telling you to do better—to study and to make sure you were disciplined. After the first quarter, I didn't want to be there and I didn't want to study, so Woody just moved me into his house.

Undeterred, I failed all my classes spring quarter on purpose to get out of there and go play professional baseball. Woody moved me back in, and I stayed for the summer quarter. I got to play that sophomore year. Then I wanted out again. I rebelled my winter and spring quarter of my second year. Then I became more dependable until I got out. It was probably illegal to have me at his house, but in hindsight it saved me. I have no idea what the rules were.

After winning the football national championship in 1957 and finishing up in 1958, I was ready to get out of there. I just did not care to get an education. I couldn't see the value of it. My dad was a farmer. My friends were all farmers or construction workers.

Professional football was not in my mind at all. My goal was to go back to farming if I couldn't get back to baseball. Baseball didn't look good to me, though, since I'd missed four years, so I was planning on being a farmer. But a week after the Michigan game in 1958 was draft day, and I was drafted by the Cleveland Browns. It took them a week to find me, and they told me I was drafted in the second round. I'm 215 pounds, and what am I going to play? Paul Brown said, "Offensive line."

Nobody worked out then. Nobody lifted weights then. You were just normal size. He said to me, "I think you'd better get a little bigger." I was the first NFL ballplayer that I know of that lifted weights. Dad made me weights out of tractor wheels and axle weights, and I lifted weights and went up to 270.

I made only $600 a month back then. There was not much money in football, even if it was everybody's goal. Out of our 1958 Ohio State team, I would say 15 guys were drafted by the pros. I don't know how many of them played very long. Dick LeBeau, Jim Marshall and Jim Houston all played, the same as me.

> **"I had run 62 miles from Cleveland Stadium to Wooster on a bet years earlier."**

I became a state senator and a lot of other good things happened, but I knew I lost a lot of good opportunities through my life. The missing piece to the puzzle was the college degree. So one day, I'm sitting with Jim Tressel, and he didn't understand that I didn't have my degree. We started talking about what it would take. It took six months for them to really figure it out.

I guess they put all your records in some kind of lockbox. They couldn't figure out, first of all, where I was going with my degree, and then how many hours I would need. After five or six months of playing around with it, we decided that there was a program for former scholarship athletes that would help me. To qualify, I had to have 45 hours or fewer remaining and a 2.0 GPA. Well, I needed *46* hours, and I had a *1.99* grade-point average.

Jim Tressel and I had a common friend, Bruce Zoldan, out of Youngstown, and another, Jim Ward, who was from Columbiana County, and the two of them helped me get back on the scholarship. They paid for me to go back to school. But once I got back in school, I wasn't sure if I wanted to do this or not because, at almost 70 years old, things are a little different. You can't think the same. You can't see the same. You can't hear the same. You don't react the same. And you're surrounded by geniuses with computers and e-mail—all 18- and 19-year-olds, so it's a little intimidating. I talked to myself many nights about why I was doing this, but Mom and Dad and Woody Hayes and his wife, Anne, spent so many hours and so much of their time, I said I was going to go on through with it.

I had always liked a challenge. I had run 62 miles from Cleveland Stadium to Wooster on a bet years earlier. A car dealer told me he would give me a car if I could make it, so I said, "OK." So, I made it. He didn't make it easy. He had a policeman follow me the whole way.

Then one time, I canoed 78 miles across Lake Erie without stopping. I liked doing things that I had never heard of anybody else doing. I had never heard of anybody canoeing Lake Erie, so that was interesting. The thing about canoeing—I get seasick and I don't know how to swim. That made it more of a challenge.

Then there was the **BEAR***. During the '70s, when I had my recreational place, we would go to sport shows to advertise my place, and one time I saw my brother wrestle a bear. I thought, "Man, I've got to do that." I did it, and the bear seemed to like me. Usually a bear will just flatten a person down in two seconds, but he'd waltz around with me, rolled with me. The owner said, "Would you come back and do that again in the next show?" So we did. As soon as I came close to the stage, the bear stopped what he was doing and looked for me, and he brought me up and we rolled and played. He said, "I'll tell you what—just come to all the shows." So, I did that for five years until the bear died.

You would think all of that would soften the fear of going back to school. The other students in my classes didn't know who I was until the professors, about halfway through the courses, would somehow bring up the fact that I used to play football here at Ohio State, or that I was a state senator. We were studying history, and the guy would say, "This guy *is* history." A girl came up to me after class one day and said, "Mr. Schafrath, are you some kind of big deal?" I said, "I don't understand what you're getting at." She said, "My great-grandfather wants your autograph." You get into some unusual situations.

I got a little more comfortable after a course or two. Then, the instructors would say, "Is there anybody in class who would take notes for this guy?" I had people who would help me by taking notes. I told each one of the profs, "Can I try to do this without e-mail and computers?" They all said, "I doubt you can make it." I said, "Well, I'm going to try."

In the TV show "B.J. and the Bear," Bear was a chimpanzee named after ***BEAR** Bryant.

So I was in the library a lot. My daughter did most of my typing. I did make it.

I met Jim Tressel when he was at Youngstown State and I was a state senator. I'd go to some of his games with Bruce Zoldan. Then after he got to Ohio State, I helped out a little bit in the 2002 national championship season, volunteering and doing what I could do. I was still state senator. I started writing inspirational messages to try to fire up the offensive line, and he liked it, so he started sticking them on the bulletin board. I've been doing that ever since.

When I came back to finish my degree, I got to go watch football practice a few times, but I didn't spend a lot of time with it. Every time I was there, I would come in, and we'd study film. I could go to the games. It was really nice. Tressel and his staff leaned over backwards. After so many years, nothing had changed. I could still remember the same thrill. I ran out on the field following the team a few times before I'd go up to the coaches' box.

I have a heart condition with a pacemaker and a defibrillator, too. That happened about seven years ago. I died on the street and they put that in. It goes off once in a while when I stretch it. I shouldn't be running, but, anyway, I thought it would be neat to run in with the team. So I did that six or seven times, and all of a sudden Tressel asked me, "I saw you on the film running out with the team? It was pointed out to me by athletic director Gene Smith and a few other people. We don't want you doing that anymore. What would ever make you want to do that?" I said, "Well, coach, it's kind of fun to run out there with 105,000 people—what better way to go if I was going to die, than running out with the team in front of all those people?"

AT LEAST HE ADMITS HE'S A MICHIGAN FAN. THAT'S OFTEN THE FIRST STEP ON THE ROAD TO RECOVERY.

JEFF REEVES

He is a Michigan man with a twist. Oh, former Michigan standout defensive back Jeff Reeves loves to needle Buckeye fans every chance he gets, even though he is from Columbus and ended up moving back there. But the executive vice president at Allianz Life Insurance Company has a place in his heart for former Buckeye coach Woody Hayes, especially after seeing what the relationship between Hayes and rival Bo Schembechler was really like beneath the surface.

I'll never forget my last face-to-face conversation with Woody Hayes. We had been very close at one time, when I was growing up in Columbus, playing sports at Linden-McKinley High School. But now I was in Ohio Stadium wearing a Michigan uniform. It would turn out to be his last game in that stadium.

It was 1978 and my freshman year at Michigan, and we were warming up in Ohio Stadium. I had been injured a couple of weeks prior, and I was standing on the sideline. Woody walked over to me and said, "You should have kept your a-- in Columbus." I said, "Thank you very much, Coach. I'm proud to be a Michigan man. Good luck to you today, too, Coach." He looked at me, and gave me that look, and I said, "Thanks, coach."

My coach, Bo Schembechler, looked at me and smiled. I said, "Bo, Woody's messing with me." He said, "I got you, and he didn't." They looked at each other and gave that little smirk. That began the rivalry between **OHIO STATE AND MICHIGAN*** as far as Jeff Reeves was

****OHIO STATE** beat ***MICHIGAN** 50-14 in 1968. Ohio State went for a two-point conversion in the fourth quarter. When asked about it, Woody Hayes said, "I went for two because I couldn't go for three."*

concerned. I determined this "Michigan boy" made the right decision to go north, and I've been grateful for it ever since, and I'm proud of it.

The rivalry didn't end after my playing days at Michigan were over. After I left Columbus in '78, I never went back until 2003. My dad was severely ill, so I moved back to Columbus to help take care of my parents. Ironically, I went to work for Ohio State. I was the chief human resources officer for the medical center at Ohio State University. You talk about abuse. Oh, my God. That was a year and a half of abuse.

After a year and a half, I did my own consulting company for about a year. Then, Allianz asked me to come and be their No. 3 executive worldwide. I'm based in Minnesota, but it's headquartered in Munich, Germany. My title is Executive Vice President. I work there Monday through Friday and then fly home to Columbus on Friday night. During football season, I come home every Friday night to watch my son's games. My son, Darius, a running back who is being recruited by everyone, went to junior high school in Bentonville, Arkansas.

When we moved, he wasn't happy but he went out and became one of the first freshmen ever to play in Gahanna Lincoln High School history. He's been doing his thing ever since. But when I go to watch him play, the people are rude. They've got their Ohio State Buckeye crap on. I may wear a Michigan cap but I try to stay neutral, but every once in a while, I like to p--- them off. They all know who I am, so I don't have to wear anything. They'll just wear stuff and say, "Mr. Reeves, how do you like this coat? How do you like this and that?"

When they make comments, I say, "Obviously you guys aren't a real program, because you've got to brag about it all the time. I'm humble. I don't talk about it, because we have academic success, and you guys don't have any of that." We get into the zings every once in a while. They shut up when I get on academics because they know they're agriculture, and we're a top-five business school. So, when I get into academics, that p----- them off.

I've had my yard toilet-papered. I've had bricks thrown through my windows. I've had people scratch my cars—write 'Michigan sucks' on my cars. One of my cars was spray painted "Michigan sucks." I've had people rip off my Michigan trailer hitch from my Hummer. I've had people egg my truck. It's usually worse during football season, especially up to game week. They're obnoxious. They're very condescending. They're very rude. They're anal about Ohio State football.

They eat and sleep football year round. They have nothing else to do. They have no life. That's what gets me about Ohio State fans. That's their "pro" sport. All they want to do is drink and party and have a good time . . . and act a fool. I'm not going to say that doesn't happen in Ann Arbor, but it doesn't happen to the extreme that I've seen it happen in Columbus. It's just out of control.

I was heavily recruited for baseball and football. I had about 100 scholarship offers at D-1 schools, I would say 70 percent football and 30 percent baseball. Baseball was my better sport, but I had played football all my life, and I loved contact. In football, I played every position, never came out of the game. I was the punter, the kicker, kicked off, returned punts and kickoffs. I was the quarterback and started at safety.

In the summer going into my senior year, I started hearing from some of the bigger schools—the Auburns, the Texases, the Oklahomas—as a defensive back, not as a quarterback. I had a good senior year, and schools just started coming out of the woodwork. I talked to Woody Hayes when I was a junior. He said, "You'll be here in Columbus." I said, "Coach, I will not. I'm not coming to Ohio State."

Woody started talking to me when I was in the ninth grade, because I had been playing sports all my life. Woody would invite me to practices. I remember back to Leo Hayden and Jim Stillwagon and Rex Kern. And I was a die-hard fan of John Hicks, Archie Griffin. My good buddies were Archie and John and Pete Johnson. I remember I loved Ohio State—*loved* Ohio State, up until my junior year of high school. Bo Schembechler appeared in my gym one day. Jack Harbaugh, who was one of his assistants, and Bo came to watch me play basketball. I had a rule—this was my senior year—that I didn't talk to coaches, didn't interrupt the team. So they would talk to me on my terms, not on their terms. Gene Davis, the coach there, said, "Jeff, do you want to take a breather? These guys want to see you." I went up in the stands.

When they introduced themselves, I said, "Huh?" All I ever knew in my life was Woody Hayes, and that him and Bo didn't like each other, from what I read in the press . . . until I learned the real story. I told them, "Guys, I don't talk to coaches during practice. If you'd like to talk to me, wait for me after practice, and I'm more than willing to talk to you." They waited. That started our discussion. What they said was "We've heard a lot about you from the coaches in the city, and they rank you as the No. 1 athlete in the city and central Ohio." Granted, Art Schlichter was coming out, as well. So, me and Art were competing for the top-player status in central Ohio. Art was playing games with the press that if I went to Michigan, he was going to Ohio State. I did vice versa . . . if Art goes to Michigan, I'm going to Ohio State, even though I told Woody that I would not go to Ohio State.

Let me tell you why I would not go to Ohio State. Two reasons. One, I figured I can't grow up as a young man if I stay in the same environment. Two—I have to be able to grow up and fail, make some mistakes, and not depend on mom and dad. I had to culturally learn to deal with a diverse mix of people. The only way I'm going to learn that is to get out on my own and grow up from a boy to a man. Staying in Columbus, I figured that I would have the same friends, same environment and that the opportunity for me to be the man I am today would not exist had I stayed in Columbus. I still believe that.

> **"Let me tell you why I would not go to Ohio State."**

When I was being recruited by Michigan, my family got a lot of negativity. This is where some of my bitterness comes in—I won't say bitterness, it's where my dislike for Ohio State comes in, and it carries over to my kids, because they get the same treatment today. People were very negative. "How can you even consider that?" "Traitor."

My mom and dad would get verbally abused at work. Literally, they would get "How in the hell can your son even consider that?" "Has your son lost his mind?" "How can you allow him to even look at that opportunity?" "They don't exist." "You guys have got to move—you can't stay here in Columbus."

I had teachers telling me, "Do you really want to pass this class?" I was a 3.9 student. I had some brains, too. I was the No. 1 student in the class. I was valedictorian. I was head of honor society. I had a 3.99 GPA as a three-sport high school All-American. And a teacher asked me did I want to graduate? She was a die-hard Buckeye and threatened to rate me down because she hated Michigan.

I made a decision on signing day. I had a press conference. Woody

Hayes and Bo were there, and I had Bear Bryant from Alabama there, too. I had Johnny Robinson, from SC, there. I had Barry Switzer from Oklahoma there in my high school library. I pulled a hat and said, "I'm going to Big Blue." Woody Hayes hollered, "Son of a b----." Bo looked over to him and winked and said, "I got you again, Woody."

George Chaump and another guy recruited in the Ohio area. Woody went back and had a meeting with his coaches and threatened them that if another player got out of Columbus and went to Michigan, he would fire all of them. That's how the story went

I will say this, though. I grew up as a die-hard Buckeye. I loved the Buckeyes until my junior year. Let me tell you what was impressive about **MICHIGAN***, because I don't want people to lose sight of this. Bo Schembechler never, ever, for about nine months when he started recruiting me, talked sports. What Bo Schembechler did was he would determine and figure out what was important to the kid's family.

My dad was big on academics. He was firm on academics. What Bo would always stress was academics and you being a better man coming to Michigan, having a degree from Michigan, having the largest alumni base in America, and what a degree from Michigan stood for versus anywhere else in the country. He said, "If you come to Michigan, you'll be the best man you've ever been. I'll guarantee you if you do the things that I ask you to do, I'll take care of you for life." And he kept his promise.

I spoke to Bo the Monday before he died. We were scheduled to meet on Saturday at the Ohio State-Michigan game in November of 2006. He called me on Monday here at this office, and we were talking about my son. He was getting on my son the last two summers at camp. He was mad because Notre Dame was talking him, and he knew that. He said, "Reeves, I got a problem with you. Why is your son still talking to Notre Dame?" I said, "Coach, he can talk to whoever he wants to talk to. I'm open." He said, "He's a Michigan man, and G-- d--- it, don't you forget that."

The ***MICHIGAN** fight song, "Hail to (the Victors)" was written in South Bend, Indiana in a house where the College Football Hall of Fame is now located.

I said, "Bo . . ." He said, "Reeves, let me talk to your wife." So he called my wife and asked her what my problem was and did she not understand that our son had no choice but going to Michigan. She said, "Coach, I'm not in it. It's between you and Jeff." He'd grab my son in the summertime and poke him in the chest. "You're a Michigan man like your daddy. Your dad was a great Michigan man, and you're going to be a great Michigan man. Son, are we clear?" But Bo was a guy who, if I needed him, I could pick up the phone and call him. I had his home number in Florida. Whatever I needed, he was there for me. I'd call him at home.

After Woody was gone, the rivalry was different. The Ohio State rivalry is always tough. I would say Earle Bruce was a little more laid back. He wore his little black cap like he was a bellman at the door. We used to laugh at his hat all the time. He was a short, pudgy little guy. He didn't speak good English. He didn't have a real strong track record in our mind. We didn't give him a lot of respect.

After Woody was fired and was in declining health, Bo talked about Woody all the time. That's one of the things people don't understand, and that's why I have so much affection for Bo and Woody. I love them both. Those two loved each other. They literally loved each other. They were best friends. They were humanitarians together. They cared about their kids. They cared about their community. They cared about their schools, and they genuinely loved each other.

Bo used to always talk about his affection—that everything he knew, he learned from Coach Hayes. He said Coach Hayes coached him and gave him his start. He said if it wasn't for Coach Hayes, he wouldn't be half the man he was or half the coach he was—that he learned it from Coach Hayes. When Woody was ill, he left town to go to be by Woody's side. Michigan flew Bo down there in a special plane to be with Woody. We were in the middle of a meeting, and he found out that Woody was ill. Bo left the meeting, flew to Columbus—he was back the next day, but that was more of a priority than him staying at practice. People don't understand that these guys genuinely loved each other.

I can remember when I was playing in the NFL, and I was back working out. It was when Bo was being recruited to coach Texas A&M. Woody and Bo met at the state line. They both drove to the state line, got out of their vehicles, and they talked about Bo leaving Michigan. I remember

Bo telling me what Woody said to him that helped convince him to stay was "You're the pride and joy of Michigan. You've built this program. This is your legacy. Don't interrupt your legacy."

I would send my son to play with either one of them any day, and I wouldn't worry about it. I believe in coaches that have that credibility and respect and integrity. They can get more out of an athlete than an athlete can get out of himself. That's my kind of coach.

The one regret I have is not closing up with Coach Hayes. I was never able to tell him how much I appreciated him and thought of him. The last interaction we had was my freshman year when he told me, "Son of a b----. You should have kept your a-- in Columbus." He sent some messages to me over the last few years that he was disappointed that I went to Michigan, but I never had a chance to address him directly. One thing I wish I could have done was have closure with Coach Hayes, because I cared about Coach Hayes.

What's the difference between Maurice Clarett and government bonds? Government bonds mature.

THE OHIO STATE GOSPEL: KING JAMES VERSION

LEBRON JAMES

In the rare quiet moments, when the Cleveland Cavaliers' next immediate crisis or challenge isn't being pushed in front of him for a sound bite, LeBron James lets himself think of what might have been. What if he had worn an Ohio State basketball jersey coming out of Akron St. Vincent-St. Mary High School rather than leaping straight into the NBA? It wasn't that far-fetched at the time. In the spring of 2007, he finally got a chance to be in an OSU jersey—or rather on it. The No. 1-ranked Buckeyes donned new Nike uniforms for the Big Ten Tournament that featured a LeBron James logo on them. The stuff that dreams are made of? Actually, LeBron James' first dreams were about football, not basketball. The 6-foot-8 wide receiver kept college recruiters hopeful for a change of heart until just after his junior year at St. Vincent-St. Mary. In the end, his only post-high school connection to football is being a fan, and he wears it well.

When I was a kid, football was my favorite sport, and that's what we played. I loved to play quarterback. I didn't play basketball on a team until I was 10 or 11 years old.

I wasn't really a *fan* of any sports, I just played them. I didn't watch them on TV or anything. When I did start watching football, I got to be a Florida State fan, because they had the best team every year. They had some great players, so I followed them and became a fan of them. If I would've played college football, I would have wanted to play at Florida State—Florida or Ohio State. But I never ever really thought about it.

With Maurice Clarett being a friend of mine, I definitely started watching Ohio State, because I was following him. We had a good relationship in high school, but I haven't had the chance to talk to him much lately. Since he is a friend, he is a person I will always support. He's had some bad times and maybe got talking to the wrong people. I wish him the best.

I went to a few OSU games to see Sian Cotton play. Because he was a friend, I was always cheering for Ohio State. That is my hometown team. You're always going to pull for your hometown team. Coach Jim Tressel does a great job with that program. It is something we in Ohio are proud of.

Being a football player made me tough. But I didn't go across the middle unless I had to. I probably went out of bounds instead of getting hit a few times. There was a worry about getting hurt, but you can't live your life in fear. Whatever is gonna happen is gonna happen. You might not wake up tomorrow. So you have to live every day.

Wisconsin: First in Beer, First in Cheese, Last in the Big Ten.

HIS JOB IS LIKE PLAYIN' HOOKY FROM LIFE

TOM LEMMING

Tom Lemming has crisscrossed the country over the past three decades as the nation's foremost college football recruiting authority. The CSTV analyst and editor and publisher of the Prep Football Report *has seen his business boom from a hobby with no budget, while working for the U.S. Postal Service, to a full-fledged industry. But one thing hasn't changed: talent-rich Ohio continues to be one of the more intriguing stops for Lemming in his perpetual travels.*

Of all the major names—Woody Hayes, Ara Parseghian, Bo Schembechler and Bear Bryant—Woody Hayes was the best recruiter of the bunch, actually. He was the first of the major names to make visits in the home. Ara Parseghian didn't do that, and Bear was reluctant to do it. Woody was the guy who forced Schembechler and a lot of other people to change their recruiting ways. Parseghian was forced to go see Steve Niehaus in his home or else lose him to Woody.

I was just getting into the business when Woody was leaving it. Earle Bruce was next in line. He was an old-school guy. He did a lot of yelling. He was emotional all the time. When I talked to him, he was gruff and to the point, just acted like an old-school guy. When I watched him, in recruiting, he really put on the charm. He had another recruiting personality when I'd see him in Chicago or even Columbus. He went with the flow.

It was tough for him to change, but he tried. Being head coach at Ohio State has its built-in advantages already. He did a good job in-state, like Woody did. I don't think they ever had anybody who didn't do a good job in-state. Tressel's taking it to another level and getting almost everybody he wants. I thought Earle Bruce was good. He worked at it.

He didn't have that personality like Woody and that charm that **PETE CARROLL*** has or even Tressel has. In his own style, he was effective.

John Cooper was an excellent recruiter. He knew how to get the big ball players in. If you look back on the glory days, I think Ohio State and Notre Dame had more players in the NFL than anybody else. His big thing, I thought, was bringing back Bill Conley as recruiting coordinator. That really saved him. Conley was there with Earle, and then, for a while, he wasn't there with Cooper. Cooper brought him back in, and that's when Cooper started having his glory days in recruiting.

The one constant under the three staffs—Bruce, Cooper and Tressel—had been Bill Conley. I always ranked him as among the top five recruiters in the country every year. He not only has Ohio ties, being a former high school coach from Ohio himself, which are invaluable to have, but he also knew south Florida, and he used to bring in a lot of their top guys from there. Cooper relied on him. Cooper himself was an engaging, funny, personable guy and did a very, very good job in recruiting.

Tressel may be the best of all of them as far as recruiting is concerned. I was watching him work during the spring. He's not as aggressive as Earle Bruce, or old-school rah-rah, and not as corny as Cooper, but, in the long run, he's probably got it better than all of them. He's his own guy, more like a professor type than a football coach, and it goes over well. His mild-mannered, pleasant, engaging personality is very effective in Ohio. You don't see them losing many guys, although they lost tight end Kyle Rudolf to **NOTRE DAME*** in the spring of 2007. For the most part, they'll get almost everybody they want in Ohio.

> USC coach ***PETE CARROLL**'s roommate at the University of the Pacific was Scott Boras, the mega sports agent. Boras played minor-league baseball for the St. Louis Cardinals . . . as did former Illinois basketball coach Lon Kruger.

> When Tom Zbikowski, an All-American defensive back at ***NOTRE DAME**, made his professional boxing debut in Madison Square Garden in the summer of 2006, his opponent was Rober Bell from Akron. Bell entered the ring wearing an Ohio State jersey. Bell was knocked out 49 seconds into the first round.

When you consider all the rule changes and everything else, he's the best of the four. He's even better than Woody Hayes, because things were different back then. Those ties were developed over a long time when Tressel was at Youngstown State and he's continued to nurture them. Head coaches like Ted Ginn at Cleveland Glenville and Thom McDaniels from Warren Harding, and big-name guys in Ohio that year after year send their players to Ohio State—Tressel works real hard to keep those friendships going with these coaches. I think the only thing considered a weak spot could be maybe the Cincinnati area, where you'll still see players leave, like Rudolf this year and Ben Martin last year. Maybe if they go to Catholic schools, Notre Dame will get a couple. Michigan's always very strong in Cleveland.

Universities have to have assistant coaches with connections to recruit out of their area. That's a major part of it. They might have come from that area and recruited the area for a while and have earned the trust of the high school coaches. Geography plays a bit of a part. Michigan will recruit Toledo through Cleveland—the northern part, guys that aren't that far away. You don't see Michigan getting guys much from southern Ohio, unless it's Cincinnati. Cincinnati is the wild card in the whole state. You don't see them going into Columbus with much success. Notre Dame got Brady Quinn, because Ohio State had gotten Justin Zwick, who was supposed to be the all-everything the year before, or Brady would have wound up at Ohio State. Michigan has always been Ohio State's biggest thorn when it comes to recruiting Ohio players.

Notre Dame has always been sporadic. Under Parseghian, they were strong in Ohio, but after that, Dan Devine, Gerry Faust, Lou Holtz, Bob Davie, Tyrone Willingham, Charlie Weis—none of them are strong in Ohio. Notre Dame has not been strong there since the early '70s. Michigan has been consistently strong in Ohio. Some years they get better than others, but they've always gotten players out of there. Both of their recent Heisman Trophy winners, Desmond Howard and Charles Woodson, are from Ohio.

One of the greatest Ohio prospects to push football away was Cleveland Cavaliers star LeBron James. I went to meet LeBron at Akron St. Vincent-St. Mary High School. He came and met me in the football office there with Stan Cotton and his dad. We sat there and watched film on LeBron. LeBron was the best wide receiver in Ohio that year and would have ranked among the top five or so in the country—6 feet, 8 inches, 240, ran about a 4.6—4.7, and he had a vertical of 40 inches. If he had wanted to play football, he could have gone anywhere nationally. Wherever he was going, he'd be the go-to guy. If he wasn't playing basketball, he would have been offered by everybody.

He was serious about football when I saw him in April of his junior year. He was just coming off of a real good football junior year where he had 62 catches for 1,200 yards. He told me he was probably going to play as a senior, but then he broke his wrist, playing basketball, in August in Chicago. That game forced him to miss his senior year for football. He would have been invited to the U.S. Army All-American Game—he was *that* good.

Traveling around Ohio, the best player I ever remember seeing on film—well, Charles Woodson was one. Chris Wells was a great one. And Maurice Clarett, Korey Stringer, Ted Ginn Jr., Chris Spielman and Orlando Pace. If I would say seven, it would be those seven. They were all on my All-American teams.

One of the more intriguing guys I came across in Ohio was Spielman. When I showed up to meet Chris in Massillon, his dad had me sign a thing to get him on a Wheaties box. He did get on it. He just needed a lot of signatures. I was just one of many. I thought it was a strange request when I went to the house for the interview. Spielman did eventually get on the Wheaties box, so they knew what they were doing. Spielman's dad, Sonny Spielman, was athletic director at Massillon Washington High School at the time. He was one of those fathers who knew how to promote his son. It worked out. But Spielman, also, was a great player. It turned out he was just an absolute fantastic player.

My worst experience in Ohio was the one time I almost froze to death. I used to sleep in my car all the time. I remember being down in Cincinnati in early November of '81 looking at a kid in Cincinnati by the name of Arnold Franklin, a tight end at Princeton High School. He was my Midwest Player of the Year that year. He signed with North Carolina over Notre Dame, Ohio State, Michigan and UCLA. Arnold was the all-everything, the top tight end in the country and the most-recruited player. I went down to see him. I'd already seen him in the spring, but I went down to interview him again and then watch his game.

It got unseasonably cold that day. I slept in my car in the Denny's parking lot, just about a block north of Princeton High School. I woke up the next day completely frozen—my lungs, everything. I always brought a blanket and a pillow. I drove a Chevette back then, and I would put the seat back. I remember telling Arnold, "You'd better really make it, because I don't know if this was worth it for me."

I got out of my car about 6 in the morning, and I tried to walk on the ice outside, and I fell down. People thought I was a homeless guy crawling. I went into the bathroom there at Denny's and sat on top of the toilet for about an hour with all my clothes on just shivering. I couldn't move my legs. My legs froze out there just doing that. Franklin did turn out to be a great high school player. He played well at North Carolina, but he never made it in the pros.

Ohio's known for some quarterbacks who didn't make it big—Kirk Herbstreit, Scott Grooms, Justin Zwick. Brady Quinn was one of the few Ohio quarterbacks who did make it big. So did Troy Smith, but coming out of Glenville High School, he wasn't that heavily recruited. He had a strong arm but was scattered—kind of a scattered arm, more of a runner-athlete, wasn't real tall. That wasn't your prototypical type quarterback, although Ted Ginn was pushing him. I didn't give him a high rating, because I thought he was the kind of guy who was an athlete that would play another position. I didn't think he was the type. So I made a mistake with him.

I can remember talking to Troy Smith, and he was a bit cocky. He wasn't a bad kid, but my thoughts about him were that he was just one of several Glenville guys I was interviewing that year

A guy I didn't know a lot about coming out was Eddie George. He attended a prep school that I didn't visit in my scouting, so I never saw him. He was at Fork Union in Virginia all four years, never went to high school. He came out of Philadelphia, but his mom was smart enough to get him out of the neighborhood and send him to a prep school like that. That's what saved him. He was not a heavily recruited kid. He should have been, but wasn't at the time.

Maurice Clarett almost didn't end up at Ohio State. He committed to Notre Dame and **URBAN MEYER***, who was an assistant coach under

*__URBAN MEYER__, raised a Catholic in Ashtabula, Ohio, was named for Pope Urban.

Bob Davie at the time. He was committed for a bit. Jim Tressel got the Ohio State job a month or two later. Tressel, who knew him from Youngstown, got him turned around quickly. Plus, Urban was leaving Notre Dame.

I got to know Maurice, and he called me a lot. I was the one who recommended him for Offensive Player of the Year to *USA Today*. He would call me after every game and give me his results. He had 400 and something yards rushing in one game. I said back then that he looked like a young version of Jim Brown, a power back, ran through tackles, 10.8 hundred-meter speed as a freshman. Remember, he might have been the best back in the country as a freshman. He had everything going for him, would have been a No. 1 pick in the whole draft . . . and threw it all away by bad advice or his own advice, which was to leave as a freshman.

Then he didn't work out for a couple of years, and he lost it. After what would have been his senior year at Ohio State, I brought him down to the U.S. Army game in San Antonio, but he refused to play in the game because he was upset with the other backs getting too many carries in practice. He sat out the whole game, told them he wasn't going to play. He left a few days later. The rest is history.

He was good with me, but he was surly, and he didn't respond to a lot of people telling him what to do. I saw that right away. He liked to be the boss, and that carried over into college ball, too. He had problems with the coaches down in San Antonio at the Army All-American game. I knew he was a great talent, but also I knew that he was the kind of guy that unless you gave him whatever he wanted, there were going to be problems.

I think it was a little bit of both—not listening to his supports and not having good supports around him. There were people clinging on from the Warren area that were trying to make money off of him and just clinging on thinking that he was a money machine, or was going to be. He got bad advice from friends and family who wanted him. What a silly idea leaving after his freshman year, even though he had a great year. He was going to have to be the one testing the waters and getting the rules changed, and that was going to hurt him to begin with. It wasn't a sound response to having a great freshman year. To be honest with you, I liked him. He certainly was a guy who could be saved. Life piled up on him here in the last couple of years.

HOOPS, THERE IT IS

CLARK KELLOGG

There were times growing up when Cleveland native Clark Kellogg found himself rooting against Ohio State's football team, but mostly he felt indifference. That's hardly the case anymore for a man who helped put OSU's men's basketball program back on the map and who currently serves as a college basketball analyst for CBS Sports. Kellogg comes back to Ohio State now for the football, and he returned also for something very important that he missed out on when he left for early entry into the NBA Draft—his degree.

Football is the first child at Ohio State There's no harm. Basketball can coexist. There are great other sports programs, but the two highest-profile sports programs at any big university are the revenue generators. That's football and basketball most of the time. Football, by virtue of its numbers, by virtue of the tradition and history—six Heisman Trophy winners have come out of here, countless All-Pros, countless All-Americans. You can't just erase that. And you can't ignore it . . . and you shouldn't. The fact that football is what it is—you just have to accept that and understand it. It benefits everybody in the athletic department in some form or fashion.

Sure, there are some additional perks—the attention, the notoriety, but hey, there's additional pressure that comes with being part of the football program, too. To me, they can coexist.

Football is always going to be king, just by the nature of what it is. It's every Saturday—one game a week. People can get jacked up for that, because they can wait for seven more days before they have to get jacked up again. You can't do that in basketball. It's impossible. The nature of football tailgating, six, seven home games a year—every game

carries significant weight. You can't duplicate that in a 30-game basketball season. You can't put 102,000 people in a basketball building.

For people to get bent out of shape about it frustrates me. It really does.
It's chasing after the wind, and it's a useless waste of energy. Understand that football is different here. That doesn't mean basketball can't
be great and appreciated and supported and given its due space, but
it's not football, and it won't ever be, not at Ohio State, not at Tennessee, not at USC, not at Alabama—they had 90,000 at the spring game
at Alabama. Then somebody is going to argue that football's not bigger
than any other sport! Are you crazy? Come on, man.

I grew up in East Cleveland, a little suburb of Cleveland. Growing up, I
was more of a Browns fan from the football side. I really didn't have
any allegiance in terms of a college football team. I actually enjoyed
watching the West Coast squads a little bit, UCLA, USC, **O.J. SIMPSON***
 and Charles White and Marcus Allen—those guys. So growing up, on
occasion, I was actually cheering against the Buckeyes . . . until I ended
up getting in school down here. I'd heard about Coach Hayes and the
football tradition but, again, my football allegiance was more on the
pro side with the Browns.

Ohio State basketball really wasn't on my radar screen until really my
junior year, when I started being heavily recruited. At that time, the
Big 10, as a conference, was highly thought of, but Ohio State was in a
period of downward momentum. Larry Bolden, a guy from Cleveland's
East Tech, a little older than me, played on some middling-to-average
Ohio State teams. But the fact was, he was a Clevelander who had gone
to Ohio State. And then Kelvin Ramsey was there, then Herb Williams,
Carter Scott, Jim Smith, Todd Penn, Marquis Miller—that group was
the beginning of things starting to turn. They had a couple of big wins.
That created some momentum, and those guys were all Ohio guys.

It seemed like the timing of them starting to get better and me being a top
recruit coincided. Those guys, the whole state of Ohio really, recruited
me. Four or five of those guys actually came to my house in Cleveland,
and my mom cooked for them. They told me how much they'd like to
have me down there, and I could fit right in, and we could do something

*O. J. SIMPSON's cousin is Ernie Banks. Their grandfathers were
twin brothers.

special. It was pretty impressive so I ended up going there—I picked Ohio State over Michigan, Notre Dame and **KENTUCKY***.

As a 17-, 18-year-old kid, I didn't give a lot of thought to the fact that Ohio State was considered a football school. I didn't really appreciate how rabid the fans were about Ohio State football or what the great tradition was of Ohio State football. I was new to the whole aura of Ohio State football, and it took me a while, even after I enrolled here, to get fully indoctrinated.

After I was drafted by the ***PACERS**, my knees gave out and my broadcasting career started kicking in. I was busy during the hoops season, but I would follow Ohio State and keep track of them through the paper and on television as much as I could. That's when I really began to be a football fan, when I left. Herb Williams and I were together with the Indiana Pacers*, and we'd be talking about games on Saturday if we were around watching and pulling hard for the Bucks, wanting to see them do well. When I came back here in '93 to live, then obviously I got more involved in keeping track of what's going on and trying to get over and be involved in practice a little bit more.

Actually, it dawned on me how unique football was here. When you live in Indianapolis for 10 years, you're removed from the mania. They're a pro sports town there, with the Colts and with the Pacers, so it was a little different. I'd forgotten how maniacal the folks are about football around here. Actually, it was a little bit of a shock when I came back. I had gotten so used to looking at it from a distance and not being involved in the daily scrutiny of talk radio and everything being football. I said, "This is ridiculous."

In the 1970s, ***KENTUCKY** basketball recruited 6-foot 10-inch Parade All-American Brett Bearup from Long Island. After a high school game, Bearup was approached by an up-and-coming coach who said, "Hi Brett. I'm Jim Valvano, Iona College." Bearup looked down and said, "You look awfully young to own a college." Later as a lawyer Bearup represented OSU hoopster Lawrence Funderburke.

When Steve Alford was a senior in high school in 1983 in New Castle, Indiana, his high school team averaged more people in attendance per game than the Indiana ***PACERS**.

IF LIFE WERE FAIR, THERE WOULD BE NO WHEELCHAIRS

HEATH SCHNEIDER

When the deluge of get-well letters was reduced to a trickle, Heath Schneider kept sending paralyzed Ohio State football walk-on Tyson Gentry words of encouragement, hope and yes, even sometimes his take on the current state of OSU football. Today, those heartwarming gestures have come full circle.

Yet Schneider, a 36-year-old ROTC instructor at Fayetteville State University in North Carolina, keeps pushing for a miracle.

I can still remember exactly where I was, what I was doing when I got word that Tyson Gentry, a walk-on punter on the Ohio State football team, broke vertebrae in his neck and lost feeling below his waist.

"A player got hurt and was taken by ambulance to the hospital."

I was stationed at Langley Air Force Base in Hampton, Virginia. It had happened at the end of one of their practices. I was at a Buckeyes website and it was on the message board, stating that they had shut down the practice and "a player got hurt and was taken by ambulance to the hospital."

It was the spring of 2006. Tyson was a punter but was asked to convert over to wide receiver. They needed help at that position over spring practice, and it was during one of those practices that he got hurt. At first, from the waist down, there was nothing. As it stands right now, he has movement in his arms, not so much in his hands, and he can wiggle a couple of toes on one foot. He's really excited about that, because you can't get any further away from your spinal cord than your toes.

Somebody posted on the board that Tyson was going to be at the Ohio State Medical Center. And somebody threw out the idea that it would be good to send him a get-well card. At this point, no one knew the extent of the injury. You just knew it must be pretty severe, since they had shut down practice.

I sent him a get-well card. Then a few days later, I sent a letter of encouragement to let him know "we're all pulling for you." At that point, we knew he had broken vertebrae and didn't have movement. I could envision what was going to happen—that a lot of people would send letters and cards at first and then it would be, like we say in the military, "fire and forget." It would just dwindle. I had a vision of this guy sitting in this hospital room for a long time with nobody but his family there and getting no words of encouragement.

I decided to send a letter or a card every week. It was not like I was going around saying, "Hey, I'm sending him a letter or card every week!" It's a pretty sick man who tries to draw attention to himself like that. He didn't respond, because he was going through quite an ordeal at the time, and he still is. But about six weeks later, his dad sent me a handwritten letter—sent from their house in Sandusky—that said how very much he appreciated what I had been doing. That just fired me up because, at that point, I wasn't sure if they were looking at the letters as something really corny or wondering, "Who is this goofball we've never heard of?"

His letter was very sincere about how appreciative he and his wife and the whole family were that I had kept on sending letters. That fired me up and I said to myself, "Okay, they don't think I'm a goofball. I'm going to keep on doing it." I've sent at least one letter or card every week. They're not always words of encouragement. I took my daughter to the Ohio State-Cincinnati game in 2006. One of the letters was just telling him "I took my daughter, and here are pictures of my daughter at her very first Buckeyes game."

I've moved assignments since then and am now teaching ROTC at Fayetteville State University in North Carolina. I use Tyson—what he has gone through and the positive attitude he has—as inspiration for my cadets. When they're struggling, I say, "Hey, here's a guy who is paralyzed at this point, for all intents and purposes, and he pushes through every day and goes to therapy, has a great outlook on how things are going." He's just a real inspiration for the way he's taken this. The whole family is just fantastic.

In August 2006, they had a press conference, which was Tyson's first public appearance after the injury. Bob Gentry said he wanted his son to walk, and they wanted to be an All-American family. I immediately wrote a letter to them and said, "You've got that box checked. You are an All-American family in anybody's book."

There came a point where I had hoped we could meet face to face. I ended up winning a pair of tickets to the Ohio State-Michigan game last fall in an online contest through AT&T. This was great, because it would have taken a second mortgage for me to be able to afford tickets.

I do a blog for the *Columbus Dispatch*—which came about from another contest I won—and wrote that I had won a pair of tickets and was going to be able to go to the game for the fourth year in a row. I mentioned that I would be in Columbus on Thursday night and Friday night before the game on Saturday, and on Friday night would be down at the Buckeye Hall of Fame Café. Unbeknownst to me, Tyson's parents, Bob and Gloria Gentry, were reading my blog from time to time, and they read that one. So they called the *Columbus Dispatch* and said, "Oh my gosh, we live real close to the Buckeye Hall of Fame Café. Maybe we can meet up."

They contacted the *Dispatch*, got ahold of the sports editor, who got ahold of the online sports editor, who got ahold of me and said, "Hey, here's their number. Give them a call." Friday night, I was able to stop over and meet them at Tyson's apartment. This was the first time we'd met. I found them to be a truly inspirational family.

I have a little checklist of things to do before I die . . . riding in a hot-air balloon, going deep-sea fishing once—stuff like that. On that list, as silly as it sounds, was "storm the field" or "flood the field" after a big win. I was able to check that off on that Saturday in November when the Buckeyes won. We were in the south stands, and we flooded right onto the field. We each got a big hunk of turf, which I have planted and on my window sill at the house . . .

I'm Buckeye born and Buckeye bred, even though I never went to school there. I'm from Wellington, Ohio, and it's tough not to be a Buckeye fan when you grow up in Ohio. I'll never understand people growing up in Ohio and being a Michigan fan. I can't fathom that. I was actually lucky enough that when my two kids were born—they are now 10 and 12—we were stationed at Wright-Patterson Air Force Base in Dayton, Ohio, so they were both Buckeye born there in Dayton, so . . . lucky for them.

Ohio State was the only place I wanted to go my entire life. Just like everybody else, I wanted to play football at Ohio State. But as you get a little older, you realize "Yeah. I'm not that good." I wanted to go to Ohio State, but, for a variety of reasons, finances being one of them, I went to a community college, Lorain County Community College, the Harvard of community colleges. When I got in the Air Force, I went to 10 different schools to get my bachelor's degree

No matter how far away from Ohio life has taken me, I've never lost touch with Ohio State football. I was in Afghanistan from June to November of 2005. I had a blast there. It's every airman's right to complain, but just about everybody out there will tell you that when they're deployed, that's the most fulfilling time of their career—maybe not personally, because your wife and kids or your husband and kids are back in the States and are worried about you, but professionally, you can't be doing more for your country or more for the mission than when you're deployed in a war zone. I had a very, very fulfilling time over there.

Through the modern advances of the Internet, I was able to follow the Buckeyes. The first time Ohio State played Texas, in 2005, I was in a panic, because I had no idea how I was going to watch the game. They have the Armed Forces Network, but you are never guaranteed what game is going to be on. I talked to the services commander that serves at the organization at the base, who would know what's coming on. They told me that would be the game that would be on. I asked where we could watch it and was told they had a little 19-inch television that everybody could huddle around. I said, "That's just not going to work. Can we do something a little better than that?"

The Air Force really takes care of their people. We organized it so that the civil engineering guys took two huge sheets of drywall, four feet by eight feet, and built a wooden frame. They put them together to make an eight-by-eight screen, which they painted white. They got a projection screen from the wing conference room—there are only two or three projection screens on base. They wired it with the communications squadron guys so they could hook it up to receive the game. Then we set it up in a big tent and watched the Ohio State-Texas game on this makeshift 8-by-8 screen in the middle of the desert. We had a blast—a really big morale booster. There were a couple of Texas fans there, but we tried to drown them out.

> **"Then we set it up in a big tent and watched the Ohio State-Texas game on this makeshift 8-by-8 screen in the middle of the desert."**

When I was deployed, I had intermittent access to a website called Bucknuts.com. I would get on there once a week and would post a weekly update about all the stuff that was happening in Afghanistan that week: "We had 16 Navy Seals die." Or two Marines. Or there was a prison break here at the base. Or whatever the news was . . . "But I'm doing well," etc. I would post weekly for people to read. I'd been at Bucknuts for about five years. You know how it is online. You get a little community going. I found out how big a community was.

When I got back in November of 2005, I posted that I was back. I got back just in time for the Ohio State-Michigan game, which I went to up in Ann Arbor, and we won. Right after that, we got picked for the Fiesta Bowl against Notre Dame. One of the guys on the Bucknuts message board, in an offhand, flippant remark, said, "Why don't we send Heath to the Fiesta Bowl?" Somebody else said, "Oh yeah, I'd give money for that."

I hadn't even seen the thread, but the guy sends me an e-mail and says, "I don't want to do this for real if you don't want to go." I didn't want to make him feel bad, and I honestly thought, "This thing isn't going anywhere." So I said, "Sure, I'd go. Do what you want." I was just trying to make him feel good. When somebody is trying to do you a favor, you don't say, "No. I don't want the favor." I didn't think it would go anywhere, but about 72 hours later, maybe 96 hours later, they had come up with $3,000 to send me and my wife to the Fiesta Bowl. They bought a pair of tickets to the game, three days at a resort in Scottsdale and round-trip airfare. I was just absolutely shocked.

I'm just a guy. I don't do anything special. "Next thing you know, *old Jed's a millionaire . . .*" And I'm on my way to the Fiesta Bowl with Mike Ruth, another friend of mine, because my wife was unable to go. That's one of the best stories of the "Buckeye Nation giving" kind of stuff. But *the* best one involves Tyson.

I did get to see Tyson's parents again at the BCS Championship Game in January of 2007. A buddy from kindergarten, John Rugg, was in Reno, and he sent me an e-mail in early November and said, "If Ohio State makes the BCS Championship Game, I'm going. Do you want to go?" I said, "Heck yeah, I want to go." We made all the plans.

About eight days before the game, I got a call from Tyson Gentry's dad, Bob. He asked me if I was still coming out—he had seen on my blog that I was coming out but didn't have tickets yet. He asked if I had tickets, and I said, "No, I don't have any yet, but something will come up." He said, "I think I have a pair for you." What happened was Tyson and his family all had tickets to go out there and be in the players' family section. The NCAA had cut through whatever red tape was there, and Tyson and his dad were going to be able to be on the field. So they took their two tickets for seats in the stands and gave them to me and my friend, John Rugg. That's how we were able to go to the BCS Championship Game.

Tyson is still on the team, so we stopped in at the team hotel and sat with the whole family for a couple of hours. They met John, who is a good guy, a former Naval officer. The day of the game, we met the family—his mom, Gloria, his sister, Ashley, who has put her life on hold to take care of Tyson, his sister Natalie and her husband, Bob—outside the stadium. Ashley and Tyson live together in Columbus, and she tends to his daily needs. She's a great gal. Tyson and his dad were with the team, so we didn't see them then. We had a good time, except, of course, for the final score—Florida 41, OSU 14.

I still send a letter or card to Tyson every week. He e-mailed me recently that he's doing well in terms of mental outlook. As a matter of fact, there's a spinal cord injury support group or interest group that called Tyson and asked him to contact a couple of other folks who were having a tough time dealing with their injury and/or their recovery process. One of them was a 40-year-old father of two. Here Tyson's 20, 21 years old and he's trying to give support to this man who has the same injury. A very impressive kid, this young man. An Ohio State man.

He said he wants to pursue some aggressive therapy, one of which is a restorative therapy bike. It's an electrotherapy bike—they can strap your legs to the pedals and make it move. I don't know how to explain it. The problem is that it's a $15,000 item. We're not even sure that the insurance, or the NCAA or Ohio State, which had a catastrophic injury thing, would cover it. Just like any other HMO out there, it only covered certain things. My wife, Karen, said, "What you ought to do is the same thing the folks on Bucknuts did for you two years ago. Do a grassroots thing." I said, "Well, I'll see if that will work"

I posted it at Bucknuts and at a couple of other sites. I said to myself, "I expect maybe $2,000. I'll be really happy with $3,000, $4,000—$5,000 is a near impossibility." Well, before Ohio State took the field for spring practice, we were at $7,800, more than halfway there. All my post said was "This is an update on Tyson Gentry. Two years ago, you guys sent me to the Fiesta Bowl, when I got back from Afghanistan. Here's something that's a heck of a lot more important than that. Let's see if we can help him get this bike." Next thing you know, we're at $7,800. I'm just absolutely in awe of the way Buckeye Nation is rallying around Tyson Gentry and coming up with all this.

> **"Woody Hayes always talked about not paying back, but paying forward. I guess this is what he meant."**

I got an e-mail from one of the former players saying that he's working with the players' parents association. I got another one from an elementary school principal in Norwalk, Ohio, that said that every year they have a spring pageant and they charge admission and donate the proceeds to a cause. This year, Tyson's the cause. It's all going to go into the Tyson Gentry trust fund to help them get that bike. I got an e-mail from his dad who told me Tyson knows nothing about it right now, and he was sure that Tyson would feel guilty that people were going out of their way to help him. He said he and Gloria are just in awe of what's going on. That's probably the best word I could use to describe it for me, too.

Woody Hayes always talked about not paying back, but paying forward. I guess this is what he meant.

Chapter 4

Ah, a Female Buckeye Fan—One of Life's Most Misunderstood Creatures . . . No Man Is Worthy

Ginger Rogers Did Everything Fred Astaire Did, Except She Did It in High Heels While Going Backwards

A BUCKEYE IN THE SKY

NANCY CURRIE

For all the exotic places the Ohio State University flag has flown around the world, Nancy Currie found a way to top that. The former NASA astronaut has taken it into space with her—four times, no less. The 1980 OSU grad plans on giving the flag as a gift to her alma mater. And the ardent Buckeye football fan can never forget the gifts Ohio State gave her—among them the hope to fly someday, the experience of being part of Block O and having a larger-than-life guest lecturer surprise her by showing up in her ROTC classroom not long after his coaching reign ended.

I was watching the OSU-Clemson game when Woody Hayes threw the punch in late December of 1978. I distinctly remember turning to a group of friends sitting around watching television and everybody said, "Did he really just hit him?" It was at the end of the game, and the announcers didn't talk that much about it. Of course, as soon as it went over to the local news, then it was everywhere. There was this letdown, like "Uh-oh, there may be some real fallout from this."

It wasn't long after, I was sitting in class as a student and member of the Army ROTC at Ohio State, when Woody walked into my classroom and introduced himself as our guest lecturer. When Woody was reassigned—I guess that's a good way to say it—he was a professor emeritus and they had had him come over and give talks on military leadership.

He was a big military history buff. He was always pretty close to the ROTC detachment at Ohio State. He actually set up his office in the ROTC building. He became a real friend to ROTC cadets. In fact, one of my friends was killed in an automobile accident while going through some ROTC training out of Fort Lewis in Washington. Woody came to the funeral. And he just really had a passion for military history. He just embraced the ROTC cadets like he did his athletes. I always thought that was pretty unique.

I met him several times. He was as passionate about the military as he probably was about Ohio State football. Of course, taking a leadership course from Woody Hayes was really cool. I don't know how else to say it. That's one of my fonder memories, having him guest lecture on military leadership to the ROTC cadets. I felt, at the time, like you are meeting one of your heroes. He was . . . even to the college students . . . a larger-than-life kind of guy.

I try to describe this to people, especially in Texas—there are a lot of professional sports teams down here. In Ohio, there were the **BENGALS*** and, of course, the Cleveland Browns, the first set of Cleveland Browns when we were growing up. In the center of Ohio, from Dayton to Troy to certainly around Columbus, I don't think there's a person in the state—I haven't really met one—who isn't a Buckeye fan. There's this pride. You can go to downtown Troy, Ohio, and find as much Ohio State gear as you can probably on the streets of Columbus. There are Ohio State fans all over the state of Ohio.

We had moved from the state of Delaware to Troy, Ohio, in 1973, and it didn't take me long to adopt Ohio State as a passion. My other passion, being an astronaut, was a little more gradual, because of the times we were in.

The space program was always an interest to me, but you have to remember that, at that time, and even up until the time I entered Ohio State in the fall of 1977, there were no women astronauts. There weren't women astronauts until 1978. So when I was in high school, there weren't even military pilots—that didn't occur until around '75, and then female astronauts in '78.

So it's not like some of the male astronauts who talk about "from the time I was a little kid, I wanted to grow up to be an astronaut," because that wasn't a realistic goal at the time for a young girl growing up. But I always wanted to be a pilot. From the time I could walk, I wanted to fly. In high school, I really, *really* wanted to fly, specifically MedEvac helicopters in the military. Luckily, nobody discouraged me and said that

The ***BENGALS**, owned by the Paul Brown family, were named after the Massillon (Ohio) High School Tigers, where Brown coached before he became head coach of Ohio State and the Cleveland Browns.

females can't do that. I was very fortunate in that the rules changed, and females were allowed to fly and all those doors were opened about the time I was in high school and college.

"One of the things that drew me to Ohio State in the first case was the esprit de corps and the pride in the university."

I went into ROTC while I was at Ohio State, because of these new opportunities. I actually went through Army ROTC, because I was too short to fly in the other two services—the Navy and the Air Force. They had a minimum flight requirement of 5 feet, 4 inches and wouldn't relax that requirement. The Army was different. About the time I was getting out of Ohio State, they were making changes. As long as you met three requirements—which were seated height, leg length, and arm reach—they would allow you to fly in the Army. It was only by virtue of that change, which occurred when I was a senior at Ohio State, that I was able to go on to flight school in the Army.

One of the things that drew me to Ohio State in the first case was the esprit de corps and the pride in the university. The size never intimidated me at all. I had a part-time job in the college of medicine. I was in ROTC. I was briefly on the OSU swim team, and then played water polo throughout the rest of the time. You are involved in enough activities that I describe it as a small town of 50,000 people, because a town of 50,000 people is relatively small. So when people say, "Wow, how did you go to a university so large?" I say, "There wasn't a day that I didn't walk across campus that I probably didn't know every fifth person that I passed, because it is a small community." It is a very tightly knit community. I used to joke for many years that the saddest day of my life was the day I graduated from Ohio State. I loved my time there. I just really thoroughly enjoyed my time there.

I'll tell you one of the things that drew me to Ohio State. When I was in high school, I was nominated by one of my teachers to attend a one- or two-week-long science summer camp. We stayed in the dorms at Ohio State. We were taught by the professors and did a lot of experiments. At that point, I was sold. Again, I came from a family that wasn't very wealthy. I've often gone back to Troy and thanked the teachers who nominated me for that who are still in the town. Without that experience, I'm not sure I would have been inspired with that love of Ohio State and that passion for higher education. It really gave me an exposure that I probably wouldn't have had otherwise.

While I was a student at Ohio State, I don't think I missed a single football game. As an ROTC cadet, many times, I marched down the field and helped put up the flag. A lot of times, we would go in uniform and help put up the flag and stick around for the games. When I was a freshman, they used to have Block O, and I was part of Block O.

I'm a huge fan. I've carried that tradition on. There's hardly anybody here at the Johnson Space Center that doesn't know that I graduated from Ohio State. In fact, in December of 2006, when the shuttle mission landed on December 23, a lot of people were wearing Santa hats, hoping that the shuttle was going to land before Christmas. I was wearing a Santa hat that had a big "Ohio State" across the front.

My most memorable game would be the Ohio State-Michigan game in the fall of my senior year. There was just total mayhem in the streets after the Buckeyes won 18-15 in 1979 to earn a trip to the Rose Bowl. That was just awesome. I was pretty sedate. I was the prototypical geek so I was observing the celebration on High Street, but it was really neat. That was Earle Bruce's first year as head coach.

The school newspaper, *The Lantern,* did this cartoon on selecting Earle Bruce around the same time they were selecting a new pope. So—this is probably not politically correct at all, but the *Lantern* comic at the time, when they finally selected Earle Bruce to be Woody's successor, showed the smoke coming out of the OSU smokestacks there near the gym. They showed it changing from black to white. In Rome, when they select a new pope, they eject white smoke—that was the takeoff on "we finally have a new coach." There were mixed emotions about the Woody thing. There was a sadness that this era was gone. There was optimism for the new coach, as well. It was pretty interesting.

I've gone to many games since I graduated from Ohio State. I received an Alumni of the Year award in 2002. I got to go to the game. They had us come out on the field before the game started. At halftime, they flashed our names up on the scoreboard and the displays surrounding the stadium. That was really cool. Typically, I try to get back for one game a year. Almost always, my husband and I just go and sit with the fans in the stands. I'm only recognized if I hang out at the ROTC building.

Ohio State has just had some fantastic teams in the last few years. I attribute that again to the tradition—the tradition of not only Ohio State football, but of Ohio State. It always cracks my friends up when all of the professional players announce themselves as being from "The Ohio State University," with the emphasis on the *The*. So I make sure that when people read my bio, they emphasize the *The* in *The* Ohio State University. I got my graduate degrees from other universities, some of which also have, at times, had pretty fantastic football teams, but what I say is "once a Buckeye, always a Buckeye." My allegiance is always to The Ohio State University.

I flew an Ohio State flag on each one of my shuttle missions—the same flag. I plan on presenting it back to the university. I have now flown my last flight and so there will be no need to keep the flag. There will be no more trips into space for me. The same flag flew on all four flights, and I want to present that back. What I said from the start was that I wanted to take a piece of Ohio State University into space with me, because that's what helped me attain the profession that I have today.

I beat Maurice Clarett in the 40-yard dash

SHE HAS IRISH EYES
AND BUCKEYE TIES

ROBIN QUINN

Robin Quinn married an Ohio State grad, watched with pride as her daughter married an Ohio State star football player and grew up sitting across the supper table from a man who worshipped Woody Hayes. But when her son, Brady Quinn, became a star at Notre Dame and was vying for the 2006 Heisman Trophy with OSU's Troy Smith, suddenly she felt like she was living behind enemy lines.

It's funny and sad, because I've had Ohio State connections around me my whole life. I think when people look at you from a distance, they come up with certain preconceived notions. And usually, they're way off base.

I remember meeting Teddy Ginn's dad, Ted Ginn Sr., after Brady's junior year in high school. We were in South Carolina, me with Brady at a camp and Mr. Ginn taking all these kids to camp like he always does, helping them. He came over and shook my hand and told me what a fine kid Brady was. I didn't really know the connection or why

> **"It's funny and sad, because I've had Ohio State connections around me my whole life."**

Brady really knew Mr. Ginn at the time. Mr. Ginn has always thought the world of Brady and I'm sure Troy Smith, who played for Ginn Sr. in high school, and Brady did camp together, so they always knew each other. And through the years, there has always been great respect.

Long before A.J. Hawk married our oldest child, Laura, our son Brady and A.J. really hit it off. There was never the animosity there that some of the fans were feeling when Notre Dame was getting ready to play Ohio State in the Fiesta Bowl at the end of the 2005 season.

And to this day, A.J. has helped Brady so much. Sometimes too much.

When Brady was getting ready for the NFL Scouting Combine in February of 2007, A.J. told Brady that not only would he be measured to the eighth of an inch in height and to the half-pound in weight, but the combine workers would also measure his biceps and announce the results. He told Brady that he might want to do some curls just before the measurements. And Brady was like, "Really, they measure your biceps?" And A.J. said, "Oh yeah, they measure your calves—everything." Brady was taking that all in when A.J. starts laughing and says, "Nah, I'm just kidding." Then Brady tries to talk A.J. into pulling the same trick on Notre Dame running back Darius Walker. It was so cute.

Those positive experiences with people from OSU, that maybe a lot of Ohio State fans didn't know about, are some of the reasons it hurts living in Buckeye country when your son is going to Notre Dame. They incorrectly assume you don't like Ohio State. It was really only bad from the Fiesta Bowl on—that last season and a half.

I think the low point was Halloween 2006. We live in a neighborhood where every single house has Ohio State flags up. They get the drift of who we are because we've had so many kids who want A.J.'s autograph or Brady's autograph. They got wind when Laura and A.J. got married in the summer of 2006, of course. We've had the TV trucks here too many times. These three kids were getting ready to come up to our house. And their dad says, "No kids, you're not allowed to go trick-or-treating at that house."

I really believe the first couple of years Brady was at Notre Dame, this town was very proud of Brady. The *Columbus Dispatch* put a lot of stories in about him and would always have a picture or something. There wasn't a week that went by, win or lose, but they always would try to write an article as nice as possible.

Ever since the Fiesta Bowl with Ohio State, after the over-bombarding of that, the *Dispatch* came and did an interview with me at the end of the summer of 2006. They came over and took a picture, because it was all about the Heisman hype for Brady, and they wanted me to do a pose and talk about it. I said, "No. I won't do that, and I won't talk about the Heisman. He's got a lot of football to play before . . ." So they respected that. We did this article. It turned out that it came out on a Friday on the front page of the sports pages in the *Dispatch,* the same week that Ohio State had a home game.

I didn't even know about it for about two weeks until someone made me aware of it. The first week after that picture, people from this area who were Buckeye fans retaliated, writing letters to the editor that said the last thing they wanted to see was Brady Quinn's mom on the front of the sports page when Ohio State's playing at home, and we could care less about Brady Quinn or his family. They should pack up and go to South Bend, too.

There were just endless comments. Then I'm like, "Whoa, OK, sorry, I'm not the one who called down there and said I'd like to do an article." The next week there was retaliation again, more comments. Then Notre Dame fans and other people were starting to defend me . . . and I didn't even know who these people were. It became one of those back-and-forth things in the letters to the editor, where someone responded to this girl from Hilliard, who had said "blah, blah, blah." This went on three, four weeks. I almost called down and said, "OK, Uncle! Enough already." So then I never was in tune to wanting to do anything more.

It just went on, and it was just rude. I'm used to hearing bad things about my son, you get that all the time, and I've got broad shoulders. I just take it with a grain of salt. You have to, especially as a quarterback's mom. But Ohio State has always been like family. Even now, it's the school we always root for.

Brady's father, Ty, graduated from Ohio State after serving in Vietnam. I am from Ohio, growing up in a burg below Canton. When Ty and I met, obviously Ty was a Buckeye fan. My mom moved down to Columbus and started businesses, so I moved down after high school and worked in her business. She had retail stores. And when I came down here, we always watched Ohio State. I had girlfriends from high school who went to Ohio State. I hung out with them and would go to games with them. We had a retail ladies' clothing store, so some of the girls worked part time for us on the weekends or nights. They dated guys like Jimmy Karsatos and Art Schlichter. Those guys used to come to our employee Christmas parties.

Earle Bruce shopped in our stores. He would come in and have Mom or I pick out something for his daughters, his wife. My mother had a store at Worthington Square and Earle lived in Worthington, so we have all these other connections, too.

I grew up in a small town. My brothers both went to college, but my older brother, being two grades ahead of me, played for the University of Kentucky. My youth of going to football was pretty passionate, because we were just a big football family. I cheered for football. If the Cleveland Browns played, I'd get a group together. My dad always had four tickets to everything Cleveland—basketball, baseball—whatever it was, we had four tickets.

But I always watched Ohio State, because I always knew kids from Ohio State. I lived in Arlington for 10 years. Our oldest child, Laura, went to high school with Freddie Pagac. We knew Coach Pagac and all of them. Then Brady, of course, went to camp with many of these guys—he'd been going to football camps at Ohio State from seventh grade on. Every summer.

"Growing up, Brady was always an Ohio State fan."

Laura would go to field-hockey camp at Ohio State. Our youngest daughter, Kelly, would go to *SOCCER camp at Ohio State. All my aunts and uncles and cousins—anyone who has a degree—all graduated from Ohio State. My uncle, John, was a trainer for Ohio State. My father, Scott Slates, was a huge, huge Ohio State fan. For my dad, the sun rose and set with Woody Hayes. John Cooper was my brother Steve's defensive coordinator at UK.

Growing up, Brady was always an Ohio State fan. He loved Notre Dame, too, as a kid. When Brady started being recruited by Ohio State, he'd had a lot of offers. It boiled down to Ohio State, Michigan and Notre Dame. I went with him on most of the visits. When it came down to the three, it was really up to Brady. We backed off at that point and let him decide, because he's the one who ultimately had to be happy. He's the one who had to make the decision.

When he chose Notre Dame, I asked him why, and he got upset with me. I said, "Brady, it's not that I care. I'm asking the question to know what your reasoning was behind it." Notre Dame was late in the situ-

> **More U.S. kids today play *SOCCER than any other organized sport, including youth football. Perhaps, the reason so many kids play soccer is so they don't have to watch it.**

ation. Ohio State the same way. They were late in the interest in comparison to a lot of other schools. Being a hometown kid, going to their camp since seventh grade, I thought, "How did they not pick up on it sooner than they had?" I know Earle Bruce did tell Jim Tressel he should be looking at Brady.

After he made the decision to go to Notre Dame, all the Ohio State fans in the family—all the ones who cared about football—were into it. They knew that's what Brady wanted. They were excited about that. It was more his uncle Dave's buddies that would make funny comments. It's so funny they all ended up watching Brady every Saturday. As the years went on, they just became so excited and so proud of him.

Laura met A.J. Hawk through Freddie Pagac. She dated Freddie a little bit her freshman year in high school, when he was a senior at Dublin Coffman High School. She stayed real good friends with him and his family. She would go down to campus when she was old enough—probably when she wasn't old enough, too. Then, when she went on to college, she'd be home at Christmas break, and she'd go see everybody.

She had met A.J., and the following year, before her senior year, they re-met. I don't think he remembered her, but he texted her and one thing led to another. Then, all of a sudden, she's flying home every weekend she had a chance. She started going to his games. Then, the Fiesta Bowl came up and that whole craziness.

The fact that Ohio State and Notre Dame were playing each other made it such a big deal. That became the biggest story. Truly, that put them in such a celebrity status. People were so interested in all that. Once something becomes a hot topic, it just becomes a really hot topic. What were the chances of that happening? She's dating A.J. They're getting serious. Here he's a linebacker, and Brady being the quarterback on the other team. So that definitely became a great story for everybody. Brady liked A.J. He had met him a lot. We had a Christmas thing that year before everybody went out to the bowl game. They were together, and they laughed and talked.

Brady, when he was home, if somebody had tickets to Ohio State games, he'd go down and watch them, even all through college. It was just pretty funny and not a lot of people knew about that.

Laura got sick out there at the Fiesta Bowl. She ended up with laryngitis. The media was just endless. When we got home, a couple of our friends said, "Oh, my God, if we had to see your daughter one more time on TV . . ." I'm like, "Sorry, we didn't get to see her like you guys did. She was doing that and we were off doing other things, so we didn't get annoyed by it." Now, that's some of our best friends, so that tells you something.

Brady and Troy have great respect for each other. Even throughout the Heisman race, Brady would watch him and root for him, and I think Troy feels the same way. I know it's sincere.

We're Ohio State fans when we're not playing them—we played them once in the four years Brady played college, so why are some people so vindictive about a kid that has worked really hard to have great accomplishments? You're always going to be in competition. Even if there wouldn't have been an Ohio State person going for the Heisman against Brady, it's like you're going to get in the NFL and you may play with someone from Ohio State or you may play against somebody from Ohio State again. It makes no sense to me. I would never put Ohio State down. I want them to do well. There's only one time I wanted them to lose, and that's when they play Notre Dame.

Other than that, I'm scarlet and gray all the way.

The BCS formula is actually a recipe for chili.

IT'S HARD TO CHEER WITH A BROKEN HEART

MITZI (SCHLICHTER) SUBRIN

She has found normalcy as an advertising copy reader back home again in Indiana. She is no longer Mitzi Schlichter. She is Mitzi Subrin, but the ex-wife of former Ohio State star quarterback Art Schlichter never ran away from her past or anybody else's. Instead, Subrin first tried to reframe the past by throwing herself into raising awareness of and expanding treatment options for gambling addictions. She even co-founded a treatment center in Indianapolis. So what started as a promise to herself became a movement, but it still needs more momentum, more resources than Subrin or any other single voice can muster. Art Schlichter himself, now 46, also talks the anti-gambling talk these days. But his message is diluted by skepticism. In a twelve-year period that ended with his early release from an Indiana prison in the summer of 2006, Schlichter spent time in 44 prisons or jails. Most of the convictions were for fraud or forgery to feed his addiction, and many of the victims were members of his own and Subrin's families. The cause no longer defines Subrin, though. She is a wife and mom first. She has varied interests and balance. The everyday urgency and all the pangs that came with it are gone, but her legacy lives on.

I don't think it's realistic to think you're going to eliminate gambling in the world. It's just not going to happen. I also don't think every person who goes in and gambles is going to end up having a gambling problem. . . .

Most people don't see this coming, I never did. I was born in Toledo, Ohio, and moved to Indiana at a young age. I went to Carmel High School and then to Ball State to study journalism. I was a senior at Ball State when I met Art. I had no idea who he was then. I didn't follow sports at the time. Some friends introduced us.

At that point he had already been suspended and reinstated in the NFL. I knew when we met he played for the Indianapolis *<u>COLTS</u>, but I just didn't know any of the other background. But he told me that first night. As we talked, he disclosed quite a bit of his history to me, and I respected that. We dated about five years before we got married in 1989. While we were dating, I went to the meetings for gambling. He went to Gamblers Anonymous. I went to Gamb-Anon.

We got married and went to Jamaica for our honeymoon. On the way home, on the plane, Art told me he was in debt, and so we mutually decided—and I was all for it at the time—to use our wedding gifts, just return them all and use that money to help him get out of debt. Looking back, that's not the advice a gambling counselor would give you. That was bailing him out and enabling him, but at the time, I didn't look at it that way. But that is what happened.

I continued with the support from Gamb-Anon during the full course of our marriage. We moved around to different places, so my support came from different people at different times in our lives. I've had great constant support from family and friends who helped me, and I have strong faith. It was a combination of things that allowed me to deal with this and still stay emotionally and mentally strong. But it definitely wasn't easy. Addiction involves a lot of emotional ups and downs. I had many downs during my time with Art also.

As the addiction continued, I didn't want to be a quitter. Out of loyalty to Art, I wanted to keep trying. It's just a struggle, such an incredible struggle. The first time he got arrested, I waited before I got divorced, because I thought, "OK, finally this is going to do it. This is going to change everything." It was almost like I was waiting and hoping that it really would. It wasn't until it became apparent that he hadn't changed that I finally felt like, "OK, if you can go that far down and nothing's changed, then maybe it's bigger than I can ever handle."

> Tony Dungy, Indianapolis *<u>COLTS</u> coach, is the last NFL player to throw and make an interception in the same NFL game. He was a defensive back and a backup quarterback for the Steelers . . . Peyton Manning's father, Archie, is regarded as the greatest football player in the history of the University of Mississippi. In honor of Archie's uniform number, the posted speed limit on the Ole Miss campus is 18 mph.

I left Art right before he was arrested the first time, but I didn't divorce him right then. I waited for a while. I waited two years. It was just a very hard decision.

The whole Ohio State experience was foreign to me until we started going to some games. We actually lived in Columbus for a short time. As our relationship progressed, I became fully aware of what's involved and how avid the fans are.

Whether we were at the stadium or just out around town, people would constantly come up to Art. People knew him everywhere. There were those people who were very supportive and there were other people who were very angry at him. They felt that he had betrayed them by not doing better after he left Ohio State, as if he had wasted his talent. They took it personally.

Sometimes they would say it right to Art, but more often they would say something to me. It was tough to hear, because although he played for them and was a figure in their life, he didn't really have an obligation to them. It's something I struggle with sometimes with sports. I do understand that public figures are role models. But sometimes that role can hinder their progress as people.

Art's family was not immune to any of this. You look at the time when all of this was happening, in the '80s, when things were unfolding. Gambling addiction just wasn't nearly as accepted as it is today. It was a foreign concept in some ways. There were a lot of people who didn't believe it could be an addiction, because there was no substance involved. Treatment was pretty scarce around the country.

"They felt that he had betrayed them by not doing better after he left Ohio State, as if he had wasted his talent."

His family was struggling to understand and manage something that is unmanageable. In addition to that, they were being highly criticized publicly at different times. It was as if everyone was pointing fingers and saying, "If you just did this, it would have been different." I don't know that you can really look at it that way, because there's such a large combination of factors that contributed to what happened. You can't single one thing out and say, "It was because of this."

Art's family went through a lot of pain and a real struggle to try to help and understand. Even back then, you would get different advice from different people, depending on who you were talking to. Just to sort through it all and figure out what direction to go was very difficult.

When people ask me about recognizing gambling addictions in someone else, one of the first warming signs is just following the money. When money appears and it doesn't make sense where it came from, or the opposite, your money is taken out of accounts—usually families find out through some financial stress. A mortgage payment isn't made and you find out that money was taken to a riverboat or something along those lines, and then you can unravel it from there. There's a lot of secrecy, a lot of lies, a lot of phone use, a lot of unexplained absences. When you look at the money, when you start there, it all usually falls into place. If you don't start there, or you don't have a real account of your money, or you don't know where it's going, it's very difficult to trace everything back.

When it comes down to this being a public fight or a private hell, a lot of times I had no choice. Early on when Art was originally arrested and things were happening I remembered thinking, "If it wasn't me, I'd be talking about this. I'd be saying, 'Wow, what happened? What's the story?'" So it didn't bother me much that people had questions for me. But what I never wanted was to feel like a victim or feel like people felt sorry for me. I really didn't like that. So I took the role that, yeah, this was a part of our lives. Yes, I went through this experience.

Sometimes people want to paint Art as probably a terrible husband and a terrible person. And in many, many ways, he really wasn't. He still isn't. He still has some wonderful qualities. I felt it was important to participate in portraying the real picture, which is not black and white on so many of these issues.

Now, you are a victim for a while. That's part of the process. But the magic in going from a victim to survivor is that you take action. That is the other reason I felt it was important to do this. If you take some sort of action in a positive manner, you're on the right path.

You can't change the things that happened to you. You can't change the early decisions that you make, but if you can do something that helps you to grow and learn from it and helps you to do something good for other people because of it, then you're no longer a victim.

Then you move into survivor mode or you move into a place where it's just one piece of you. It's just one of your experiences, but it doesn't define you.

I got to the point where I had turned the page and I didn't want to relive it. What happened with me is early on you're spewing all this information, and that's healing. But at a certain point, it's no longer healing, and you do feel like, "I just want my life to be about something else now. I feel like I've contributed. I feel like I've done some good work, but I don't want to live this every single day forever." For me, there came a time where I was just ready to move on.

I still have people who know who I am and approach me, and I'm very, very happy to spend time and talk to them and do whatever I can to help them. But you don't want to live it every single day from 9 to 5. I don't want to live it anymore.

At this point in my life what I'm about is my family and my kids. One is 17, soon to be 18, and the other one is 13. These are important years to be really present for them. I've remarried. I spend time with my husband and my family. I work and enjoy the work that I do. My degree was in advertising and journalism, and that's the field I'm working in. I enjoy the creativity, but I like the fact that I have other people, friends, relationships, things that I can spend my time with that are really important to me. So I'm much more balanced right now.

Art is out of prison now. I know he's been on the radio a lot and has done some interviews. I know he has some sort of foundation. I know he's done some speaking. I don't know if he aspires to start a treatment center or aspires to connect with one. But I do know that's what he's spending his time on now. I don't know the details and that's not an accident, because I want to keep my life separate. I wish him well, but I don't want to work jointly with him on that.

A lot of times people will still point out when there's an article about Art. When we were together, those were some of my worst times, when you knew an article was on its way out and you didn't know what it was going to say. You'd get this anxiety about it. Now when I know, I tell the kids. I tell them, "I think Dad did some interviews" or "Dad was in the news." Again, I somehow have been able to stay even with all that.

The way I look at it is people have talked about this story for a long,

long time and people will continue to talk about it. It's a fascinating story. It really is. It's fascinating to think about what potential is there and what could possibly happen. I personally look at Art, and I know some people feel so angry at him and they feel so disappointed that he didn't fulfill his potential after he left Ohio State. I look at him as an individual, and I hope for his sake, as a person, he goes on and can have a good life, because he did pay a pretty high price. He did many things that were very, very, very wrong. So I'm not, by any means, excusing anything that he did. But I think it's time for him to be able to contribute something good, and I hope that he's able to do that. For himself, for his children, for society, I hope he's able to make a good contribution.

I think the girls and I can have a happy ending regardless of whether he does. Part of the reason is we have been fortunate that throughout this process, it has been a constant dialogue—understanding the addiction, understanding what he's done, understanding how we're affected. My kids have been disappointed numerous times by him getting rearrested. If you know his history, you know it wasn't a one-time thing. It was in and out, and in and out, and in and out.

It's been such a long time, and the girls are old enough to accept that maybe this won't turn out great for their dad, and maybe it will. They realize they can't control someone else. As much as we want him to do well and hope he does well, we have established our own life. And our life is solid enough that I think, yes, we will all be fine.

YESTERDAYS TOMORROW

STEFANIE SPIELMAN

In the darkest moments, Stefanie Spielman not only found hope, but she made a promise to spread that hope, spread the light. The wife of former Ohio State All-American linebacker Chris Spielman refused to fight her battle with breast cancer in private. And by doing so, she not only showed the world her courage and saved some lives, she also revealed that Chris Spielman's strongest suit wasn't football after all, but heart.

When I found the lump in early 1998, I had just miscarried our third pregnancy. I think I was looking for something to blame, so I went in to the doctor and said, "Hey, I need you to look at this. Maybe this could explain some things."

He said, "Probably not, but I definitely am going to look at that anyway." So I was fortunate. I would like to make a point of saying I was fortunate I had a doctor who didn't dismiss me for only being 30 years old and not having a family history of breast cancer. He sent me on my way to get a mammogram. He saved my life.

> **"My husband, Chris, told everybody he was taking a year off from football."**

This was in 1998. I can remember the exact moment. My husband, Chris, told everybody he was taking a year off from football. He didn't want to go up to Buffalo, which was the team he was playing with at the time. He had this press conference where he said that he didn't want to leave me, under the stress we were in. He had the press conference over the phone, and he was sitting in our sunroom, which is connected to our kitchen. I was in the kitchen. He covered the phone up, and he turned to me and said, "What am I going to say once this starts? Do you want me to say it's because of health reasons, or family matters? What do you want me to say? How vague should I be?"

Immediately, I thought, "Wow. There's a life lesson here. We can be teaching our kids this—that you can make lemonade from lemons. You can turn a bad situation around and make good come from it. We may have one guy go home that night and say, 'Honey, my favorite football player's wife just was diagnosed with breast cancer. She's only 30. Have you done your self-exam?' Or 'Have you scheduled that mammogram lately?'" At that moment, when I knew he had everybody's attention, I saw an opportunity to serve. I knew that it could cause some good.

In 2001 and 2004, again there were problems. For a number of reasons, these were totally different. The first time I was rediagnosed, I had just had our third child. She was 7 weeks old. During that pregnancy, I'd had this horrific cough that would not quit. As soon as I delivered that baby, it was gone. I thought, "Whoa! That is just too weird."

Even though I was in the bliss of having the child we always thought we'd have, I said, "I need to get a checkup." I got a scan done. That showed that the cancer had traveled to my lungs. It was the baby pressing on my lungs, giving me that symptom of a cough. Had she not been inside me, I would have had no symptoms. So, again, I felt like I was saved. I still feel like she was my little angel.

After that, I did chemotherapy again. The spots in my lung shrunk and remained stable. They never completely went away. Once you're rediagnosed with cancer, it's a common fact that cancer's never going to go away. It may be in remission. It may disappear for a while. In my case, it shrunk and remained stable, but, you know that this is a lifelong battle.

During my first battle, Chris shaved his head so we would match. It was pretty cool. The day he did it was the day the hairdresser was to come over and cut my hair off. The two oldest kids were 2 and 4 at the time. In order for them to feel comfortable and for it not to be scary, we went outside—we had a picnic. We laughed, giggled and took pictures as she was shaving my hair off. It was fun. But the one key thing missing during that special time was Chris. We couldn't figure out why daddy was not home. Where was he?

Chris walks in the door 15 minutes later . . . with his own bald head. We were just floored! We laughed. It was a sign of support for me. He thought if we were walking down the street together, people might notice the big football-sized player who was bald, more so than the fragile lady with the hat on. He wanted to do that for me. It was wonderful. It was fun having him bald with me. We got some good photos.

I met Chris in our hometown of Massillon. I went to Massillon Jackson High School and Chris went to Massillon Washington. We had a mutual friend who knew we should meet. We met at a teenybopper dance club place one night . . . and it was history after that. I was a sophomore and Chris was a junior. Chris was already well known then, and I was a cheerleader. He was definitely more focused than the other guys. I liked his confidence. I liked that he had a passion about something.

I would say that, at that time, I was not so focused. I was a **CHEER- LEADER***—my big thing was dance, and I competed in dance. Outside of those two areas—Chris is walking in the room laughing at me right now reminiscing about my past—I was very much social. I loved the boys. I wasn't very focused on my studies, either. Here, all of a sudden, I start dating this guy that had it all—on the football field, as well as at school. That made me want to succeed, too.

My father passed away Chris's senior year. I really felt like all the coaches were nice and went out of their way to support Chris and reach out to me, too. Earle Bruce was Chris's coach, so I held him up very high, and still do to this day.

I knew Chris had two sides to him. I was thankful I was in his life *on the softer side.* I don't know what he thought of in college getting prepped for a game, but I know what he used to tell reporters would go through his mind before a pro game—that his wife and his children were being kidnapped by the opposing team. He would work himself up into this frenzy of how he wants to just get at them, because they've taken his family away from him. I can't honestly say that I understand all that, but if it got him to where he wanted to be on the football field in competition, acting out those thoughts are different than having those thoughts, I would think.

There are lots of crazy stories about Chris, like when he was a kid, if he couldn't find other kids to play football with him, he would put bologna in his pocket so the dog would try to tackle him. There's the story

When the Dallas Cowboys ***CHEERLEADERS** started in 1972, each earned $15 per game—the same amount they receive today.

about Chris tackling his grandma. He *really* did that. His grandma used to talk about that all the time. I think he was in second grade when he did this. It's crazy. You know, people are destined for certain things. He must have had this inner strength where he knew he was destined for this life of professional football. Even at a young age, when we were dating, I knew that he was someone special.

When all this started with the breast cancer, I don't think I thought I was going to become a public figure. I thought maybe at that press conference that hearing about our story might save someone's life. That's as far as I thought it would go. When people started finding out that Chris was taking a year off from football, on different media outlets, it received national attention.

"In a matter of six months, we raised $1 million. It was crazy."

We were on *Oprah, Good Morning America* and different places. We had no clue that was going to happen. It was just bizarre for us, although it was great because, we were getting awareness out. Now, I'm not really a public figure—I just donate my time and some of my energy to raising money and try to continue to raise awareness for breast cancer. In central Ohio, people may recognize me as someone who helps the breast cancer cause, but Chris is definitely still the one who is the public figure.

I had started chemotherapy, and the attention to Chris for taking a year off was surrounding us. Our local grocery store here, Big Bear, called Chris and said, "We really want to do something for Stefanie to show our support for her. We want to do this thing where people can buy a paper football for one dollar at all our grocery stores in Columbus, and we'll hang all the footballs on our windows."

Chris said, "Well, that's great, but you have to do two things. You have to give the money to where Stefanie is being treated, and to name the fund with her name." They said, "Sure." We had a press conference, and Chris made the announcement that we hoped to raise $250,000 for breast cancer research with this. In a matter of six months, we raised $1 million. It was crazy. We had Brownie troops. We had midget football teams. We had golf tournaments. You name it—people in our community were wrapping their arms around us. It took on a life of its own.

I do not deserve any credit for that, because really it was Chris seeing an opportunity and just having it be in my honor. Then it just boomed from there. Since then, we've put time and effort into it, but it really is so much our community, and we've raised over $4 million since that time.

A couple of years after the fund started, we thought to ourselves, "Here are all these wonderful folks in the community raising money for our fund. What are we doing to raise money for our fund?" We came up with this idea of how Chris and I could personally put on an event that went toward our fund. It is an event that honors support systems of cancer survivors. The support systems are what we call "The Champion."

The James Cancer Hospital is a separate comprehensive cancer center, but it is part of Ohio State, so we feel like Ohio State is part of our team for this breast cancer fund. They always do wonderful things. One year, at one of their games, they had Spielman Fund pins everybody bought, and we raised money that way. Another thing they have done is all the proceeds from the spring game have gone to our fund.

I do a commercial every year with Coach Tressel about our October awareness event that we do. Big Bear, the grocery store, went out of business, so Kroger picked up fund-raising for our fund. They do this breast cancer awareness campaign, where they have some in-store promotion that tries to raise money for our breast cancer fund. Coach Tressel is very nice to donate his time and do this commercial with me every October. There are a number of things the team has done. Once you're part of that family over there, it's a good tie to have throughout your whole lifetime.

Chris knows Coach Tressel better than me, but I think I know him pretty well. We socialize at different events. I very much respect Coach Tressel. He is a Christian man, and that makes me respect him. He has high standards for his players, not only on the football field, but as far as their education goes. He never gets out of sorts. I like that he's always calm and collected. He's a family man. There's lots I admire about that. He and his wife, Ellen, are both very good people.

Life sometimes doesn't turn out exactly how you thought. Whatever you're given, you're supposed to do something with. This is what we were given. It's my hope that some good has come out of it.

What's the definition of gross sports ignorance? IIII Michigan fans

Chapter 5

That's Entertainment

Actually, There Are a Lot of Businesses Like Show Business

A VISIT TO PLANET SCHEMBECHLER

BO BIAFRA AND THE DEAD SCHEMBECHLERS

Upon discovering the existence of the band Dead Schembechlers, the real Bo Schembechler was quoted as saying, "Holy smokes, I couldn't believe it. They're all dressed like Woody. I think it's crazy. I still matter in Columbus!" Their identities are secret, their future uncertain, their lyrics edgy, their legend growing. They've actually found their way into everything from the pages of **PENTHOUSE*** *to the Web pages of ESPN.com, but never* Tiger Beat, *says lead singer and band spokesman Bo Biafra.*

It was rumored the concert in Newport Music Hall in Columbus was going to be the band's last appearance. That would have been the Friday night before the game, November 17, 2006. To look into a crystal ball . . . I don't think there's a man on the planet who can tell you anything that is going to happen into the future. I would never take it upon myself to try and make genuflections of the forward recessions. It's a difficult period for the band.

We began playing in 1990. We were just young lads at that point. We were playing what we called the Wolverine Hate Music, not punk rock music. Punk rock is sharp. It's catchy. But all our lyrical content has to do with the evil of The International Wolverine Conspiracy. Because, as you see, the Michigan Wolverine football program is just the tip of the foul spear of The International Wolverine Conspiracy. It's aimed at enslaving mankind . . . every man, woman and child is drawn under the foul yoke

When former ESPN and current NFL Channel anchor Rich Eisen was in college, his stand-up comedy routine included reading "Letters to ***PENTHOUSE**" using Howard Cosell's voice.

of Wolverine football. Every supposed natural disaster is the fault of the Wolverines. Rumors of fake moon landings feed the Wolverines.

Take World War II—not many people realize it. The state of Michigan was actually on the Axis side. They sided with Italy, Germany, Japan. As a matter of fact, many of those planes that bombed Pearl Harbor were made in Detroit. They were supposed to be punching out cars, but they were punching out dive bombers. Dive bombers stabbed into the very heart of our proud United States of America. All this has gone on without anybody in the media stepping forward. It's a mystery unless you know the machinations of The International Wolverine Conspiracy. The Dead Schembechlers have been the only thing standing between this nation and disaster since 1990.

Historically, our band has only played once per year, on the night before The Game. It is *always* that Friday night before the OSU-Michigan game. It has always, pretty much, been in Columbus. We were, in fact, banned from the late '90s up until the early 2000s from actually playing in the city limits because of the violence that would break out around our performances. The violence, of course, was not the fault of the band, even though that's what you would read in the lying liberal Wolverine news media papers. Not the fault of our fans, God bless them—the backbone of the republic of Ohio. I would never lift a finger or even a word against the law enforcement. No! The violence was started by agents. Agents working on behalf of the Michigan Wolverines to destroy us, to destroy our fans, to destroy our show.

There's nothing funny about this. This is just as deadly serious as anything on this planet.

There was a band in Ann Arbor trying to do some of the same things we did, "The Dropkick Woodys." Once again, you see, just as Satan created things in mockery of the creation of God, we see the Wolverines come up with a cheap knockoff, a rip-off, just a falsification of the real band. We are familiar with the Dropkick Woodys. We invited them to share a bill with us a couple of years ago at a Hate Michigan Rally, 2005. They were so p--- poor, they were booed off the stage. They didn't even perform. They did a bad lip-synching job. They were met with a hail of bottles, broken glass, jeers, curses. Bodies burned and the flesh scattered.

We stay up all night before the game. After the Hate Michigan Rally, we will normally repair to some great vacation hotspot, like Sandusky.

We'll party all night and then be back for the game the following day. We normally fly in and out of Worthington International Airport. We have a private landing strip there. We often get an air escort from the Ohio National Guard to protect us in flight. We've had dozens, perhaps hundreds, of attempts on our lives and our livelihood.

I met Bo Schembechler once in my life. I was just a young lad, a spry young Buckeye lad, growing up off the fat of the land in Ohio. My family was having dinner at a restaurant. We heard a whisper go amongst the folks there having their supper. Coach Schembechler was there at the restaurant. My daddy urged me to go over and ask him for an autograph. I did so. I didn't know any better. I walked over and said, "Excuse me, Coach Schembechler, could you please sign this for me?" Instead of signing the paper, he covered me in kerosene and set me on fire. The man was pure evil.

> **"Instead of signing the paper, he covered me in kerosene and set me on fire. The man was pure evil."**

It is, in fact, true that in the last couple of weeks before Coach Schembechler passed, he was very vocal about our band. He may have, in fact, said some positive things about us. I believe, in hindsight, he was just trying to lull us into a false sense of security. What this was, this was just another plot, another insidious plot against our persons to find out our true identities, to bring us to the surface so we would let our guard down, and pay the ultimate price for the Buckeye Nation.

Does anybody know our true identities? Absolutely not—I don't even know who I am. It's too deep of a secret. It would be a pretty safe assumption that all of us are from Ohio, but I don't wish to say "yea," nor do I wish to say "nay." The smaller the amount of information known about our personal lives, the safer we will be. I can't answer questions about our past. It's too easy to check records, transcripts, grades, class photographs. I would love to be able to share that information with the community at large. Certainly, many of our millions of fans would be very excited about these personal tidbits. It can be so dear to them. But I would have to say what I said to *Tiger Beat* magazine when they wished to put us on the cover; I'll say, "I can't help you there."

What we do when we are not playing in the band is not important. The only thing that is important is when the four of us are together as the Dead Schembechlers, fighting the Wolverine menace. We could be beggars, lawyers, policemen. We could be soap-opera actors. We could be anything. It doesn't matter. It's not important. The only thing that is important is that we are a vessel representing the spirit of the Buckeye nation.

It's too dangerous for the Ohio State coaches to acknowledge us. Certainly, if they acknowledge us, given some of our strong adult lyrical content, they would be brought to the mat. Chastised. Ostracized. Omni-romanticized. There is no way in hell that they could even acknowledge our existence, even a smidgen, not even a modicum. Let us not mince. Let us not waffle. Let us not mince nor waffle together. There is no way they could ever, ever pay any attention to us, but we understand that. We work in the darkness, the shadows, the underbelly of the rivalry. It's our job. It's not always easy. It is not filled with glory. Somebody has got to do it, and we're gonna do it ourselves.

Some of our songs—"Bomb Ann Arbor," "I Don't Want to be a Wolverine," "Schembechler Kicked My Crippled Dog." If I had to pick a favorite song, I would probably say, "Stukas over 23." The vision of using a vintage World War II dive bomber to strafe, mutilate, destroy and otherwise incapacitate the Michigan Wolverines as they drive on the approach to the stadium, God Almighty, I get excited just thinking of it.

Our band members are absolutely the same members, always the same members. Dead Schembechlers—it's like a mafia. Once you're in, you're in for life. Our band members are: Bo Biafra; our guitar player, Bo Thunders; our drummer, Bo Scabies; and our bass player, Bo Vicious.

You'd have to be out of your mind to think that any of those media conglomerates like MTV or VH1 are going to put the Dead Schembechlers on their air. It was almost a mistake that we ended up on ESPN. We were the No. 1 story that week, around the clock. But whatever, they were reporting about us after all these years. Why suddenly, it's the force under the American media. It was to destroy us. It was to lead us in—lambs to a slaughter. We are not lambs, and we were not slaughtered. We survived to this day.

Certainly, the biggest show we played was the 2006 Hate Michigan Rally. It was the biggest game in the history of the rivalry. It was the biggest gig in the history of our band, our group. This was the largest attendance ever—1,500.

We play to audiences as small as two. We sometimes didn't even have all the band members there, because the danger was so acute. We couldn't tell anybody where the show was, including the band members. Sometimes, the show just had to go on without us. Good Lord Almighty. Do we live in an age where a man and a band singing about football fears for his life?

The profits from the last concert we did, we did indeed give all the profits from that show to the "Heart of a Champion" fund, one of Bo Schembechler's charities. We wuz duped. We wuz duped.

I honestly can't say, at this point, what the future of the band is, if any. I've been spending most of my time getting some rest and relaxation at the Athens (Ohio) Lunatic Asylum. It was very hard after the Bucks lost to Florida in the national championship. That was, of course, due to the fact that the band was not there to support the team.

We hate Florida. We hate all other non-Buckian teams. The fact of the matter is this. There is no greater, more dangerous threat—not only to the Buckeyes, not only to football, not only to the state of Ohio, not only to the United States of America, but to mankind in general . . . There is no greater threat than the Wolverines, and the avowed belief that the Wolverines should rule the world. They are now led by a bloodthirsty b-----d by the name of **DAN DIERDORF***. He is a gentle giant in the broadcast community. He is now the head of the international Wolverine conspiracy. He has sworn death to the Dead Schembechlers, death to Ohio State Buckeyes, death to the sovereign nation of Ohio.

Marion Motley, Alan Page and ***DAN DIERDORF** are all Canton natives and are enshrined in the Pro Football Hall of Fame in their hometown. Page worked on a construction crew that built the Hall while Dierdorf and his father attended the groundbreaking ceremony.

BIG DADDY'S IN THE HOUSE

DADDY WAGS

For the better part of three decades, Mark "Daddy Wags" Wagner has lampooned Ohio State football coaches as part of his shtick working on the air for QFM-96 in Columbus. The longtime morning host even dressed up as Earle Bruce one Halloween. But behind the punch lines beats the heart of a serious Buckeye fan and one who helps keep alive the "pay forward" philosophy that was so much a part of who Woody and Anne Hayes were.

Being the kooky, morning-type program that we are, we have fun with the coaches. I've been here through Earle Bruce, John Cooper and now Jim Tressel. You lampoon them when it all becomes necessary. Like making fun of the way Earle Bruce's sweatshirt didn't quite reach the top of his trousers sometimes. That's always fun to do. But we are unabashedly "homers."

When I went on the air at QFM, Earle Bruce was the football coach. Apparently there was some concern on behalf of the board of trustees or the athletic director at the time, so he decided to overdress. I always felt bad for the guy, because how do you take over a program from Woody Hayes? If you remember that one Michigan game when he came and he dressed up with the fedora and all that stuff, his team carried him off the field. That was the year I went to our Halloween bash as Earle Bruce.

I grew up in Columbus and went to St. Francis DeSales High School. Back in those days, WOSU television televised the Buckeye games on Saturday afternoon, before the networks really got all that interested in college football. I can remember my parents taking me down on campus to see all the homecoming floats when I was a little kid, basically riding in the back of the car.

I started at Ohio State in the autumn quarter of 1971. Here again it's kind of indicative of my attitude back then. Ohio State *had* to take me. I had a valid diploma from an accredited Ohio high school. At the time, it was a land-grant college, and the way they had it set up at the state university was if I showed up, which I did, they had to take me. I didn't take the ACT test. I didn't take the SAT test. I had nothing, other than an application that I filled out and sent in, going for me. That was pretty much my mentality back then.

When I was in college, I got this gig at the Jai Lai, parking cars. It's now the Buckeye Hall of Fame Café. That was the part-time job I used to support myself. First of all, you were working at a restaurant . . . so a meal came with it. The Jai Lai had pretty good meals, so you could not only work students' hours—go over there and work lunches, go over there and work some of the evenings, work on some of the weekends, and make a nice little piece of change—but you also got a meal that went with it. That, too, did a lot to enable my lackluster academic career at Ohio State.

The cool thing was that on Mondays after the games, Woody Hayes had his press conferences there. It was always important that you worked on Monday, because it was always busy with all the press coming in and all the TV stations showing up and unloading their equipment. Then, of course, Woody would show up and jump out of his car. We'd park his car, and he'd go in and have his press conference. We always knew to expect Woody.

Usually, one other day of the week, one evening, Woody would come in and meet his lovely wife, Anne, for dinner there at the Jai Lai. They never arrived together in all the years, and I parked cars there on and off for five or six years. I never saw the two of them arrive together, and I never saw the two of them leave together. They always met there to have dinner once a week.

He drove a white Ford El Camino, the half pickup truck, half station wagon, with wood paneling on the side, and a big old piece of Astro-turf in the bed. She would show up, usually a little bit after him, and go in. Then he was always first to come out and get in his car and go back over to campus, and then she would come out and chat with us and then drive back to their home in Upper Arlington.

When Woody came, he was always in a hurry. He would show up, get out of his car, go in. And when he would walk out, we always would have his car waiting there, because he was a busy guy, and he was always in a hurry. Now, his wife, Anne—different story—she always took the time to say hello and chat with us. That was always really cool. We always used to joke that if Woody came out and there was nobody else on the walk when you brought his car around, you got a quarter for a tip . . . but, if there were people standing on the walkway, you got a dollar. I think there may have been a little *image* thing there—I don't know. Let's just say, we would sometimes wait a little bit before we brought his car around . . . 'til there would be a crowd of people on the walkway.

One time, we did bring Woody's car around and one of the guys was down in a three-point stance on the Astroturf in the bed of his El Camino there. He thought that was pretty funny. That was about it. The guy was all business, man. It used to make us laugh because, like I said, when he'd meet Anne for dinner, they'd have a nice dinner and I'm sure they chatted the evening away, but when it was done, she was headed home, and he was headed back over to the office.

I still do a charity event today for a local charity, Heinzerling Foundation, a private nonprofit organization dedicated to the care, education and treatment of individuals with multiple disabilities, including severe or profound mental illness, which was one of Woody's pet charities (heinzerling.org). It's a fund-raiser I do every year the Friday before the OSU-Michigan game. I do it just because I want to do it. Anne used to attend it after Woody passed away, and it was always sweet to be able to see her again and support one of his pet charities. I don't want to say I feel obligated, but, to me, it's a part of that whole "pay forward" thing he used to talk about. To me, personally, it's an honor to be a part of an event that helps out a charity that was near and dear to his heart.

From my experience with Anne Hayes, she didn't appreciate these kids as football players, she appreciated them as kids. As much as football was a big part of their lives, and all the rest of it, there is a real community on any college campus, even on a big college campus like Ohio State. I don't want to use the term *inbred* here, but it is very supportive. Very inclusive. I think that was her thing—it wasn't just a football team. A lot of times, people consider it a football college. Well, that's not how she saw it. She saw it as a really big family.

When I got to college there, Woody was exactly what you saw. I'm sure you're going to find people who will say, "Well, I knew him as Dad." Or "I knew him as grandpa," or something like that. I'm sure there are people who saw him that way, but, no, what you saw was what you got. Whether he was teaching a history class or teaching a freshman football class, he was exactly what he was. He always had a white shirt on. I never saw him show up at the Jai Lai with a sweatshirt on. Maybe sometimes he'd be dressed up in a coat and tie, but I don't recall that. It was always that short-sleeved white shirt, the dark trousers, and the Spot-bilt coaching shoes and a hat, or the hat would come off and stay in the car, but that's the guy. That's who you saw. Was that who he wanted you to see? Maybe. I don't know. There were no two faces of Woody Hayes.

"There were no two faces of Woody Hayes."

I joined QFM 96 in October of 1979. I was still in college. I had a rather extended college career, let's say. The only reason I left college was to take my job here. If you look at my transcript, you might argue that I actually walked away sooner than 1979 . . . but I got a job working at a small radio station outside of Columbus, up in Johnstown. That began to distract me. When I was offered my job here in 1979, that's when I was willing to admit the fact that I was done with college.

As much as I might have been lackadaisical in my efforts, the bottom line is when I returned to school, I only lost five hours out of all those years that didn't quality for my degree, and was able to graduate. I needed 55 hours, when it was all said and done, to finish up. I'm a proud member of the class of '06. When I graduated, I was 53 years old . . .

I was asked to introduce John Cooper to the young alumni club when he first came to town. He seemed genuine. He was from Arizona State. He might have been a little overwhelmed with the intensity. He certainly knew what he was getting into—the history of the program, the legend of Woody Hayes and the rest of it. But I don't think anybody who comes in from the outside can gauge the intensity that you are faced with. He was bowled over by how much attention is paid to this team in this town.

Coach Tressel is so quietly effective. Our sports guy will go over to the press conferences and he always comes back with his "Jim Tressel nugget of the week." Riverboat gamblers don't play their cards as close to their vest as Jim Tressel does. He doesn't give you *anything*. He talks, and everything is a learning experience, but behind that is the mind of a true tactician. He doesn't get up, but he doesn't get down.

He is cool as a cucumber. One thing I really love about the guy—I was so impressed when he instituted the policy of after the game the players all go over to Block O, the student section, and sing the Alma Mater. That touches me so. Maybe that's been done at other schools before. I know it's being done at other schools now. Whether that's their response to the Buckeyes' doing it or not, I don't care. It is just such a cool thing to remind these kids that as big as the football team is, they're genuinely a part of something bigger than the football team.

There are all kinds of stories about how Woody would break things that were conveniently weakened so that they would break easier, whether it was a table or a chair or something. He was like a good baseball manager, who, rather than let the kids take the brunt of an official's wrath or whatever, he would step up. He would do things to motivate them. He felt that was his job. When you develop that "bigger than life" persona, it's no surprise that that persona lives on long after the man.

Does
your
alma
matter?

BRACE YOURSELF, BRIDGET
HOLD TIGHT, CARMEN
HANG ON, SLOOPY

JOHN TAGENHORST

Professionally, John Tagenhorst is a composer, songwriter, arranger, music and record producer, author, consultant, publisher and business executive (John Tagenhorst Music, Inc.). Growing up in East Liverpool, Ohio, he was a child prodigy who studied music from age 5 and wrote for instrumental and vocal ensembles in high school. In between, his persistence helped bring "Hang On Sloopy" to life as a staple at Ohio State football games.

It was raining. I can't even remember the opponent that day in 1965, but I do remember the rain. And I remember Coach Woody Hayes wouldn't allow the Ohio State Marching Band on the field. The band had black raincoats and played their whole show on the sideline. The audience had raincoats or umbrellas. It was the day the song "Hang On Sloopy" was going to become something special to OSU fans, I thought.

But the rain changed everything. The band played the song and it absolutely died. All that work was for nothing, and I had hounded the band director for months to do it.

I first heard the song "Hang On Sloopy" by the McCoys in late August of 1965 at the Ohio State Fair on the **P.A. SYSTEM***. I used to "hear" things for the band. I wanted to arrange it for the band. I called the director of the band and he said, "The Ohio State band would *never*

The ***PUBLIC ADDRESS** announcer for the Houston Astros (Colt '45s) in 1962 was Dan Rather. John Forsythe, the actor, was the P.A. announcer for the Brooklyn Dodgers in 1937 and 1938.

play that kind of song." I called him every couple of weeks, and then I worked on the assistant director. Finally, about the last week of September, 1965, he called up at 8 o'clock at night and said to go ahead and arrange that song.

"Wow!" I couldn't believe what I heard. By 9:30, I had started arranging the song and finished it at one in the morning, in the key of F. I laid down for about a half hour. I was really, really tired. I was in a band and had to get up at 7 to be on television in the morning. I finished the arrangements and then told myself, "get up, you lazy so-and so," and modulate it. I redid it and went to the key of C-flat, which is six flats. That's a no-no in marching band language, but that's what I wanted to do. The first time the band tried it was on Tuesday morning before the game, and Fred Dart, the assistant director, called me and said, "God, they just love it. They just love it. They're wild about it."

So we're at the game and they played it on the sidelines, because Woody wouldn't let them play on the field. I thought of all that work and all that hassle, and it died. But the following week they played it again. And this time the sun was shining and the students just went nuts—up on the top deck, where they put the students, pretty much, other than Block O. Then they asked for "Sloopy" again, and they started standing students on top of each others' shoulders and rocking back and forth. Each week, it got more of an ovation.

Woody Hayes knew I did "Sloopy." We had a meeting with the band directors. Woody had been there a couple of times. He'd walk over and say hi. One time, during a game, the team wasn't doing so well, and Woody left the team and walked over and told me and the band director to play "Sloopy." Honest to God.

The band, for a while, hated "Sloopy," because they got sick of playing it, but that didn't last. Now they think nothing of it. It's for the fourth quarter, and they play it when the team needs an extra push to get the fans going. I'm pretty proud of that—I love it. I never, in a thousand years, would have dreamed that the song would be lasting.

WARM BEER, COLD PIZZA . . . STAY TUNED

JAY CRAWFORD

He wakes up with a smile and brings it to work each day, even though his co-host on ESPN2's First Take *(formerly* Cold Pizza*), Dana Jacobson, is a graduate of "that school up north." Crawford himself is a Bowling Green grad, but came to appreciate the Buckeye culture growing up in northern Ohio and during his stint as sports director at WBNS-TV from 1993 to 1998. His favorite Buckeye memory, though, has nothing to do with broadcasting, and everything to do with a father-son road trip, and—oh yeah—taking a few jabs at Jacobson in the process.*

I grew up in Sandusky, Ohio, rooting for both ***NOTRE DAME** and Ohio State, but probably more for the Buckeyes, even though I consider myself a good Catholic. I worked in the Columbus market as a sportscaster at WBNS-TV. We'd even gone back to Columbus with the *Cold Pizza* show a couple of times.

But the best experience was just being a fan. A dad and his son. It happened in November of 2006, the biggest Ohio State-Michigan game ever. And it came so close to not happening.

My son and I had booked flights. Mike DiSabato, who wrestled at Ohio State, a good friend of mine and a big supporter of the program, called me on Tuesday of that week and said, "Hey, I've got a couple of tickets for you and your boy if you want to come in." I booked a flight—2:15 out of LaGuardia, knowing that typically our show is on live 10 to noon every day and then it replays from noon to 2.

Before the ***NOTRE DAME** band marches to the stadium on game day, the sousaphone section gathers by the southwest corner of the Sacred Heart Basilica. They sing "The Victory March" . . . and then they sing it backward . . . syllable-by-syllable.

Barring any major, breaking news stories, we're done every day by 12:30. I figured that gave me plenty of time to get to the airport. Because we had waited so long to book the tickets, I couldn't even fly into Columbus—we had to fly into Dayton. We were going to rent a car and then go in and stay at Ryan Miller's condo. Ryan played on some of those teams in the mid-90s, and Ryan and I have been very good friends ever since.

At 11:30 the day before the Ohio State-Michigan game, the producer gets in my ear and says, "Bo Schembechler just died." Obviously, it wasn't completely unexpected, because we knew he had been sick and knew he had been rushed to the hospital, and we had been reporting that throughout the day.

We actually were the ones to break it nationally. My producer broke in and said this is what's going on. We delivered the news that he had passed. We were in the process of gathering up anybody we could from Michigan to do interviews and to talk about Bo and his legacy, and what he meant to Michigan. We even got Ohio State people, too, to talk about his relationship with Woody.

As all of this is going on, my son, Corey, who was 14 years old at the time and had never been to an Ohio State-Michigan game, couldn't have been more excited that we were going. He is the biggest Ohio State fan I think I've ever met in my life. But now he's realizing what's going on and that this is probably going to mean we're not going to make the flight. That was the risk I took by booking a flight at 2:15.

We ended up staying on live until 2:00, and there was no chance of making that 2:15 flight. So I'm calling the airline, trying to figure out if we can go later. There was nothing. I tried to see if we could get something out the next day. There was nothing. I could have tried standby—again, into Dayton. The flight I was most likely to get would have gotten us in at 2:30. By the time you rent a car and get to Columbus, it's going to be late.

There was a whole range of emotions. Obviously, even being a Buckeye, the news about **BO SCHEMBECHLER*** was sad. Then it became

> ***BO SCHEMBECHLER** was president of the Detroit Tigers following his Michigan career. For many years, the Detroit Tigers Hall of Fame was in Ann Arbor.

more and more obvious we weren't going to make the flight, so we went through the emotions of "we're going to miss the game." Then we decided to make a road trip out of it.

I looked at Corey and said, "Well, I just don't think there's any way we can miss this game . . . so let's just drive." He was like, "Wow, how far is that, Dad?" I said, "It's probably going to take about nine, 10 hours, but if you keep me up, I can do it." We both had obviously gotten up early in the morning to go into the city to do the show. We're talking about being up since 4 o'clock in the morning, and if we left right away, we would probably get in around 11:30 or midnight. It would be a very long day. There was just no way in the world I was going to be able to tell him we couldn't go. So we loaded up the car, and off we went.

We just talked for nine hours driving to Columbus and nine hours back. On the way up, we played the game 15 times in our minds—how it was going to unfold. Then, on the way back, we replayed every big play and remembered this, and "what about that?" I took probably 100 pictures as everybody stormed the field after the game. Corey and I were right there.

Corey grabbed some turf and put it on top of his head, and I took pictures of that. He wrote a sign, because Dana Jacobson, my co-host, is a Michigan grad. Corey wrote the final score on a piece of paper and wrote, "Sorry Dana," and I took a picture of him standing next to Brutus Buckeye. It's just one of those times that no matter what happens—I could be 85 years old, and Corey could be 56 years old—we'll talk about that Saturday afternoon in Columbus as fondly as we do right now. I know he feels as strongly about it as I do. The way it worked out ended up being better than had we caught our flight and done it just the normal way. . .

When I was working in the Columbus market, it was weird for me to be more involved, because I knew the outside portion of the program. That's the part all the people in Ohio see and know. What was fun and, at the same time, almost surreal for me was to go behind the curtain and get to know the inner workings of the Woody Hayes machine, the behind-the-scenes action you never really get to see. It's hidden 350 days out of the year. You don't really get to see it. That was a lot of fun for me.

I was like a kid in the candy store, because it gave me an opportunity to follow very closely the team I had most rooted for growing up as a kid. It was both a job—probably second—and, first, it was a lifestyle. It was a hobby. It was so much fun to be able to cover the team. They were all very good when I was there.

When I got there, I realized right away, it was a full-time job, just about year round for everybody on the team. It was a given that you didn't go home for the summer, and that always surprised me. They were all there. It was their job, as much as anybody had a regular job. That's what it was for them. It was just very much like a corporation.

We led our newscasts, not the sportscasts, we led our newscasts with Ohio State stories 30 to 45 days a year. Game day, on Saturday night, 6 o'clock, 11 o'clock, first story—how did the Ohio State team do? Oftentimes, if they were undefeated and ranked nationally, the big story on Sunday was "Where are they ranked? What does this mean, and who's next?" I did the weekend sportscasts, so I was constantly leading the newscasts with Ohio State sports stories. Not only was it the biggest sports story in town, but, again, 30-45 days out of the year, it's the biggest *news* story in town. For the most part, it's still like that.

John Cooper was the head coach during my time there, and I loved John Cooper. He was extremely accessible. He was honest, sometimes to a fault. He was an unbelievable recruiter. If you look at the talent he was able to bring to Columbus from the time I was there until I left—'93 to '98—it's almost an indictment that he didn't win the national championship.

When you're talking about Eddie George, Joey Galloway, Bob Hoying, Terry Glenn, you know the names, the list is very long. Mike Vrabel, some of the defensive stars they had there. And to think that they couldn't put it all together in one season. His legacy is he brought in so much great talent, but obviously struggled from the last game in November to **JANUARY 1ST OR 2ND*** or whenever they played their bowl games. His track record was what it was. Bill Parcells is famous for saying "You are what your record is." If that's true, John Cooper was a magnificent recruiter, a terrific coach the first nine or 10 games out of

If actress Tuesday Weld married the namesake son of Senior Tour golfer Don *JANUARY, she would be Tuesday January, the Second. (The author couldn't resist. He'll show himself to the principal's office now.)

the year and, for whatever reason, never really had that same success against Michigan or in bowl games.

We absolutely felt Woody's presence during those Cooper years. John was constantly being compared to Woody. "Well, Woody did it this way . . ." I remember having a conversation in John's office, where we were talking about the magnitude of the Michigan game. I'm an Ohio guy, and I know John wasn't. And I'm sitting there, as a reporter having just an off-the-record conversation with John. I'm not saying that he tried any less—I'm not saying that for him it was anything intentional, but I think that, for me, I was able to put it together pretty simply by saying that John really never understood the magnitude of that game.

He knew that it was a game he had to win, but I don't think he ever fully comprehended how important that game is to everybody from Portsmouth to Sandusky to Toledo to Youngstown to Zanesville and all parts in between. That's the game. He told me, "Look, I know all about rivalries." And he rattled off some of the rivalries he had been a part of in the past. I told him, "John, those are all big rivalries, but those games don't mean anything to the people here, just like the Ohio State-Michigan game doesn't mean anything to the people there."

The only thing that matters to Ohio State is beating Michigan, and now—because Jim Tressel has raised the bar even higher—"do we have a team that can compete for a national championship?" John, I think, believed that game was very important, but I think he never realized that it would ultimately define his legacy at Ohio State. John is a very bright guy. He would have loved more than anything to win those games, but to sum it up, John tended to prepare for that game as if it was any other game. That might be the psychologically smart thing to do in sports, you're dealing with kids. You don't want to tell them it's different.

But you compare that and contrast that to Jim Tressel, who, on his first day as the Ohio State football coach, stood up in the arena at a basketball game and knew exactly how many days until the Michigan game and knew that they were going to win. He proclaimed that. So for me that was kind of ushering out of the old mentality that it's just another game, and it would be *nice to win*. To somebody who was an Ohio guy, he knew the rivalry, he embraced that pressure, and stood up and faced it, and now the irony is it's kind of switched. Now, Lloyd Carr has, in effect, turned into John Cooper. He hasn't had the success in big games that he did against John and now Jim is having against Lloyd.

I remember when Eddie George won the Heisman. We were in New York. We had a great relationship with Eddie. We had worked it out with Eddie that if he were to win the Heisman Trophy, he would come by CBS on 57th Street, where we were going to do our sports show from live that night, and he would join us for a live sportscast at 11:00.

He shows up at CBS in this limo and they all come upstairs. At one point, I looked at my photographer, and we chuckled. It was about 11:05, and we had done our "top of the news" interview with Eddie, and then we teased that we were going to have more with Eddie in our sports segment. So we had about 15-20 minutes of downtime, and we had ordered pizzas to feed everybody.

At one point, I looked around and told Dave Sirak, who was my cameraman and my photographer, "Just take a look at this picture." There were probably eight people, including John Cooper and Cindy Cooper and Helen Cooper and Eddie George and his mom and all the others sitting around at desks in the CBS newsroom using telephones, calling long distance on CBS's nickel, eating pizza in the newsroom with the Heisman Trophy. It was just one of those bizarre surreal moments where you look around, and you're like, "Well, that's an interesting story to tell 30 years later."

I do remember when Eddie went back to Columbus, he had to put the trophy through the metal detector at the airport. It broke the thumb off on the hand. This was pre-9/11, and I just always remember thinking, it's a Heisman Trophy and it's Eddie George—do they really need to put that through the scanner? It actually gets damaged going through there. That was just another bizarre little tidbit from the Heisman experience.

Eddie was great. Joey Galloway was great. Bobby Hoying. Really, all those guys from that era were. And, at the time, I really wasn't that much older than all of them. I think that made it easier for me to build relationships with them. I still have friendships with a lot of those guys today, which has been fun for me, because I think they're all my kind of people. Most of us are from Ohio. We have fun stories to share. It's the same with Eddie and all the guys from those teams.

AN APPETITE FOR CHANGE

JON SELF

He wasn't even an Ohio State guy, they thought, just a man with deep pockets and a twisted vision. Here was Huntington, West Virginia, native Jon Self tearing apart Woody Hayes' favorite restaurant, the Jai Lai, and the publicity was scorching. But what Self had in mind was something better. And today the 59-year-old owner of the Buckeye Hall of Fame Café isn't just a guy with a good idea, he is entrenched in OSU culture and one of the Buckeyes' most faithful followers.

Archie Griffin means a lot to me as a friend. One of the great stories was when we opened up the Buckeye Hall of Fame Café, I asked Archie if I could borrow one of his Heisman Trophies to put in for the opening. To show you the kind of guy he is, Archie said, "Absolutely. In fact, just leave it there. Not that many people see it at my house." I'll never forget when I went out to get the trophy from him, he said to me, "Which one do you want?" I said, "Seeing how you're the only guy in the world that can say that, maybe you ought to make that decision." He said, "Well, everybody seems to like this second one better. Why don't you take it?" And it's still at our restaurant.

> **"I asked Archie if I could borrow one of his Heisman Trophies . . ."**

Archie has always been a huge supporter of our restaurant. At Troy Smith's Heisman Trophy presentation, I'll never forget they asked Archie where he kept his Heisman, and he said he had it in a friend's restaurant, the Buckeye Hall of Fame Café. I remember seeing him at a basketball game a couple of days later. I said, "Archie, you didn't mention our lunch specials, and that was the one thing I was upset about."

I remember a guy was standing there in our café and looking in awe at

Archie's Heisman Trophy. Arch happened to be in the building for something. I saw him and said, "You've got to come up here. This guy just can't get over your trophy." I tapped the guy on the shoulder and said, "You really like that, don't you?" He said, "Yeah." I said, "How would you like to meet the guy right here standing next to you?" I thought he was going to go to his knees. Archie's just that kind of person.

I was meeting with Archie one day up in their offices at St. John Arena. I was looking around at all the wonderful pictures and trophies and everything, and thinking how few people had the opportunity to come up in that area and to see that, and how much the fans loved the opportunity to see that kind of thing. I thought what we ought to do is open a restaurant and make this stuff available in the form of a Hall of Fame.

Typically, I've watched Halls of Fame not work based on the fact that you've got a charge to go to them and people may want to go once, but they don't go often, and it costs them to take people to it. I also thought that in our restaurant business, it would be something that wouldn't particularly ever go out of style, tying it to a university. The fans seem to always want to talk about the history of the team and current events, as well. What better place to do that than in a sports venue like that?

I was looking for a location for the restaurant. I was driving by the Jai Lai one day and went in. Of course, it was doing what it had in the past. It had grown old, both with the age of the restaurant and the concept itself, but it had great history for a lot of people with Ohio State. Woody used to take a lot of his meals there. A lot of ex-players used to go there. A lot of recruiting went on there. I had knowledge of all that history. It was close to the university. It had good visibility for a restaurant. It made sense that it would be a good restaurant location.

When we first purchased the restaurant late in 1996, we just got pummeled a little bit in the press for the fact that "you closed Woody's old hangout—you're closing a restaurant that had been a standard in this town for many, many years." It got a little bad press for the first few days until we made the announcement of what we were going to do there. That completely turned it around in Columbus.

In the mid-'70s, I moved to Columbus. At the time Archie and Pete Johnson were playing, and there was a lot of excitement. I was from West Virginia and an Alabama fan. I decided to throw a party at my house, where I served everything in Tide boxes and had a big picture of **BEAR BRYANT***, not realizing I would lose friends over that. It was the Sugar Bowl. Alabama beat Ohio State, 35-6, and the next day I was kidding everybody about it, and my boss walked in and said, "John, you realize where I went to school?" I said, "No, I don't have any idea." He laid a buckeye on my desk and said, "Don't forget where your bread is buttered." He walked out. I think I became an Ohio State fan that day!

> "He laid a buckeye on my desk and said, 'Don't forget where your bread is buttered.'"

When I met John Cooper, I thought he was a wonderful, funny guy. I don't call him a throwback, but John always had something cute to say. I'll never forget he recruited a great player one time—a great big kid—and I said, "John, how old is he?" He said, "Jon, I don't know his age, but he was born on the 4th, 5th and 6th of June." I remember when John was going through some hard times, and I was walking through the lobby of the restaurant with him, I asked him, "Are you doing OK?" He said, "I got two theme songs. 'Lord, Help Me Make It Through the Night' and 'One Day at a Time, Sweet Jesus.'" You always got on a personal basis with these guys. That gets hard when people get critical of these coaches when they're not doing as well as everyone wants and expects. You get a bit defensive about that, because they are your friends.

Woody really loved tradition. I really got to know Woody in an interesting scenario. Woody lived in Upper Arlington. Back then, I had a little kiosk-type ice cream place up in Arlington. Woody came in there . . . and he wasn't supposed to eat ice cream, but he would always seem to end up having some. I would join him in the seating area out there and listen to some of his stories. Woody loved his ex-players. He loved to talk about that. I think if Woody were alive today, he would be a regular guest at the Buckeye Hall of Fame Café, and he would be sitting there telling stories with the other ex-players and coaches that come

---

***BEAR BRYANT** coached against two schools three times each that he never defeated: Notre Dame and Alabama. While coaching at Kentucky and Texas A&M, he never defeated the Crimson Tide . . . Bryant often joked that if he ever quit coaching he'd probably "croak within a week." He died 28 days after his last game.

in there. That really makes it fun to be in here, when you get some of those guys together telling stories.

Whether they're about Woody or any of the ex-coaches, I'm telling you there are times you want to laugh and times you want to cry when you hear the great stories about the things these coaches did to inspire them, to help them grow as better citizens, better husbands, just better people, and how much those coaches affect these kids' lives. It is just unbelievable. I think Woody would be in there often if he lived here today.

Charlie Weis ate the Chocolate Factory

IF YOU DON'T STAND FOR SOMETHING, YOU'LL FALL FOR ANYTHING

JOHN KASICH

John Kasich, host of Fox News Channel's Heartland with John Kasich, *is a former U.S. congressman. The author of the book* Stand for Something *still likes what Woody Hayes stood for. He is as staunch a defender of OSU's academic reputation as he is of the football program.*

I've been an Ohio State football fan for a long time. It never got to the point where I painted myself scarlet and gray, but at the same time I don't like it when they lose.

In 1996, my girlfriend, Karen Waldbillig, and I went to see the Michigan-Ohio State game. We were getting beat. It just seemed to get worse and worse. That day, I was going to ask my girlfriend to marry me, so I kept saying, "Don't worry. Things are going to get better." Michigan would score another touchdown, but I'd say, "Don't worry, sweetheart. There are good things about to happen." We leave the stadium after one of those depressing losses to Michigan, which we don't have much anymore. I took her out to this piece of land I had bought and asked her to marry me. She said yes. I said, "Well, I told you things were going to get better."

What brought me to Ohio State in the first place was that I was looking around at colleges, trying to figure out where to go, and my mother told me about a lady whose son went to Ohio State. She said, "What do you think about that school?" I said, "I don't know a thing about it." So my dad and I drove to Columbus. I remember walking around inside the dorms. People had these things on that said, "Go Bucks," and I wanted to explain to them that the **PITTSBURGH PIRATES*** spell it "Bucs." It never dawned on me what the heck "Go Bucks" was.

The ***PITTSBURGH PIRATES** was also the name of a National Hockey League team for five seasons in the 1920s.

Yet it was almost love at first sight. When I got to Ohio State, I knew. Isn't that funny? I just knew it's where I wanted to go to school. My dad was a mailman. We didn't even know there was such a thing as out-of-state tuition, but they decided to send me anyway. Obviously, it costs a lot more than going in-state. Ohio State just changed my whole life. I feel a tremendous obligation to Ohio State. Now I have an opportunity to teach there.

Ohio State University has become tougher and tougher in terms of who they let in. We have to be careful that we don't tip that too far the other way. I spend time on that campus. There are two particular gems in Ohio that stand out in my mind more than anything else. No. 1 is The Ohio State University, for all that it offers to Ohio. Second is the Cleveland Clinic. I look at those two things as being just such great assets that we really don't appreciate or take advantage of.

You hear people from other schools sometimes criticize Ohio State and its academics. I'm there—I see the dedication of the teachers. People say they have big classes. Most of the classes I teach in are not very big. It's got beauty. It's got character. It's got resources. If my kids went there, I'd be thrilled. I have twin daughters. But they're little. Who knows where the heck they're going to go to college? Let's get them through the first grade, and then we can figure it out later.

I had the great pleasure of really knowing Woody Hayes. I spent a considerable amount of time with him. He was a real supporter of mine, as was Anne Hayes, his wife. I'm a disciple of Woody Hayes. It doesn't matter where I am in the country, I talk about Woody. I just think they don't make them like Woody Hayes, from the standpoint of ethics and dedication to players.

Obviously, the national media tried to create an impression about Woody, after the Clemson game, the Gator Bowl game at the end of the 1978 season that ended Hayes' career. That fades and now you can paint a new picture of him. He was an awesome, awesome man—one of my heroes. He not only talked the talk, but Woody walked the walk. I remember him telling me once they wanted to make a movie about him. He flew out to Hollywood. He was very uncomfortable, so he got on a plane and flew home. That was the coach. I loved him. He was very volatile and very opinionated, but a great teacher, too. He was a unique person.

I met Woody around 1982. The one thing I always was struck by about him, before I ever met him, was the fact that he never panicked. He had such confidence in his game plan. I can remember them punting the ball with two minutes to go, down four. "Why is he doing this?" Then something would happen. They'd get the fumble. I thought he was a good coach, but we all wanted him to pass more. Let's be honest about it.

"I thought he was a good coach, but we all wanted him to pass more. Let's be honest about it."

My latest book is called *Stand for Something*. And I think Woody could have written a book called that. I'll give you an example, a glimpse. There was a young man who was paralyzed. My wife said there would be many days when she'd be there visiting him, and it wouldn't be surprising to have Woody walk in. People have a tremendous dedication to him, because he was dedicated to people.

I'm glad I get to do my *Heartland* show on the Fox News Channel from Columbus. It keeps me close to Ohio State and a lot of great memories—and maybe great opportunities. There's a possibility that I would run for governor, but we just have to wait and see what happens.

Hey, I think Michigan's a 4-year school now

Chapter 6

Home Sweet Horseshoe

Open the Gates, and Open Them Wide . . . Buckeye Fans Are Coming Inside

YEAH, THAT'S THE TICKET
THE BOY WONDER HAD THE
BOYS WONDERING

JERRY MARLOWE

Whoever coined the phrase "Yeah, that's the ticket" definitely did NOT have Jerry Marlowe in mind, The 71-year-old pharmacist and Ohio State grad from Dover, Ohio, has been whipping up prescriptions for gate crashing the Ohio State-Michigan game on a steady basis since 1970. His disguises have ranged from a parachutist to a hot dog vendor to a nun. He has vowed to go straight, but can he?

I have been sneaking into every Ohio State-Michigan game at Ohio Stadium since 1970. The only time I had missed was in 2004, when we had an emergency at the pharmacy. And it had gotten tougher over the years . . . with the media doing stories on my gate crashing. Our paper here in Dover/New Philadelphia, Ohio—the *Times-Reporter*—had done quite a bit. The Cleveland *Plain Dealer,* the Columbus paper, a paper in Des Moines, Iowa, *PM Magazine* in Columbus and many more—and all of this publicity made it more difficult to pull it off.

I'm originally from the Dover, Ohio, area. I was born at Union Hospital at 10 o'clock in the morning on Lincoln's birthday. My brother, who was six years younger than me, always kidded me, referring to me as a "Dishonest Abe."

I've dressed as a Boy Scout leader, a pizza deliveryman, hot dog vendor, band director, a team doctor, a nun . . . The nun was one of my favorites. I ditched the costume pretty quick that day, though. I mean, which restroom would you use? I didn't want to be arrested for being a pervert.

Now, I have a few rules with this. I never impersonate someone in the military or a police officer. And I always send money to cover the cost of the ticket and then some. I've even started a scholarship at the OSU pharmacy school, of which I'm a graduate. Sometimes I've even had a ticket. I just wouldn't beat them out of the price of a ticket. That's not the idea.

It all started really my freshman year at Ohio State, 1954. Now, I didn't have a streak going then, but that's when it all started.

When growing up in Dover, there was always that interest in Ohio State football. I was never of the physical nature to get into football and play. We played in the backyard, and I can still remember Frank Elwood, the quarterback for Woody back in the mid-'50s, Danny Fronk, Dick LeBeau—all these guys in the neighborhood who would go on to play at Ohio State would come over and play. We had a big backyard, and they'd play a little touch football or whatever.

I was the little guy, but they'd let me in on it. I remember catching a pass from Frank Elwood one time, and it literally knocked the wind out of me. I caught it, but it was all I could do to hang on to it. All these guys were neighbors and would come over to our yard to play. So that they could use our yard, they let me in on it.

So it made the games all the more fun when I showed up on campus in 1954. I joined the TKE fraternity and met a guy named Harry Thoman. And Harry was the inspiration behind all this.

It started innocently enough, with no intent to actually sneak into the game. I had this tuxedo and top hat from my father. The top hat was one of those you could pop the side of and the top would pop out. You could flatten it. Then, if you hit the edge of it, it popped up. I had that top hat and his tuxedo and somewhere I had acquired a pink umbrella. This was when people didn't wear weird outfits to the game. Everybody wore ties—it was a weird era when you had to dress up and look nice to be a member of a fraternity. Now, you can be pretty scroungy.

Harry and I went to a game, and I had this whole outfit on. The gatekeeper said, "Your tickets?" I looked at him, and I opened the umbrella up and put it over my head. I popped the hat and put it on. I said, "Oh, tickets, tickets, tickets. Who needs tickets? Rubbish. Rubbish." He started laughing so hard. I had a student ticket, but when he started laughing so much, we just walked right by him. He was still laughing when I went in. I said to Harry, "My God, he forgot to take the tickets." That started it all then.

There was a break in there, but when I started it back up on a regular basis it was really to surprise Harry and his wife, Sue Dell. I'd always find out where they were going to be and try to jump out at him in some new outfit every time. It lent itself to gate crashing in different various ways. I took my inspiration from a lot of different sources.

When I was at Sinatra's opening concert, I think that's what gave me the idea for the nun. I noticed all these nuns sitting ringside. They'd just walk right through the turnstile, just walked right in, and nobody would ask for a ticket. I thought, "Well, heck, if they can do that, so can I."

The year I went in as a referee was the year Woody was tapped to go to the Orange Bowl. I'll never forget. A local guy, Les Williams, was a referee and lent me his uniform. He was a pretty big guy. I also bummed a downs marker. On the uniform I had it lettered to say "**NBC-TV*** News Referee."

I snuck in a white cane. Under my jacket, I had a tin cup and some dark glasses. Woody always invariably would get after the referees and shake his fist at them. So I was waiting for the moment when that happened. I was going to walk across the end zone with the white cane, tapping my way. And the funny thing about the down marker was we added a 5 for fifth down.

So I was going to flip to number 5 and walk across the end zone with this white cane tapping, wearing the dark glasses and holding the tin cup. I thought that if that didn't get some notoriety, I don't know what would. As fate would have it, I was up in C Deck looking for Harry up there. I heard the roar of the crowd and damned if it wasn't Woody out screaming at the refs. Here I was clear the heck up in C Deck. I raced down, risking a heart attack, trying to get down in time. By the time I

***NBC** Sports President, Dick Ebersol, recently paid $50,000 at a charity auction to have Carly Simon tell him the name of the subject person in her song, "You're So Vain." Only Simon, Ebersol and that person know the identity, rumored to be Warren Beatty, James Taylor or Mick Jagger.

got down there, it was over. They had settled it all, and the game was proceeding. It just wasn't the right time.

I wanted to go as Brutus Buckeye one year. We had made a costume and everything. But we found out someone at a pep rally had stolen the real one. **WENDY'S*** Restaurant had a big reward out for anyone who could lead to finding Brutus Buckeye for the game that weekend. I thought, "I can't go in wearing that now. They'll think I stole it." So I called one of my daughter's friends, Jan Ewing, who was a cheerleader at Ohio State.

I asked her if I got the uniform together, if I could just run in the gates with them. She said, "Yes, we'll get you a megaphone and everything." To go in front of that band and run in there with those cheerleaders in a cheerleading outfit—talk about adrenaline. I'm running in. Of course, I was much younger then. I actually, literally did a cartwheel, which I could never do. I couldn't have done it then if it wouldn't have been for the adrenaline. Then they let me lead a cheer down at the other end. I just had a ball with it.

When I was the hot-dog vendor, I had to affiliate with a church group. At that time, church groups ran a lot of those concessions. I had to go through Marriott, which was in charge of all the vendors. I told them I was doing an article for the local newspaper on what it's like to be a hot-dog vendor at an Ohio State game, and how you survive the day. The Marriott guy bought that. The church group gave me change and the apron and everything. I had taken along two jars of Grey Poupon mustard. I had a big leather hat on, and I thought that would grab attention. The church group told me I sold more hot dogs than any other vendor.

That was also the game when Harry was dying—he had prostate cancer. That's the year I got the band to play "Hang On Sloopy." I got the card section, which still exists, to spell "Hang On Harry, Hang On." There was hardly a dry eye in our group up in C Deck. Harry just about fell out of the stands.

When 2002 came around, ESPN wanted to get involved. We'd had that

Late hamburger king Dave Thomas named the company after his daughter, ***WENDY**. Wendy was once a babysitter for John Havlicek's children.

awful 9/11 thing the year before. I talked to them and thought, "I gotta stop this." It's a violation of trust of the people who are in charge of security at the stadium. What better place to blow up than an Ohio State-Michigan game. I thought it was time to put an end to it.

> ## "I'm running down Neil Avenue at break-neck speed in this outfit. I looked like an escapee from jail."

One of Harry and Sue Dell's very close friends was Russ Thibaut, an usher who always worked C Deck in the section where Harry and Sue Dell's tickets would be. He would always tailgate with them after the game. I thought, "Well, gee, I'm gonna call Russ this year. I'm going to put an end to this thing, but I'm going to do it with some class."

I went over to the costume shop and got the old-fashioned white-and-black striped suit and a hat. It came with shackles and a ball and chain. I called Russ and said, "I think it's time to put an end to this with all this 9/11 and everything. Would you arrest me if I get to the game at a time when it would work for you?"

Down at the gates, it looks like a prison. If I can get there in time, I'll get ahold of the fella from the *Times-Reporter* and tell him to be there with a camera. But I wasn't going to tell him what I was doing. Russ said, "We would be glad to arrest you, Jerry." There are always sheriffs' deputies there with guns on their belt and everything. I told him to round up one of those deputies, and we'll get some pictures.

As it worked out, I get down there and there was just mass confusion that day. I've never seen so many traffic jams. I parked far away. I ran from there on down to the gate, where I was supposed to be between 9:30 and 10, because Russ had to go up to work. The game didn't start until 1 o'clock.

I'm running down Neil Avenue at breakneck speed in this outfit. I looked like an escapee from jail. Here comes this cab away from the stadium. I yelled at him and banged on the door. "I've got to get to the stadium immediately. Can you swing this thing around?" He was from Palestine, I think, and he looked at me and said, "Ten dollar." We were only a few blocks away, but I jumped in the cab and told him to do a U-ey, a U-turn.

Apparently in Palestine, a U-ey doesn't mean what it meant to me, so

OCTOBER 24, 1955

SPORTS
ATED

25 CENTS
$7.50 A YEAR

HOWARD CASSADY
THE OHIO STATE STORY

OCTOBER 24, 1955

This section contains every *Sports Illustrated* cover devoted solely to Ohio State.

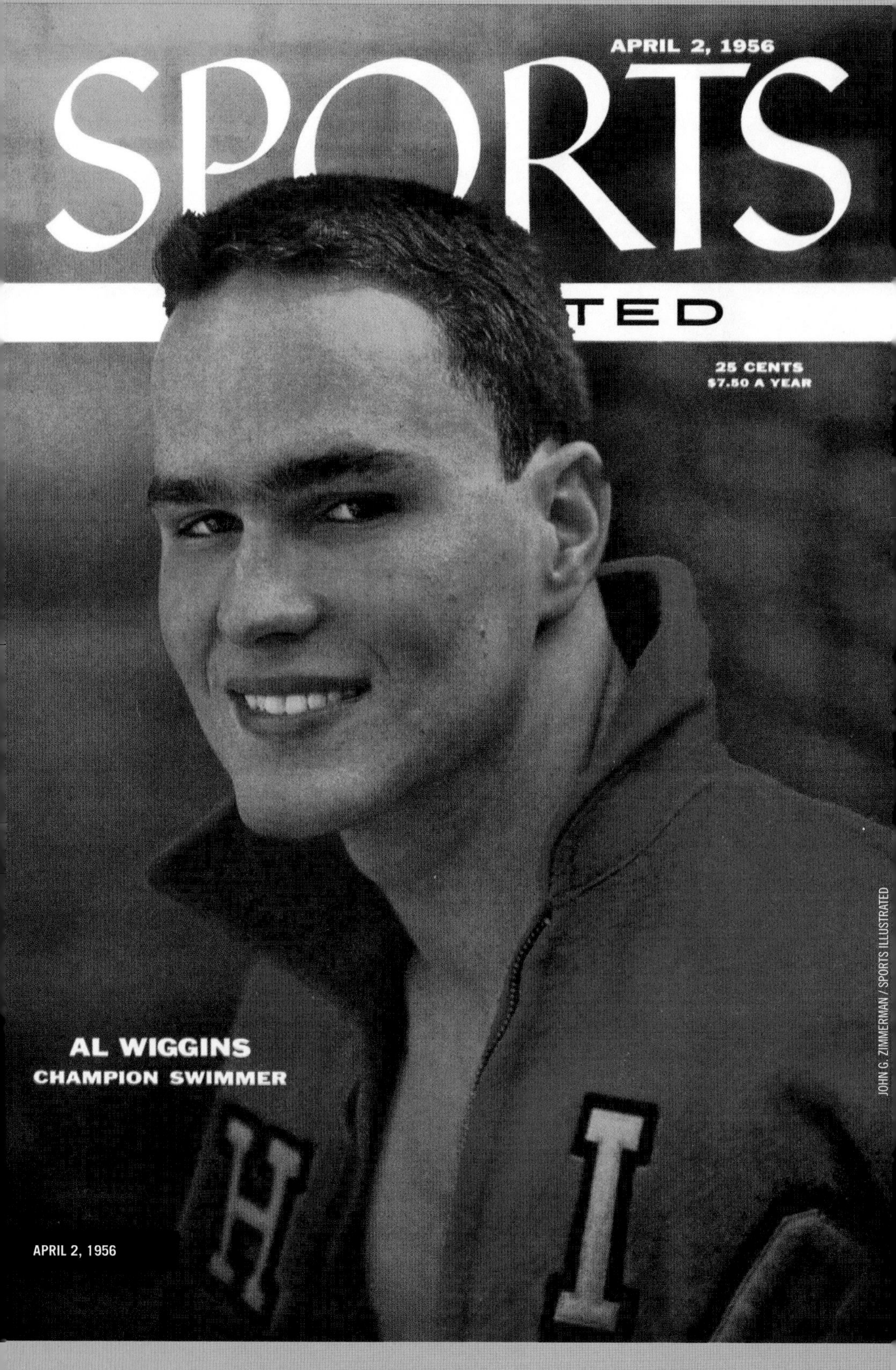

APRIL 2, 1956
SPORTS
TED
25 CENTS
$7.50 A YEAR
AL WIGGINS
CHAMPION SWIMMER
JOHN G. ZIMMERMAN / SPORTS ILLUSTRATED

APRIL 2, 1956

OCTOBER 13, 1958

America's National Sports Weekly

25 CENTS
$7.50 A YEAR

SPORTS ILLUSTRATED

THE COACH

A CONVERSATION PIECE DISSECTING THE MAN FOR WHOM THE HORNS BLOW

OCTOBER 13, 1958

OHIO STATE FOOTBALL

SPORTS
ILLUSTRATED

JANUARY 11, 1960

America's National Sports Weekly

25 CENTS

THE BRIGHT NEW
STARS
OF BASKETBALL

JERRY LUCAS
of Ohio State

JERRY COOKE / SPORTS ILLUSTRATED

JANUARY 11, 1960

Sports
Illustrated

MARCH 27, 1961   25 CENTS

**BASKETBALL'S
NATIONAL CHAMPIONSHIP**

MARCH 27, 1961

SPORTSMAN OF THE YEAR

Sports Illustrated

JANUARY 8, 1962 · 25 CENTS

BASKETBALL'S
JERRY LUCAS

Weaver

Sports Illustrated

NOVEMBER 11, 1968   50 CENTS

OHIO STATE'S JANKOWSKI CATCHES TOUCHDOWN PASS AGAINST MSU

NOVEMBER 11, 1968

COLLEGE FOOTBALL
Sports Illustrated

SEPTEMBER 15, 1969   50 CENTS

OHIO STATE
STILL No. 1

SEPTEMBER 15, 1969

Sports Illustrated

SEPTEMBER 9, 1974   60 CENTS

COLLEGE FOOTBALL/1974

Ohio State's Archie Griffin

SEPTEMBER 9, 1974

Sports Illustrated

JANUARY 22, 1979 $1.25

BIG DOINGS IN THE BIG TEN

Ohio State
Upsets Illinois

JANUARY 22, 1979

Sports Illustrated

NOVEMBER 26, 1979 $1.25

ROSE BOWL BOUND

Art Schlichter Leads Unbeaten Ohio State Past Michigan

NOVEMBER 26, 1979

724454   48   ®

Sports Illustrated

Take That!

No. 1 Michigan Flattens Ohio State

DECEMBER 1, 1997

Sports Illustrated

1998 COLLEGE FOOTBALL PREVIEW

MARK McGWIRE
Can He Break Maris's 61?

Ohio State is No.1*

*If Andy Katzenmoyer Makes the Grade

We Rank the Teams 1 to 112

How to Build the Perfect Team

Why The Option Is All the Rage

AUGUST 31, 1998

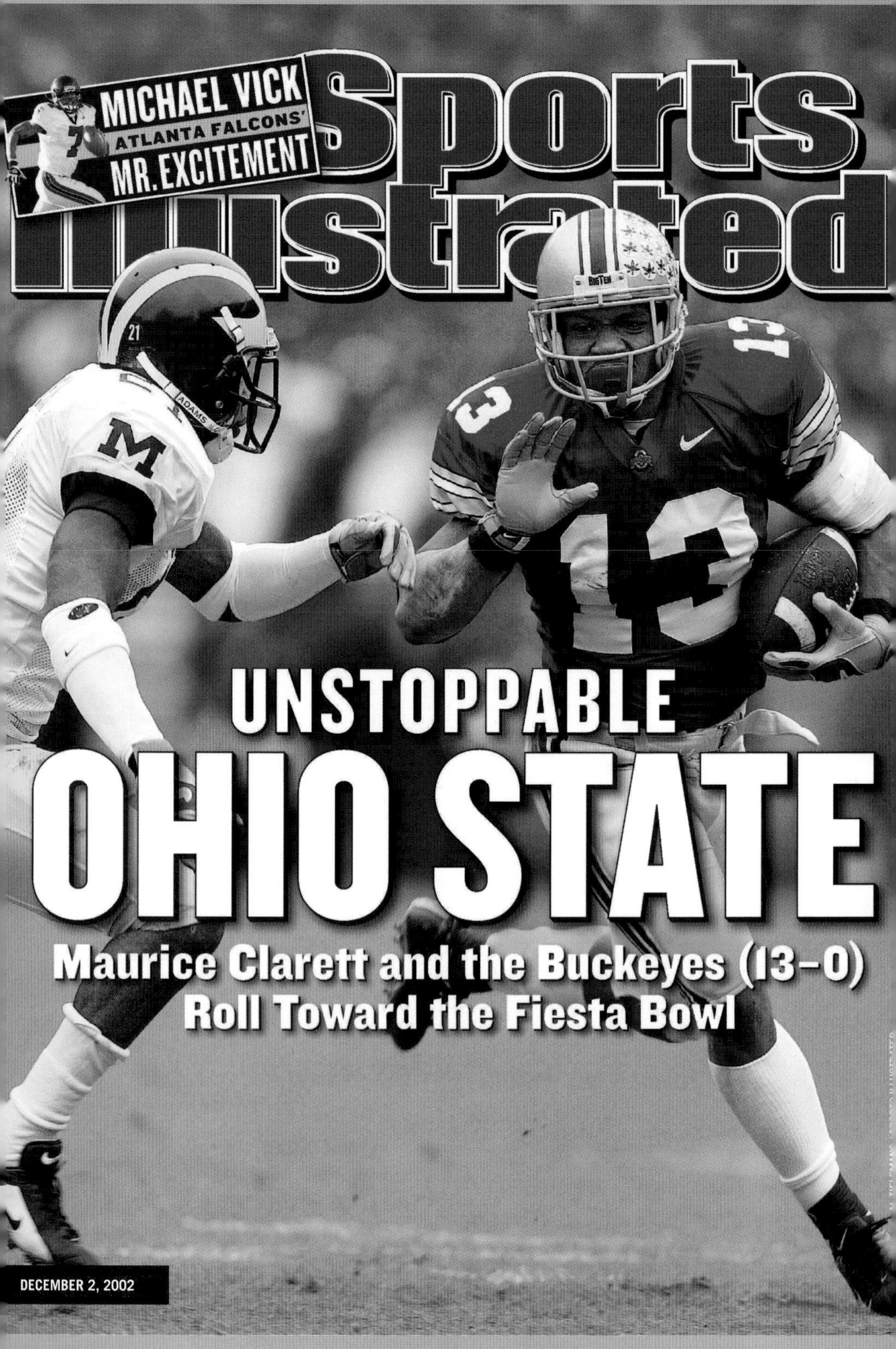

MICHAEL VICK
ATLANTA FALCONS'
MR. EXCITEMENT

Sports Illustrated

UNSTOPPABLE
OHIO STATE
Maurice Clarett and the Buckeyes (13-0) Roll Toward the Fiesta Bowl

DECEMBER 2, 2002

FIESTA BOWL PREVIEW
ARCHIE GRIFFIN: I LOVE THESE BUCKEYES!

SPECIAL COMMEMORATIVE

Sports Illustrated

PRESENTS

RUNNING BACK
MAURICE CLARETT

BigTen

OHIO STATE
BUCKEYES
2002
A PERFECT SEASON

DECEMBER 18, 2002

$5.99US $8.99CAN

0 70989 10259 0

35

COMPLETE NFL PLAYOFF COVERAGE

Sports Illustrated

HOT YOUNG QBs

CHAD PENNINGTON

MICHAEL VICK

"Best Damn Team In the Land . . ."

OHIO STATE

Shocks Miami To Win the National Title

PLUS: The Top 10 Teams Next Season

Quarterback Craig Krenzel leads the Buckeyes to their first championship in 34 years

JANUARY 13, 2003

DAMIAN STROHMEYER / SPORTS ILLUSTRATED

COLLEGE FOOTBALL PREVIEW

Sports Illustrated

SCOUTING REPORTS
117 TEAMS RANKED

SI's Top 10

1. OHIO STATE
2. OKLAHOMA
3. MIAMI
4. TEXAS
5. GEORGIA
6. VIRGINIA TECH
7. KANSAS STATE
8. N.C. STATE
9. AUBURN
10. USC

AUGUST, 2003

CRAIG KRENZEL
The Ohio State quarterback and molecular genetics major has set his mind on a second straight title

Brain Power

OFFENSIVE LINEMEN
The smartest players in football (Really)

SIDELINE GENIUSES
Best coaching minds in the game

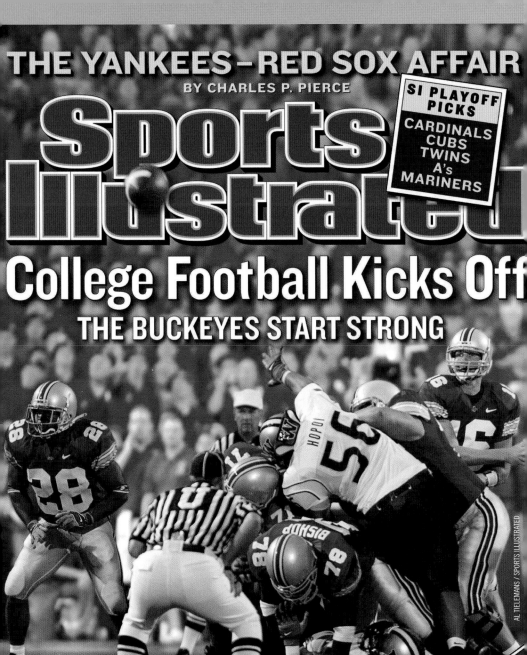

THE YANKEES–RED SOX AFFAIR
BY CHARLES P. PIERCE

Sports Illustrated

SI PLAYOFF PICKS
CARDINALS
CUBS
TWINS
A's
MARINERS

College Football Kicks Off
THE BUCKEYES START STRONG

AL TIELEMANS / SPORTS ILLUSTRATED

BIG WINNERS
USC · Georgia · Nebraska · Colora
Oregon · Michigan

Ohio S
Quarterb
Craig Kre

SEPTEMBER 8, 2003

DARK DAYS IN NEW ORLEANS

GARY SMITH · MICHAEL SILVER · TIM LAYDEN · GEORGE DOHRMANN · LARS ANDERSON · RICK REILLY

Sports Illustrated

College Football's
Fast Starts

Ted Ginn Jr. has Ohio State running hard and gunning for a shootout with Texas

SEPTEMBER 12, 2005

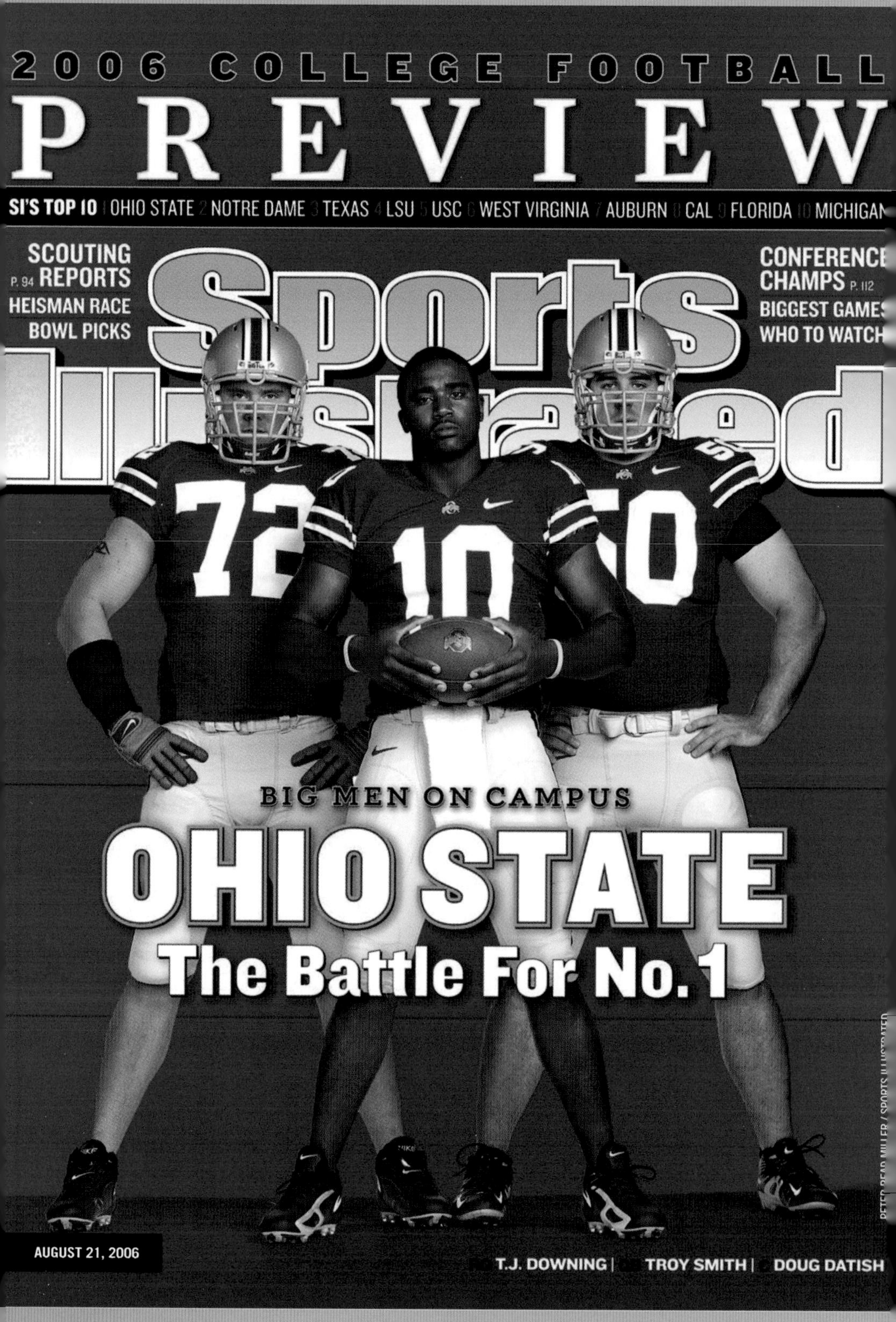

2006 COLLEGE FOOTBALL
PREVIEW
SI'S TOP 10 OHIO STATE NOTRE DAME TEXAS LSU USC WEST VIRGINIA AUBURN CAL FLORIDA MICHIGAN
SCOUTING REPORTS P. 94
HEISMAN RACE
BOWL PICKS
Sports Illustrated
CONFERENCE CHAMPS P. 112
BIGGEST GAMES
WHO TO WATCH
BIG MEN ON CAMPUS
OHIO STATE
The Battle For No. 1
AUGUST 21, 2006
T.J. DOWNING | TROY SMITH | DOUG DATISH
PETER READ MILLER / SPORTS ILLUSTRATED

Carson
Palmer

Sports Illustrated

{ U.S. OPEN }
PRETTY GREAT
Maria Sharapova
Wins Her Second Major
Roger Federer
Gets His Tiger On
by S.L. PRICE

Ohio State

TEXAS

The No. 1 Buckeyes Dominate Texas
BY AUSTIN MURPHY

NEXT: Separating the Contenders from the Pretenders
LSU-AUBURN | MICHIGAN-NOTRE DAME | NEBRASKA-USC | FLORIDA-TENNESSEE | OKLAHOMA-OREGON | MIAMI-LOUISVILLE
BY PHIL TAYLOR

A PHILLIE GOES BOOM
Ryan Howard — Chasing 60 Home Runs

NASCAR CHASE PREVIEW
Kyle Busch — Unloved and Dangerous

SEPTEMBER 18, 2006

1929–2006
Bo Schembechler

Sports Illustrated

The Best.
Period.

Troy Smith and Ohio State Overpower Michigan

BY AUSTIN MURPHY

With a brilliant performance against the Wolverines, Smith wrapped up the Heisman

NOVEMBER 27, 2006

Does Sammy Have Any Whammy? P. 44

Sports Illustrated

NFL COMBINE
The Arms Race
JaMarcus Russell and
Brady Quinn Square Off
by PETER KING
P. 48

OHIO STATE
THE PROGRAM
BIG WINS ○ BIG MONEY ○ BIG SPIRIT
BY L. JON WERTHEIM

BIG CHANGES IN COLLEGE SPORTS

Poll: New Jock Culture · Life After Football? · Pressure-Cooker Sport

MARCH 5, 2007

what did he do? He went the wrong way and got onto the freeway. I jumped out and started running in between cars—in this outfit. Here's a cop, with his car up on the berm. As bewildered as he was, he came running down and grabbed me and said, "What the hell are you doing? You can't be on the freeway on foot."

I said, "I know that. I'm trying to get to the stadium." He said, "I'm going to arrest you." I said, "Oh, you can't. I've got this photo shoot set up. I've got to get to the stadium." I tried to give him a little background on it. Finally, I said, "What would you do with me? You can't go any-where." I said, "What if I get up on the berm and run? He said, "OK." I get there. Now it's about 9:52—eight minutes 'til.

We get the sheriff, but by then the *Times-Reporter* has left, because they didn't know what the heck was going on in the first place. So I'm at the area where they have all the names where you sign in as ushers. I really wanted to still get caught, but . . . I'm standing there in this outfit and this little guy was there signing people in. I asked him if I could use the bathroom. I told him I had run half the length of Columbus and had to go to the bathroom.

He said, "Are you an employee?" I said, "Well, yes, I'm an employee . . ." And then under my breath I said, ". . . of Marlowe Drug, Incorporated." He said, "Well, all right." I went in the bathroom. When I came out, everybody was folding the tables up. They had all signed in by now. The little guy was gone when the rush was gone. I started helping fold the tables up. You'd think somebody would have inquired. But I was helping fold the tables up. They're all going off to work. I said, "Oh, my God, I'm in." I got in even when I tried to get arrested.

My plan was to go back and watch the game with my cousins, Susan and Larry. So I went back out and did some tailgating with Sue Dell and her family. Some ladies came up to me and said, "What is the significance of that outfit?" There was this crowd milling around. It was right when Martha Stewart had gone through all her problems.

I looked at these ladies and said, "Well, you know, I work for Martha Stewart. I literally took the rap for her. I've been in jail, but she got me out to come to this game. She even stenciled my cell." They looked at me, and I think they knew they'd been had. They started laughing hysterically. I said, "I'm just kidding." That was a great game. We won that and then went on to win the championship that year.

ESPN came back in 2006 and talked to me again. The producer called and said that they would like to do a piece on me. "We've done so many interviews with players and coaches, so we want something a little different." I told them I was really trying to put it to rest. But they kept bugging me, and finally I said, "Well, maybe we could try something."

So now here I am at a urinal in Ohio Stadium with an ESPN camera hidden in my cap, and I wasn't sad that the streak was coming to an end. I was concerned about what the camera would—or wouldn't—see if I looked down. So, that's what I kept telling myself—"don't look down"—as I was faking going to the bathroom.

I was an usher that day in late November 2006, or pretending to be one anyway. By this time, Russ Thibaut had retired and lived in Florida, but I still keep in contact with him. I'd never gone as an usher before. Russ is much bigger and taller than me, but he was kind enough to send me his stadium usher jacket and the hat they wore. They have that "O" on the front of the hat above the bill. ESPN wanted to monitor so they put a lipstick camera in the top of the hat.

My wife had to design a hole right through that "O" for them to put the camera. They came on Thursday before the game and were there four or five hours filming and interviewing me. They had me get in and out of a few outfits. They wanted to show it Sunday morning after the game. They wanted to follow me into the game.

On Friday night, they met me at my daughter's house in Gahanna. We did a mock-up of how we were going to do it and how we would dress. They had me wired with a battery pack, so they could tape it all. They wanted to follow me through the campus in this outfit. They had these big cameras.

You had to be there at a certain moment to get in the ushers' gate. What Russ forgot to send was his badge. They have a badge they wear with their picture on it. I said, "Well, maybe I can scrounge up some kind of badge." He said, "They never look at it anyway half the time. Just put a badge around your neck." My son-in-law had just graduated with his MBA, so he had a badge. It looked to be about the same size, so I put that around my neck.

I made the mistake of telling one of my cousins about it, because I was trying to come up with ideas. She knew an usher, and thought maybe

I would have a better chance of going through where he was. When he found out about it, he didn't want any part of it. He thought he'd get in trouble. None of them want to get in trouble and lose their right to go to every game.

I don't know if he tipped somebody off or not, but, anyway, I got to the stadium and had to be there precisely at 11. The guy down in Florida had said, "Don't sign in, because then somebody else isn't going to get to usher. Just go in and once you get in there, just go over to the table and go through the motions and you shouldn't have a problem." So I get in past the first two guards. They didn't even look at the badge.

Maybe they had high security that day—the third guy was there, and he wanted to see the badge. I whipped it out for him, and he looked at it. I said, "Oh, darn." ESPN was miking me, so they had to beep that, because I said something stronger than darn. "When I jumped out of the car, my son-in-law was parking and I had to get here, and I grabbed his badge instead of mine." I was trying to think fast.

He said, "Well, I'm sorry. I can't let you go any further." I said, "Well, OK, it'll take me a half hour to go back and get it. We parked a long way back. I'll go get it and come back." He said, "Go ahead and sign in. You're here." I said, "No, I'll go get the badge and keep it legal." But, then, I looked over and saw the men's room there. I knew if I could get in there, I could go out the other door maybe.

I said, "Look, I really have to urinate. Let me go in the bathroom there." He said, "No, I can't let you go any further." Finally he relented and told me to go ahead. I went over to the bathroom, thinking, "Oh, I'm in." I'm standing at the urinal area—I didn't have to "go," by the way—but you know how you feel somebody behind you. I turned my head a little bit, and here he was five feet back of me against the wall, waiting.

Again, I don't know if somebody tipped him or what. I had that feeling that they were looking for me. Then I flushed the urinal and came out and said, "I'll be back. Do you know a guy named Russ Thibaut? He was one of the ushers here for years and retired." He said, "No, there are 1,400 of us. I don't know them all." I said, "Well, I'll be back." Then when I went back outside, they wanted to interview me. In my opinion, it was unsuccessful. I did get halfway in. That was my last attempt—2006.

MY BROKER GOT ME INTO SOME CATTLE AND OIL DEALS, AND I'M GONNA MAKE A LOT OF MONEY—AS SOON AS THE CATTLE START GIVING OIL

TODD MCCARTNEY

Todd McCartney's decision to go through a Burger King drive-thru on horseback in his high school days actually seems like a natural transition, in a twisted sort of way to living in Millsap, Texas, and being a rancher and a cowboy and doing some public speaking, TV and promotional work in the cattle industry. But being Brutus Buckeye? Well, during the now 42-year-old McCartney's one-year reign (1986-87 school year), Brutus did ride a horse in a parade. And he did shatter a chandelier, like a bull in a china shop. And he did almost literally stumble into the role.

I've been in Texas since shortly after college. I'm in the ranching/ cattle business. I've been on both sides of the fence. I cowboyed for a good number of years. I always worked on the big ranches— made my living from my horse, made my living with a rope. I punched cows and lived in the bunkhouses and did the boyhood dream of being a cowboy. Then it came to a point in life where "maybe it's time you come in out of the weather, and let's try to do something that doesn't send you to the hospital quite as often."

It's certainly a different world from my days as Brutus Buckeye back at Ohio State. Not only are there no Ohio State fans, and no Ohio State news, there's really no presence or recognition of them of any kind. So Brutus Buckeye is far from my everyday thoughts, but I do remember I ended up being Brutus by accident.

My dream was to compete in rodeos. I'm from the *<u>**TOLEDO AREA**</u>. I was raised out in a little community called Monclova, Ohio, just a tiny little burg. My father grew up on a small farm, and he wanted that for his kids as well. We raised our own stock, and we broke and trained horses. It was a very rural setting, although, in Ohio it doesn't take but 40 miles, and you're going to be into a big town. I'm the youngest of nine kids. My older brothers rodeoed so I knew that's what I wanted to do.

When I got to Ohio State, I was very proud of my university. I was very engaged with the whole concept of Ohio State and its legacy and what it was. I was very serious about that. I embodied the spirit of Ohio State and always thought, "Man, wouldn't it be neat, your senior year, to be a cheerleader." But when I thought of being a cheerleader, I thought, "Yeah. Spirit. Lead the crowd!" So, for my senior year at Ohio State, that's what I'm going to work toward. Again, still, I have no idea of really what a male collegiate cheerleader is.

These guys are huge, and they're gymnasts. I laid off rodeo so I could be healthy for the tryouts. Then I **TORE MY HAMSTRING*** and a short while after that I snapped my ankle, ironically not in rodeo, but training to be a cheerleader. By the time tryouts came along, I was just getting out of a cast. And my tumbling was very comical. I did a routine during one of the clinics to help cheerleaders to get ready. I went across the floor and did a series of stunts. The guys laughed and said, "You sure you aren't trying out for Brutus, because you're just pretty darn comical." It just kind of hit me. I'm not skilled enough to be a cheerleader at this point, but why not Brutus?

> Tigers manager Jim Leyland was once a second-string catcher for Perrysburg High School, in the *<u>**TOLEDO AREA**</u>. The starting catcher was Jerry Glanville.

> Almost every good football team at any level in America is one play away (*<u>**INJURY**</u>) from being average . . . Average time lost due to injury in high school football is six days. . . Healing time due to injury to a high school cheerleader is 29-days. . . Among the sixteen most popular college sports, spring football has the highest injury rate.

After winning it, you go over to the athletic department, and they issue you your turf shoes. That was the big medicine. You got those Nike turf shoes that said, "Go Bucks," on them. Then they issued me these polyester pants. I pulled on a pair of those, and my buddy goes, "Brutus, you ain't gonna impress any chicks in those." So that was the impetus to make a few changes in his costume.

I went toward more of a sport pant, a cotton sport pant. I had Ohio State down one leg and Brutus Buckeye down the other. I at least brought him into the '80s.Then on his head Brutus wore this ball cap. It was a white, fuzzy, flattened ball cap. I know kids today wear beat-up old caps, but where I came from in the country, you were proud to wear the local elevator's cap or a seed corn cap, and you took care of it. It was your lid, man. So, Brutus needed a new hat. My dear old mother, bless her heart, she sat down at the sewing machine, and she built a hat for Brutus. There was pride in that for me and for all my family when they would see Brutus on TV wearing that hat that my mother made.

Ski Magazine hosted an invitational mascot ski race. I got to go to Winter Park, Colorado, and ski for three days. The other catch was you had to do it in costume. I'm an Ohio farm boy. I had never skied. They send you a plane ticket and they fly you out there and they put you up. You spend the first few days trying to get the hang of it. It's a well-attended event. They've got bleachers set up. You come out of the starting gate, where you trip the lever, and you have to go through a slalom course.

Just picture mascot dogs and cats and elephants and Brutus Buckeye and the Shockers (shocks of wheat), and ducks and every animated colorful thing you can think of trying to navigate down the side of a mountain. You make about the first two turns and then you just crater and you just roll and roll and roll. Who won it was probably some kid from Colorado. I can just remember seeing through that peephole in Brutus' head and watching things and then it just turning white, and you roll and roll. You hear the crowd. It was all a spectator event just to see which mascot could actually make it to the bottom.

The university was really cautious. I went to the athletic department all the time with some idea I had—"What about doing this, could I?" They were just very cautious about what they gave you license to do. And rightly so. They're dealing with a college kid in a costume. I can only imagine the stories of what came before, and I can only imagine what could have gone wrong. But I honored what they said, and nearly everything I wanted to do was denied.

But I soon realized that Brutus belonged to the student body. Brutus was blue-collar. He was one of them. The fans, the students identified with him. They knew he wasn't some lettered, full-ride athlete chosen out of California somewhere. He was one of them. He had burst from the ranks of the student body, and he was not at that elite athletic level. I made it personal, and I bent some of the rules . . . knowing very well that I had to be accountable and I had a responsibility. I took some chances—I took some liberties.

Brutus showed up at some parties. Brutus did some things. I always said to myself, "Is the university winning here? Am I improving spirit? Am I helping bring a fever to the game? Am I reaching out to the student body?" With that in mind, I did those things. If I were ever to be caught, I'd have been court-martialed. It was easier to beg for forgiveness than it was to ask for permission, so I did that a little often.

You go across campus as Brutus, and the student body would just holler to you. It wasn't Todd—it was Brutus. It was amazing what an important figure he was to them. I truthfully believe they didn't know our school president when he walked across campus, nor would they want to run up to him and get their picture taken. Now, they probably should have. But Brutus was different. I took that very seriously.

As the season went on, it was interesting. I was driving somewhere, and I got pulled over. It was one of those harmless tickets. You're speeding—nothing reckless, but sure enough, you're speeding. That's the law. The policeman, a county deputy sheriff, was just as nice as could be. He looked at my driver's license. He said, "You've got the same birth date as my daughter. I ought to just let you off. I'll tell you what—you got any other reason I ought to let you off on a pretty day like this?"

I thought, "Do I pull that string. Do I *not* pull that string?" I said, "Are you a Buckeye fan?" Of course he is—he's a Franklin County deputy sheriff. He said, "By golly, I am." I said, "Well, you wouldn't want to mar the name of Brutus Buckeye, would you?" He just looks at me and goes, "Are you Brutus Buckeye?" We went to visiting. I signed something for his daughter. It was just one of those harmless deals. Of course, I got a big head out of the deal.

I might have done a few other things that I needed to have been brought down a notch for. I'll never forget—about two games later, there was this very stout motorcycle policeman with the knee-high leather boots they wear, and he wore a helmet. He walked around the track during games. Brutus fell in behind him, and I mimicked him. He walked in a certain manner, because he was short and wide and was in those tall boots and that helmet. He was kind of a cartoon-character-looking fellow. I walked behind him and swaggered like he did. Now we were in front of Block O. How many tens of thousands of people are there? When he stopped and turned around, I stopped and turned around. I just mimicked him. Of course, the people started hooting and hollering. I kept it up for maybe a minute.

> **"I got close enough where I said, 'Point taken, officer.'"**

Finally, he said, "Brutus, get over here." I could tell by the tone of his voice that he wasn't happy. I jovially went over to him as the character, and he said, "You been speeding lately?" All I could think of was it was a county policeman who had pulled me over in rural Franklin County. Or maybe a city cop—different ranks of law enforcement, but word had traveled. I stayed in character and I dropped to my knees. I always carried a red handkerchief, and I pulled it out and went to polishing those boots. I never sneaked out of character, but I got close enough where I said, "Point taken, officer." I bowed to him, and I backed away on my knees, and I never touched him for six more games.

But it told me something—that I abused a privilege, and people knew it. I tell you that was a dose of humility. That was a life lesson. To this day, I don't forget that. As the season went on, I could see how that was a blessing to me, because I saw how cheerleaders began to act. I saw how athletes began to act—entitlement, almost. "Why can't I park there?" "Why don't I get to sit where I want?" "Why don't we get those free things?" You know what, that's a disease, a cancer. And I was so glad I had that early dose, because I then took my role, my celebrity status, and I was able to handle it so much better, and deal with it and use it for the good.

That's why, as it turned out, one year in that capacity was enough, and I was glad to move on and allow someone else to step into that. What a glorious role! What an honor! But for someone to do that four years in a row, it would take quite a character not to be affected by it . . . and then the ambassador role is lessened—diminished. You can sure see it in some ball players. You can sure see it in fourth-year cheerleaders. They just weren't who you'd want to sit in a pickup with and ride from here to the East Coast.

At the end of the season, we made it to the Cotton Bowl. We went down to Dallas to play Texas A&M. Of course, there was a Cotton Bowl parade. The police would bring you into that parade and then get you out of it. I remember going through a parted crowd. I remember someone in a Texas drawl saying, "Hey, Brutus." I was almost ready for—not an insult, but a jab. You're the opposing team, and there's nobody more visible than you. You embodied who the university was. If they're going to hurl anything, they're going to hurl it at you.

I remember spinning around to take it face first. He said, "So sorry to hear about Coach Hayes." It was relative to Woody's death. I thought, "Wow, we're 1,500 miles away, and he's a legend. He's not just ours, but he belongs to a lot of other people." I probably walked up to him, not comically at all, but very in character, stuck out my hand and really gave him a nonverbal thank-you that way. It was great hearing someone say, "Sorry to hear about Coach Hayes," in a Texas drawl.

I haven't been back to a game since I graduated. Here I am 1,400 miles away, and now you have to get a loan approved just to get a seat at the game. My goal is to gather up my four little kiddos and my wife and get back there someday. They've planted grass in the stadium for goodness' sake. Things have changed.

How do you make Notre Dame Cookies? Put them in a Bowl and beat 'em for 3 hours.

IT'S A JUNGLE OUT THERE. DRESS ACCORDINGLY.

PEARSON BUELL

His grandfather temporarily disowned him. His parents just naturally assumed he would be a Michigan man. Pearson Buell, now 47 and living in Lake St. Louis, Mo., started down that path, but eventually converted to being a Buckeye—a rewarding, but not always trouble-free, experience for the senior functional analyst for Citi.

I spent my early years in Michigan in Grosse Pointe. Both my parents attended the University of Michigan, though they started out at other schools. My grandfather was a huge supporter with season tickets. I went to **MICHIGAN*** games with my grandfather. I had all kinds of maize-and-blue stuff.

When you're little, you just love the team you love. I didn't really care about any other team. It wasn't until I started to gain an understanding of the whole "Woody and Bo" thing and that dynamic that I started to say, "Ooooh, Ohio State, bad, evil."

Eventually, we moved to Atlanta and then to a Columbus suburb, Worthington, my senior year in high school. I had attended three high schools in three years. Every time I moved, I would set my sights on different colleges in the area. I wasn't like my brothers, who were looking nationally. I was looking at what's easy and what's nearby. I wasn't the consummate student. At that point, my senior year, I just said, "There's a big, great school down the road. I'm just going to go there. It's easy."

That was the fall of 1978. I probably had mixed emotions leading up to that first Ohio State-Michigan game as an OSU student. But I had

Until recently, ***MICHIGAN** had more golf courses than any state in the Union.

come to the conclusion you had to be true to your school, so I decided to finally switch sides.

My senior year in high school, my uncle, who was a big Oklahoma booster, sent my mom and I tickets to the Ohio State-Oklahoma game in Ohio Stadium. We were sitting with all the Oklahoma fans. The Sooners won that one. Their kicker, Uwe von Schamann, kicked a field goal with no time remaining for a 29-28 Oklahoma win back in 1977.

I thought the stadium was awesome. Compared to Michigan, which was just a big bowl that was easy to get in and out of, this was a little bit more complicated. Back then, Ohio State hadn't closed in the end so it had a completely different feel about it. But, it was certainly loud and the fans were as ravenous as anyplace I could ever imagine being.

> **"Everybody was cheering "ATHA, ATHA, ATHA!" to get him in."**

As a freshman at Ohio State, I got season football tickets. That would have turned out to be Woody's last year. It was Art Schlichter's first year, and Bob Atha's first year—for him it was primarily as a kicker, but he was also the backup quarterback for Schlichter those four years. My recollection, as a fan, was that he was a fan favorite. When the game got well in hand, everybody was cheering "ATHA, ATHA, ATHA!" to get him in. He was at Worthington with me and had graduated there. We didn't know each other real well in high school, but we knew each other in college, were in the same fraternity, Phi Kappa Tau.

Still, that first Michigan-Ohio State game, I felt a little ambivalence. It was hard to let go of that Michigan allegiance, especially because at every other game, I'd been cheering against Ohio State—it's hard to just switch sides and say, "Oh, now, I'm going to cheer for the visiting team."

As I recall, when my grandfather learned that I was going to be going to Ohio State, he didn't speak to me for a few weeks. I don't think he was seriously angry, I think he was just making a lighthearted point. My mom later told me she had heard he had said to somebody, "Well, my grandson goes to Ohio State, so it must not be that bad of a school." He had softened his view a little bit.

I was watching the Ohio State–Clemson game when Woody threw that punch. It was during my freshman year, I mean right after the Michigan game when my allegiance finally had shifted. I was watching at home on TV, and I just thought, "Oh God." I had actually gotten to be fond of Woody. He seemed straightforward and seemed to love the university and love what he was doing. The thing about Woody you just don't see in coaches anymore is that he was a part of the campus. He taught classes. He walked around campus. He didn't just go lock himself in an office somewhere with the rest of the folks in the athletic department and look at films. He was a part of the university.

Whether he was coaching or not, he was part of Ohio State. I don't know that there are coaches like that anymore. I know that the guys who came after him were certainly not like that. Tressel may be more into the traditions of Ohio State, but my impressions of Earle and Cooper were that they were just hired hands in there to do the job and weren't integrated into the university the way Woody was. You could see Woody walk across campus. I can't imagine ever seeing any of those other guys walking around campus.

I never ran into him, or talked to him on campus. I ran into Schlichter a lot at the track—at the **HORSE TRACK!*** And Earle Bruce too, by the way, at the track.

I went to a Michigan game in Ann Arbor my sophomore year, the 18-15 Buckeye win. That made us undefeated at the end of the regular season, if I remember correctly, and rated No. 1. It came to us that the easiest way to do this—the most fun way—would be for us to rent a Winnebago, rather than for a bunch of people to drive up separately. So eight or nine—may have been more—went up there. I do remember that we filled up the shower in the Winnebago with ice and kept a keg in there, which may be in violation of some statute somewhere. We went up on Friday night, and we parked it in a parking lot on campus. We were not far from the actual stadium.

When the game was over, we stormed the field. There were people all

In what sport was Chris Evert the leading money winner in 1974? The answer: ***HORSE** racing. The owner, Carl Rosen, named his horses after tennis players. The horse named Chris Evert won $551,063 with five wins in eight starts.

over the place, jumping up on the uprights. I don't recall that security, in those days, went to the efforts to protect them the way some schools do now. I know some schools grease them. Some schools put cops all around them. I don't recall Michigan doing any of that. Clearly, there were an awful lot of Ohio State fans there, because there were a lot of people who went out onto the field. I don't remember who went up on the goal posts . . . all I remember is them starting to come down. Several of the Phi Taus grabbed onto one of the uprights and just started pushing it and it snapped right off. Here we had this long tube of steel in our hands, and we just said, "Let's go." We never could have done it, at least, not today, in Ohio Stadium, because there are very few straight ways out from the field. In a bowl like theirs, you walk straight up the aisle and straight out. People just got out of our way. Here we were, five or six guys with this upright on our shoulders just walking up and nobody stopped us. No officials. Nobody with the university. No police. People just made way for us.

We were so excited. And here we had this memento. I don't think we really even thought about what we were going to do with it. We just started walking out. I don't think we made the connection that it was something we could take home with us. It wasn't until we got to the Winnebago that it dawned on us that we had the perfect vehicle to transport it with. If we could strap this goal post to the top of the RV, we could take it home. It must have been pretty secure, because it didn't fall off.

We brought it back to our fraternity house and took it up to the third floor and stuck it under a bunch of beds. Everybody had their ideas about what they were going to do with their piece of this, but I don't think we fully knew what we were going to do with it other than the fact that we had it. I didn't really think about it until people started talking about how we were going to divvy it up . . . or where we were going to put it. Are we going to hang it on the wall? . . . or we going to plant it in the yard and make it a flag pole—what are we going to do with it? I think the agreement was that if we could cut it up, we'd split it up. To the best of my recollection, they did cut it up . . . but it was *much* later. It literally sat up there, and I guarantee you that a good number of people who were in and out of that third-floor room had no idea what this big piece of metal tubing on the floor was—the significance it had. Except Bob Clegg, a fraternity brother of ours. He knew what significance it had, but it had nothing to do with football. Some stories are better left untold.

We were all initially excited about it, but then it just sat there, for at least a year. When we were carrying it out of the stadium, we didn't have a plan. In the parking lot, if we decided it was too heavy, we could have dropped it in the parking lot and walked off and never thought about it again. We really were never thinking much beyond the moment. As we arrived back in Columbus, it was all very exciting that we had this trophy, but things move on, and it's quickly forgotten. I did not ever get my piece of it. I have no idea who has pieces of it. But it is my recollection that, after a year or so, it got cut into pieces . . .

I guess I never got the desire to make a big splash out of my system, because in the fall of 1982, **JOHN ELWAY'S*** senior year, Stanford played at Ohio State in a nationally televised game on ABC. Ohio State lost that game, but I wasn't there for the end of it. They were winning when I left. You see, the splash I made was in jail.

This was the third game of the season, the second home game, and Ohio State had been winning pretty handily, building up a pretty substantial lead by halftime. That's when Atha was getting to play a lot, because they were pounding teams pretty good. I don't want to say we would get bored, but we just felt like the games could be more entertaining if we found a way to entertain ourselves and the people around us.

We had been coming up with different themes for different games. There was one game where we all wore tuxes. For this particular game, somebody said, "Let's rent gorilla suits." So, about seven of us went to various costume shops around town and everybody ponied up their money and rented gorilla suits. Maybe only five or six of us went to jail, but there were seven or eight of us who had the suits. I know that Craig Little wasn't one of them, because he was president of Block O at the time. He was leading the cheers when we were led out. When we were arrested, we were hauled underneath the end of the stadium where Block O was at the time.

In the 1979 baseball draft, the Kansas City Royals selected Dan Marino in the fourth round and ***JOHN ELWAY** in the 18th round. That same year the Royals hired Rush Limbaugh for their group sales department. Limbaugh left in 1984 for a radio opportunity in California.

Our plan was just to wear the gorilla suits to the game and hang out and cheer. I know a lot of people would leave at halftime, probably because they'd had too much to drink. There were cameras everywhere because this was such a big game. We felt like the game needed something beyond all the usual hype so somebody suggested we go down by the field and make a pyramid of gorillas, and maybe we'll get on TV. We all thought this was a fabulous idea—"why not?"

We headed down, further and further. We got to the edge. At that time, there was a track that ran around the field. We were in the stands, but all the way at the edge of the stands—just stepping over the little railing would have put us onto the track. There was an usher there in a red coat. He asked us what we were doing, and we said, "Do you mind if we go over here on the track? We're just going to make a pyramid and get on TV and then we'll leave." He said, "Fine. Go ahead. Just don't cause any trouble." We did that. We went over and made our little pyramid, and there was a camera on us, but I can't say for sure we were on TV, but I believe that we were. We made our little pyramid of gorillas and we did our dismount and everybody turned around.

We were getting ready to walk back out, and we looked and Ohio State was on the 2-yard line—right there getting ready to score. We're there, just feet away from this football team that's getting ready to score. We're not going to walk out of here. We're going to watch them score, because we're so close. Some gentleman came up to us and told us to leave. We said, "OK, just a second." He didn't even say another word. He just turned around, and went over, and we saw him talking to a police officer, one of Columbus' finest. As soon as we saw this, we said, 'Uh-oh. We should probably get going."

> **"Our plan was just to wear the gorilla suits to the game and hang out and cheer."**

We started to go, started to head back the way we came. This policeman came over to us and said, "You guys were asked to leave." We said, "We are leaving." He said, "You're leaving with us." He marched us out underneath where Block O was. It's also where the band comes in. Of course, Craig Little had all of Block O booing as we were being led out. We hadn't been handcuffed or anything like that, but we were led out.

As we got outside the stadium, there was what looked like an old school-bus style of bus, but it had "Columbus City Police Department" on it. We were told to get on the bus. There were no police on the bus. He just put us on the bus and then walked away. We thought, "This is a hassle. We're missing this incredible game." It didn't really dawn on us that this was a big deal. We thought they would talk to us, and let us go. Neal was a little concerned, because he had a lot of beer inside his gorilla suit. That was how he had smuggled it into the stadium.

He had to figure out a way to get rid of this beer because we were now stuck in this paddy wagon, where if something happened or if they decided to frisk us now, we didn't want to have this added to the list of charges. I had asked the police officer what the charge was and the police officer couldn't really narrow it down. Ultimately the charge was "failure to disperse during a riot." I asked if we were being charged with impersonating an endangered species, which may not have helped our cause.

In any event, Neal took the beer out of his gorilla suit and then literally ripped open the seat he was sitting on and stuffed the beer inside the springs of the seat he was seated on. Someday those cops were going to find out they had a bus full of beer. Eventually some guy came and drove us all to the jail downtown.

We got off and there were several cops waiting for us. They apparently had seen it on TV and also had heard the radio calls that these bunch of guys dressed as gorillas were coming in. They thought this was very entertaining. So as we got off the bus, they were quite amused by it. The Columbus guys had much less of a sense of humor than the sheriff's deputies. They seemed to think this whole thing was pretty funny.

We got in and they told us the first thing we had to do was take off the gorilla suits and that they would put them in storage along with anything else. They usually take all your stuff before they put you in jail. That was all fine and good. We all stripped down. Most of us had shorts and a T-shirt on underneath . . . except when we got to Neal. It turns out he had nothing on underneath. They had to get him one of the orange jail/prison jumpsuits to wear. We all got fingerprinted. They put us in a jail cell.

At some point, they came and said, "OK, you guys can go. Except you." And they meant me. There was some kind of traffic ticket on my record that I had evidently failed to pay. They asked me about this thing and I said, "Well, it rings a bell, I suppose, but I thought I'd paid that." Which was probably a lie, but . . . They had to keep me in for several more hours while they decided what to do about this, because I had this unpaid ticket. The other guys were all free to go.

Eventually, they did let me go. They gave me back my gorilla suit. This was probably four hours after everybody else had left. This was still Saturday evening. I was on shaky ground with my girlfriend at the time, partly by choice. When I called her up to pick me up, she would have nothing to do with it. She was not at all amused by it. Her younger brother had been at the game and she didn't think I was being a very good role model for her younger brother—getting arrested and all. Another nail in her coffin, as far as our relationship went. She would not come and get me.

So I had to walk from downtown Columbus with my gorilla suit on—I had the head under my arm. I recall that we had pillows in them because the gorilla suits were huge. Some of us had put pillows inside to fill them out like you would a Santa suit. Here I was . . . walking down the street . . . in a gorilla suit . . . with a head under one arm and a pillow under the other arm. I walked all the way from downtown where the jail was all the way back to the fraternity house—a several-mile walk. It was at least an hour.

This is a dejected, lowly walk for a man who thought he had triumphed by doing the gorilla thing, and it had turned out to not play so well. We were having a party at the fraternity that night. When I got back, I was heralded as a hero—anytime you're arrested, in the fraternity you're considered a hero. As it turns out in real life, it doesn't always work out that way . . . but in the fraternity world, getting arrested is a badge of honor. So that cheered me up, but I had really lost my enthusiasm for the idea of dressing up for football games during that long walk back.

I was charged with "failure to disperse." Because of my separate ticket, the other guys who were arrested all went together and I think one of them hired an attorney who convinced the judge to expunge their records. They may have had to pay a fine, but I don't know. They went through this thing pretty much scot-free. I, on the other hand, had to have a separate trial, or hearing, with the judge. I didn't have a bunch of co-conspirators with me to make it look like "hey, this was all just a bunch of good clean fun." He said, "I'm going to let you off with time served, having spent a good number of hours in the jail." He confirmed with the clerk that I'd paid off my other fine that had kept me in jail those extra few hours. I pled no contest, so I was convicted of the crime, but not fined—just the time served in the jail. He let me go.

Other than the fact that it was an amusement, I wondered if this would ever show up somewhere down the line. It never really dawned on me that this was anything that would come back to haunt me. Until I ran for public office. It didn't show up during the campaign. It showed up after I was elected as an alderman in Lake St. Louis, Missouri.

At one of our first meetings, the local police chief, whom I know fairly well, came to me and said, "You know, we have to do a background check on all of our newly elected officials." Immediately a light went on. I knew exactly where he was going. I said, "OK." He said, "Well, I found something in your record." I said, "Would that be a 'failure to disperse' charge?" He said, "Yes." I said, "Yeah, that's true." He said, "Tell me the story." I just gave him a very *Reader's Digest* short-cut version of it without any of the sordid details. He said, "Well, I'm sure, at this point in your life . . . I know some people— there's probably something we could do to maybe get this expunged from your record." I said, "Are you kidding me? That's one of my proudest college moments. I'm taking that one to the grave with me."

The best part about it was after my girlfriend told me we were through, I wasn't too distraught about it. There was a girl named Lisa Leak, who I had recently met, who I went to go see later that night. She *was* highly amused by it. She wasn't angry at me for showing up at her sorority house in a gorilla suit. In fact, it probably helped. Her first impression of me was that I was very conservative, very quiet. When I met her, I went home and told some of my fraternity brothers, "I just met the girl I'm going to marry." And I did, thanks in part to the gorilla suit.

I went to all the other football games that year. I wouldn't have missed them. And I never regretted converting from Michigan to Ohio State.

CLONES ARE PEOPLE TWO

ROGER THOMAS

Roger Thomas has been a futures broker since 1966, hedging corn and soybeans for farmers. But it was a blast from the past that pushed the 68-year-old Tipp City, Ohio, native unwittingly into the spotlight. Could it be Woody Hayes all over again? Thomas certainly has Buckeye fans seeing double.

Some people for years had called me "Woody," but I hadn't paid much attention to it. Then, about six years ago, I met Woody Hayes' high school football coach. He brought me some pictures of Woody and his father and said, "Boy, you look like Woody Hayes." He had been with Woody all his life and had some good pictures of him, so he was a credible source. I looked at them and said, "Yeah, it's hard to deny." That was when I first really took it seriously.

I auditioned for a Woody look-alike part in a benefit for the Central Ohio Diabetes Association at the Buckeye Hall of Fame Café in Columbus several years ago. Jon Self, the owner of the café, said to me, "You belong to Ohio State." He was dead serious about it. He knew Woody from years ago. He said, "You come to all the home games?" I said, "No, my wife won't pay scalpers' prices for tickets." He said, "I'll help you out." He has, and he has introduced me around and has allowed me to know some other people.

Three years ago I met Dick Guy, who played for Woody in the 1950s. He took me by the hand and looked me straight in the eye and said, "Thanks for keeping the memory of Woody alive." That's when I focused a little bit more. I said, "That's my job." So I got even more serious at that time about studying Woody and buying Woody books and reading and working on Woody's legacy—what he did . . . the kind of person he was . . . some of his history. That's basically been my job—to keep the memory of Woody Hayes alive.

I try to stay on the positive side in what I do. Woody was human. He had his faults, there's no doubt about it. I just cringe when people ask me questions about the Clemson game, the Gator Bowl game that ended Hayes' career. I remember watching that game on TV. I just felt sadness at the time, so I would rather not think about it. I would just rather emphasize all the great things he did and kind of leave the human side of him alone. I know that's slanting the news a little bit, but I think that's my job.

People call me L.L. Woody Hayes. The "L"s in L.L. Woody stand for "Looks Like." I get a lot of hugs from ladies, as Woody did—sometimes a few too many. I do all kinds of charity work. At those benefits, I'll charge $5 to take a picture with "Woody" and then give all the money to that particular charity. Almost every week, I have a Rotary Club or Lions Club where I go to speak and have a free lunch.

I've never sat in the same place twice. One of my sponsors gives me tickets, or they pay me and I buy tickets, but I'm never in the same place twice. That's a lot of fun, because when I go to my seat, it's always exciting. A lot of people get on their feet and yell, "Woody, Woody." I tell people it's best if I sit on the aisle, because usually by halftime a lot of people have spotted me, and there will be a line of people standing in the aisle wanting their picture with me at halftime.

That's one of my rules—I never ever turn anyone down for a picture. My wife understands this—how long it takes me to get out of the stadium. At the open practice last fall, they had the big open practice where they had 25,000 people there. Buckeyeman and I were standing down on the rail, around the 10-yard line. It took us 30 minutes to work our way up to the portal to get out of the stadium

My wife, Sandy, and I talked about this whole thing and said that as long as it's fun and we get to meet great people, we'll keep doing it. That's what drives it. I have never run into a Bo Schembechler look-alike, but I have run into a John Cooper look-alike, right here in Tipp City. I said to him, "Hey, I've got a great business deal for you. Let's buy one of those dunking machines that they throw baseballs at. We'll take it over on Lane Avenue on the OSU campus, and I'll sell baseballs and you can sit up there. He said, "No deal. I'd get wet, and you'd have all the fun."

HE'S THE MOST—
TO SAY THE LEAST

BOB BULEN

Bob Bulen has retired now, leaving behind his home in Canal Winchester, Ohio, and 27 years of service as a bailiff in the Franklin County court system for a new life in North Carolina. But he's taking part of his old life with him—The Streak. At the end of next season, "Buckeye" Bob will attend his 400th consecutive game, the longest current streak known to exist, and one that not even high ticket demand at the 2002 national championship or his own autumn wedding could truncate.

The streak was really in jeopardy this time. I had gone to 335 Ohio State football games in a row, and the Fiesta Bowl was coming up. From 1968 to 2002 was a long time between national championship games. Those tickets were hard to come by. In fact, they were just not available. We were calling everybody in the world, trying to get tickets. My cell phone number got published through publicity about the streak apparently finally coming to an end, so I was getting calls from all over the country—people wanting to make sure my streak stayed alive . . . but to the tune of $1,000 apiece. If push came to shove, at the end of the day, I would probably have

> **"I had gone to 335 Ohio State football games in a row, and the Fiesta Bowl was coming up."**

paid that, like we did this last time. Even Earle Bruce was working on trying to help me get a couple of seats. We actually ended up getting tickets through the Phoenix Alumni Association at face value, and they were upper deck in the end zone. We had already bought plane tickets before we got the game tickets . . .

My wife, Martha Dean, is a retired attorney. Our first date was not to go to an Ohio State game . . . but our honeymoon was in Boston, so we could go to the Ohio State-Boston College game in 1990. On our wedding day, we went to the Ohio State-**TEXAS TECH*** game, the 1990 season opener, and we left at the end of the third quarter and went to our house to have the wedding ceremony. By the time we got home, the game was so close that we, and all our wedding guests, went downstairs and finished watching the game before we had the ceremony. Between you and me, we would have finished watching the game no matter what the score. By the way, Ohio State won, 17-10.

We've recently retired and we've moved to North Carolina. It's 425 miles from our new house to the stadium, so that's a piece of cake. We'll drive to the games, and we'll move in on people in the Columbus area that we know. Since we're both retired, I don't see my streak coming to an end. We've already made plans to go out and stay with a couple in Portland for the Washington game. Then we'll start fighting for the Michigan and Penn State tickets. I'll have to start that fight before *spring* football practice even starts. I just tell everybody that if they don't want their tickets, let me know . . .

In 1968, I was in Vietnam, but I got to listen to the game with a colonel from Ohio State. We were listening to it on the radio at 3 o'clock in the morning. It was cool. Seven years later, the streak began. My best friend and I would go down, and just hold our fingers up in the air and get tickets that way. Then, there wasn't any other way to get them.

I joined the Presidents Club at Ohio State. There were about six of us couples who decided to join, because we were tired of getting tickets that way. They made us a deal where we could get four tickets between the 20s if we gave them a donation through our will and our estate.

***TEXAS TECH**'s basketball arena, the United Spirit Center in Lubbock, is on Indiana Avenue. Texas Tech's nickname is the Red Raiders. The nickname of Bob Knight's Orrville, Ohio high school was the Red Raiders. . . . In the 1962 NCAA semi-final—Ohio State versus Wake Forest—Billy Packer of Wake Forest had 17 points while Knight failed to score. It was Knight's last college game, as he did not play in the title game. . . . Bob Knight once had Woody Hayes as one of his instructors in a class at Ohio State . . . Richard Nixon gave the eulogy at Woody Hayes' funeral.

That didn't last—it went down to two tickets between the 20s. Now it's two tickets in the location of their choice. We're still able to get two home season tickets every year through the Presidents Club. I don't have a very large donation. Obviously, the larger the donation, the better your tickets are going to be.

On October 11, 1975, I went to the Iowa game in Ohio Stadium, and that was the beginning of the streak. We never really understood that we had something going. A friend of mine, John Stroefer, from Dublin, Ohio—we didn't know it, but in the '75 Rose Bowl, we probably passed each other out on the field while we were celebrating the rather large victory Ohio State had.

We met in a bar in Minneapolis. We found out he was from Dublin and I was from Columbus. There were a whole group of guys who went up in a motor home, and we met them up there. We invited them to a bar back in Columbus. This was back in my drinking days—I don't drink anymore.

We started going to the games with each other and tailgating. He graduated from Miami, Ohio. His wife, Sue Stroefer, went to Ohio State. The streak actually started with him. He went to 107 before he quit. It was one of those things where we would just get into a van and go to all the home games, and then we started going to away games. The next thing you know, here we are.

The margin of error in a college football poll is plus or minus 100%

SAY WHAT YOU WANT ABOUT MICHIGAN . . . FRANKLY, "LOSERS" COMES TO MIND

ANDREW PONGRACZ

Andrew Pongracz is a world away from Michigan, living in Chandler, Arizona, working as a real estate investor and part-time high school golf and football coach. But the 36-year-old Michigan native's dislike for the school in Ann Arbor knows no bounds, much to the chagrin of his Wolverine-loving father.

Although I didn't attend Ohio State University, I'm a big fan. I was born in Dearborn, Michigan, and went to high school in the Detroit area. Our house was pretty divided. My dad went to Michigan and is a huge Michigan fan. My older sister also conformed to being a Michigan fan. My mother's a big Notre Dame fan. My brother, God bless his soul, he's the stupid one of the group, although he's an engineer, so I shouldn't say that, but he's stupid . . . he is the Michigan State fan in the group. Why anybody would want to be Michigan State fan—I can't tell you.

We went down to a pep rally in Ann Arbor when I was pretty young. **RICK LEACH*** was still quarterback at Michigan. I sat on my dad's shoulders most of the night. At the time, Michigan had a colorful radio announcer named Bob Ufer, who was the emcee of the pep rally. He was getting the crowd all worked up. There was something about it that, at 6 years old, I just didn't like. Then they dragged out this dummy of Woody Hayes. They decided to set him on fire in the middle of a circle. When they set Woody on fire, I began to cry. My dad had to pull

Who was the only Major League Baseball player to grace the cover of the college football edition of *Sports Illustrated*? Bo Jackson? No. Kirk Gibson? No. ***RICK LEACH** of Michigan? Yes.

me out of there. I came home and took my Michigan T-shirt off, and said I was never cheering for Michigan again after they pulled something like that.

So, I was 6 years old, and who am I going to pull for? Well, I could go over to my mom's side of things, but it's like rats off the sinking ship. Even though you didn't know it yet, you could just feel the arrogance of Notre Dame.

Then, of course, there was Michigan State, but you're better off hitting yourself over the head with a hammer twice a day than being a Michigan State fan. With all the stupid things they've done over the years— good Lord, who wants that? So, what's left? Well, at that time, there was the Big 2 and the Little 8. You only had Ohio State. So, I decided I would commit myself, for life, to being an Ohio State fan . . . and that's pretty much what I did.

"I was kicked out of the house and spent the night with a friend and didn't come back until Sunday."

In '82, I got chased out of the house for waving a No. 1 finger at my dad. When Ohio State beat Michigan that day 24-14, I was kicked out of the house and spent the night with a friend and didn't come back until Sunday. That happened a handful of times. He also chased me down the street, even though Ohio State wasn't involved in the game, in '85, when Michigan was No. 1 and Iowa was No. 2. When Iowa kicked a field goal to beat them, 12-10, I started laughing so hard, again, he chased me out the front door, and I ran down the street and didn't come back until Sunday.

Drove by the Woody Hayes Museum of Forward Passing today. It's still not open.

WE'RE GONNA GIVE JOHN COOPER A FAIR TRIAL . . . AND THEN WE'RE GONNA HANG HIM

BOBBY DIGERONIMO

To this day, Bobby DiGeronimo maintains there's so much more to former OSU coach John Cooper than his smudged bottom line against Michigan. An owner in the family business Independence Excavating near Cleveland, DiGeronimo became best friends with the Buckeye coach and shares a side of him the public didn't always get to see.

Fred Pagac was the linebackers coach for Earle Bruce, and he was retained by John Cooper when he took over for Earle. Fred told me, "You're really going to like this guy." I remember feeling really bad when Earle got fired. I knew him pretty well. My wife said, "You never know. The next coach might be one of your best friends." Basically, that's what happened.

Fred invited me down, and I took one of my young sons to the indoor facility there while they were having practice. I walked over, and Fred introduced me to John Cooper. He got a practice ball and gave it to my son, Donny, and said, "Now don't put this on your mantle. Wear it out." That's just the kind of guy he was. He didn't know me from Adam. He was a very nice person, a shy person. I hear a lot of times people thought he was a little aloof or something like that, but that wasn't it at all. He was shy around a lot of people. Still, he would say, "Hey, don't be a stranger. Come around. Come to practice anytime you want."

By John's second and third years, we had become such good friends. I'd come in the locker room after the game. In those days, I'd sit in the stands. I was having some back problems. He said, "Bobby, I've had back problems, too. Why don't you stand on the sidelines?" Well, heck, what guy wouldn't want to be on the sideline during a Buckeye game?

He'd take me to some away games with the team. He was a very generous, good, loving person. He's like that with his family.

He's a tough guy, too. He just knew ups and downs are a part of the business. He did a hot tub commercial. This was not during the season. He had that southern drawl, and they knew that when they hired him. And they'd hold the commercials against him, and they didn't like that drawl when he lost.

Unfortunately—and I hate to take a shot at Earle Bruce, because I like Earle—but if you look at John's first three, four years, there weren't many guys drafted from those Ohio State teams. I'll tell you this, when he checked their recruiting lists with the coaches the year he came in, he said he about fell out of his chair. They weren't recruiting anybody out of state.

It took them a little while. If you remember Ohio State history, when they lost to Air Force in a bowl game in 1990, a lot of people thought that was going to be it for him. But he was starting to recruit real well. He used to say, "Give me a few years here, and I'll start making some inroads in recruiting, and we'll build a picket fence around Ohio." And he did. If you really look at it, there were a few years he lost some people to Michigan or Penn State, but after he got established here, he didn't miss many big players in Ohio.

Again, I don't want to be against Earle in this, but you look at the weight program. The weight room was big in a lot of schools back then. The Ohio State weight room wasn't that big a deal. When John came in, he brought Dave Kennedy. By the way, when Dave came to Ohio State, he loved John so much he turned down a four-year deal with Bill Belichick—that was probably about $1.2 million over four years—to stay with John for $125,000 a year. Coaches loved to coach for John. If John had a fault, I would say he was too loyal to his assistant coaches. Elliot Uzelac got him in trouble during the Robert Smith era.

Andy Geiger had to eat crow after he had said that "John Cooper was going to be my coach no matter, win or lose, in the bowl game against Lou Holtz' South Carolina team." Then, after they lost the game, he probably got pressure to get rid of him. So now he had to impugn his character and say "The program was getting out of hand." Well, that's bull.

All the criticism John was getting bothered me. We had about 300 people in our construction company at the time. I'd go on jobs. The guys knew that on Monday morning, I'd be in a bit of a bad mood if Ohio State would lose. So if somebody would say something derogatory about him, I would really get upset. I'd say things like "Hey, when you get to the point in your career when you're at one of the top 10 places in the country, and you're as successful as John Cooper, then tell me about it. But, don't dislike him because of his southern drawl . . ."

Basically, people want to beat Michigan. John acknowledges he didn't do it enough. It took him a little bit to equal the talent level, and I think that game got bigger and bigger for a lot of the coaches. You lose the first two, three games when there's a couple there they could have easily won. Players have to make plays. I loved the players that played for John, but a few of them, in those Michigan games, they didn't make plays. I just think sometimes you get too much credit when you win and you get too much blame when you lose . . . and that's just the way it is.

I had a three-year-old grandson die from bacterial meningitis. John and the strength coach, Dave Kennedy, came up during the day to spend the whole day with me. I know he and Coach Pagac came up when my mother died. They came to Mass. I don't think I'll ever have a relationship with another coach like that. He's just a great person. After John left football, he used to tell me, "I don't have a bad day. I wake up in the morning. I'm fine. I've lived a good life. Ohio State's been good to me." Andy Geiger treated him like crap, the way he let him go out.

I did not go to Ohio State. I got drafted and sent to Vietnam, so I wound up getting out of the service and going right to work. Seven of my eight kids went to Ohio State. They all loved John Cooper. They think he's the greatest thing. My daughter, Lisa, cried when he got fired. She's 26 years old, and she'll never think about Ohio State quite the same ever again.

Greg Oden suffered from Anorexia Ponderosa

YA GOT YER SUPERMAN
YA GOT YER BATMAN
YA GOT YER SPIDERMAN
YA GOT YER BUCKEYEMAN

LARRY LOKAI

It's a bird. It's a plane. No, it's an adjunct professor and a city councilman in Urbana, Ohio. It's Buckeyeman. The 65-year-old grandfather of 16 is perhaps Ohio State's loudest fan, both in terms of decibels and dress. His game-day garb includes 7 pounds of buckeye necklaces and, seemingly, a like amount of makeup and face paint.

Most definitely being Buckeyeman has helped my political career. I lost every election I ran in before that, and in different areas of the state. It might be a coincidence, but maybe not. You equate Buckeyeman with somebody who is doing good. I attend parades. I've been to all the universities here, speaking to groups as Buckeyeman. I've been to church functions. I've been to nursing homes. When I go, I put a smile on their faces. And all these places have voters.

Before I started doing the Buckeyeman, I would go to games dressed pretty normally. And at first it was very much a challenge for me to wear a wig. It was by accident that I decided to do the Buckeyeman. In 1998, we had this real good football team. We were picked No. 1 in the polls. Joe Germaine was the quarterback. Michigan State upset us in a home game. Later that year, the final game of the year, I didn't get any tickets, but my son was able to get two tickets to the Michigan game.

I looked at the ticket and thought, "Holy mackerel. We're right smack dab in that corner, back where the Michigan fans sit." I thought, just for the heck of it, I'm going to put a wig on. I didn't do any face paint or anything else. I put the wig on with a jersey and walked into the stadium. Face painting and wigs weren't quite so big back then. From there, we got a few little catcalls and everything. That triggered it. That was November 1998. I just had a jersey and wig.

The next season, 1999, we're coming down to a game, and I couldn't find that wig. I went over to Conrad's and, for one year and one year only, they sold the real long, ugly red wigs that I have. I looked at them and thought it looked like they were for some gay girl. I thought I'd try it just for one game and then try to find my other one. I put it on.

I knew some teachers down in Canal Winchester, south of Columbus there. I was going to meet them at a sports bar for supper. I said, "I'm going to surprise them. I'm going to wear this long wig." I painted half my face red and half my face gray. I walked right into the restaurant. I sat down and had a heck of a good time. They go, "That looks kinda weird." I said, "Well, I might want to improve on this. Let me think about it a little bit."

By the fourth game of the year—this is how Buckeyeman officially became Buckeyeman—I got to thinking about it. Neutron Man always danced all the time. He's passed away now, but we used to do a lot of things together. Then Brutus Buckeye was like the team mascot. I thought I would combine those names. I took the "Buckeye" from Brutus Buckeye; I took the "Man" from Neutron Man and combined those names to come up with Buckeyeman. Nobody is called *Buckeyeman.*

When I first started visiting with the fans, I always took 10 buckeye necklaces with me to the games to give away, and that really became a problem. You give one person one, and another person wants one. For away games, I take five or six necklaces with me. Those are primarily for negotiating purposes, so I can negotiate and get a low seat. When I get down to the low seats, I chit-chat with people about "Let's work together here. Slip me in here, and I'll get the TV cameras here and you'll be on TV." And that usually works.

BUCKEYETEMS

I've been a stadium usher since the mid-'80s, and not even moving to Georgia could stop that. I tell people I do it for the money, which is $6 a game if you're a supervisor like I am. If you're not, well, then you don't get paid, but I wouldn't trade it for anything. I live in Alpharetta, Georgia—near Atlanta—and I drive to every home game, 600 miles, which takes about 11 hours. One time, I tried to see how fast I could do it, and I did it in nine and a half hours. I figured I was averaging about 70 miles an hour, and that was way too fast.

When I got transferred away from Columbus, I thought I would have give up the ushering. A lot of people said, "Well, it's been nice knowing you, Dave. We really liked you doing it. We're sorry you won't be able to do it anymore." This would have been February or March. But over the summer, I

> **"I drive to every home game, 600 miles . . ."**

got to thinking how much I was going to miss the Buckeyes down here in Georgia, where it's all Bulldog Nation and Georgia Tech. Oh man, I decided I would try to go back to some of the games.

Several years before they redid the stadium, my job was at the visiting locker room before the game. At halftime and after the game, we would take nylon ropes and run them from the field back to the locker room so the team could get on and off the field. I remember once just before the Michigan game, the ropes were back. Michigan hadn't come out of the locker room yet. There was an ABC cameraman standing there, and he started to walk back between the ropes toward the locker room.

I told him, "You'd better not stand there." He said, "No, no. I'm fine. I've been doing this for many years." I said, "Well, I'm just warning you. This Michigan game is different than other games." He said, "OK, I'll be fine."

Well, wouldn't you know—Michigan came out of the locker room and went charging out onto the field and just ran right over him. His television camera and everything went flying. He went down on the ground. After the game, my family and friends were saying, "Did you see the guy who was standing right there?" He busted his camera. He was hobbling around the rest of the game. They gave him another camera to use. The Michigan game is different.

—**Dave Mumma**, 62, commutes from Atlanta
to usher every Ohio State home game

We would always wander through the stadium at our leisure on days other than game days. There were all kinds of little nooks and crannies. There were a few back, hidden stairwells. If you go to the other end of the stadium, the curved closed end part of the horseshoe, there's a little balcony that looks down on the formal entrance to the stadium. You could walk out there and stand on the balcony and watch people come and go. You could sneak in and watch practice.

We used to play football on the **ASTROTURF*** at night. We had access to it all the time. They just couldn't keep us out. We'd go out the fire door onto the ramp and then go out onto the field. The police never said anything. If it was game day or if something special was going on, you didn't go running out on the field. Other than that, you could go out and wander around and take your friends on a tour of the inside of the stadium.

I didn't go to practices myself. Right on the river side is where the marching band always practiced. Most of us would sit in the windows and watch the band practice in the late afternoon rather than go watch the football team practice. The band would play right outside your windows. We used to watch the tryouts. We used to watch them practice all the time so could see them practicing Script Ohio. It was impressive to watch that practice.

—**Keith Blatner**, Washington State professor,
lived in a dorm room at Ohio Stadium in the early '70s.
The dorm rooms are closed now.

It's hard living out of state on OSU-Michigan week. In 1988, I was living in Maryland. Both the Virginia and D.C. ABC affiliates did not

An announcer once asked Tug McGraw about the difference between ***ASTROTURF** and grass. Tug replied, "I don't know. I have never smoked Astroturf."

broadcast the game. They broadcast the *Virginia-Maryland game* that day. I just remember when I found out, I called both stations. I didn't know what to do. I was at work. I was in a panic. This was the day before the game. I didn't know what it was like to not watch that game.

I called my parents and said, "Look. I'm hardly making any money, and I've got to watch my phone bill, but can I call tomorrow every 10 minutes and just somebody answer the phone and give me an update and hang up, so I don't run up my bill." I'd hit redial. Somebody would answer the phone at my house. I'd say, "Update." They'd just go, "Buckeyes on the 35. Third and three. They're down 10-7 with two minutes to go in the first quarter." That went on for three hours.

The day of the Michigan game, I take all the furniture out of my living room and put it in my bedroom, so I don't throw anything, hit anything. I want a clear path. I get a can of Skoal. I don't chew any time other than that day. I don't smoke. I won't drink during the game. So I get a can of chewing tobacco, with a spit cup, and I just pace back and forth and basically—I know I sound like an idiot—I yell at the TV. I coach the game. And in 1988, we lost. When I called to get the final update and to see that the game was really over, I just told somebody, "Tell the old man—don't call me. I know they lost."

—**John Karliak**, Cleveland native,
now living in New Hampshire

Most people don't know that I'm the guy who came up with the name "Brutus Buckeye," and I'm more than OK with that. In fact, for a few days after the contest, I kind of wished people didn't know. I was a member of Ohio Staters, which was a service organization. The Ohio Staters did sponsor a contest in 1965 to name the mascot, which was the creation of another student named Ray Bourhis. When the contest was announced, I went to the university library and checked out some books on names and submitted four different names. The other three I don't even remember. Brutus then was selected by the panel that chose them. I don't even know who sat on that panel.

A few students wrote in to *The Lantern* complaining that a member of Ohio Staters, a student service group, had won the contest *sponsored* by Ohio Staters. That was in *The Lantern* for a few days, but nobody ever called me and threatened to take my gift certificate away or any of that business. I was given a $50 gift certificate from the Union Department Store, and I bought myself a new blazer. That was pretty much it. I really didn't dream it would take off like it did . . . and it didn't, for a while. It was just there. Brutus made his official debut in the fall of '65. There has been a change from the original model. There was a handle to move the mouth from a smile to a frown. There were handles to move the eyebrows. It appeared, and people applauded.

—**Rev. Kerry Reed**, pastor, Canal Winchester, Ohio

If you watch the tape of the 1975 Rose Bowl when we beat OSU 18-17, you'll see **JOHN MCKAY*** not going over to shake Woody Hayes' hand after the game. He's running off the field with about four policemen. And what happened was, before the game, he had a death threat.

It was interesting, because ordinarily, the assistant coaches always used to stand next to the head coach in big games, because they knew they were going to get on television. It's funny now, because it *was* a hoax, but each of our coaches knew there was a death threat. You did not see an assistant coach within 10 yards of him. They were all scared stiff that they were going to get shot by mistake.

Another funny thing about that game, I saw with my own eyes Woody Hayes stomp on his glasses. And then I saw, like, a little team manager hand him another pair. I don't know whether he had eight pairs and this was an act or whatever, but he certainly had another pair ready to go. For me personally, I thought it was going to be my last football game I ever played. I accepted a Rhodes Scholarship a few weeks before and was going to be on my way to Oxford.

I grew up in Southern California watching the Rose Bowl games. I threw what turned out to be the Ohio State game–winning touchdown pass to lifelong best pal—still my best pal—J.K. McKay, and then threw the two-point play to Shelton Diggs, which ended up winning the national championship for us. The last pass you throw wins the national championship and the last touchdown you throw, you throw to your lifelong best pal, so you're thinking it's your last game. You grew up dream-

After the Tampa Bay Buccaneers were trounced by the Giants, a reporter asked Bucs' coach ***JOHN McKAY**, what he thought of his team's execution that day. McKay replied, "That's a good idea."

ing about playing in the Rose Bowl. It was a special time and moment for me.

—**Pat Haden**, former USC star quarterback, Rhodes scholar

I don't fly the Ohio State flag anymore. I got into a ruckus with my neighbors, actually not about the flag, but about the flagpole. That became the big issue in the neighborhood. It actually got very ugly. Many times, I've thought, "If it had been a Florida flag, would the pole have been an issue?" My neighbor claims that the flagpole devalues his house, which is a joke to me. But the bottom line is he swayed enough people on the architect committee to vote against it. I am allowed to fly the flag, but would have to put it on a flagpole *on* the house. I looked online and there's actually been all kinds of legal issues on flagpoles at homeowners' associations all over the country.

You want to tell these people to get a life. It really went on for two years. I just said, "I don't have time to deal with this. I've got better things to do." This is so petty. I said, "Look, I'll take the pole down, to settle this issue—I'll take it down." It really wasn't worth the aggravation for me.

"If it had been a Florida flag, would the pole have been an issue?"

My best football memory at Ohio State—next to the great Oklahoma game in 1977—wasn't even at the football stadium. While I was in college at Ohio State, one summer I was driving through the McDonald's parking lot one day. This old man walked up in front of me. I pulled up behind and motioned for him to veer to the right or to the left. He kept on walking right down the middle of the parking lot. I thought, "Come on, pal. Move out of the way." I was a little disjointed, so I just kept following him out. I thought, "That's kind of ridiculous."

I looked in the mirror, and it was Woody Hayes . . . so I thought, "Oh, Woody Hayes—that's OK." This was while he was still the coach. I will always regret—always—that none of us ever thought about getting a picture with him, getting his autograph and that kind of stuff.

—**Pete Nash**, OSU grad, Gainesville, Florida

Block O was started in 1938 by the head cheerleader at the time, Clancy Isaac. He made a trip to see the USC student section. They had a spirit section and did stunts and cards. He was really excited by it and wanted to create that here at Ohio State . . . and actually created Block O.

We hold up placards and banners and spell out words and form pictures. A long time ago, they would use paper bags and would paint each paper bag a different color and would have to line them up in the section. Other times, they would use little pieces of plastic. Eventually, it progressed to where there's an online grid, so we could actually plot out and come up with our own design online rather than sit down and do them on paper.

We go into the stadium on Friday afternoon to sort the cards out and organize them, We usually show up about 3½ hours before game time. We will actually set them in each seat. That way when the students come in, placards are right underneath their seat. A lot of people don't really realize how much actually goes into the planning and the setting up and all that, but it's pretty neat when it actually comes up.

We do run into the problem of Block O, a student section, being general admission seating. The fans who are most excited and are ready to be there and want to be up front close to the field will show up as soon as the gates open. There are also those students and fans who do some tailgating beforehand, do some drinking before they come, and they will fill in as kickoff nears and fill in the top of the section. So you also can find that sometimes when we do our stunts, especially some of the more complicated ones, that the top part of the section and the top part of the stunt itself doesn't look quite right. That's because they either just don't want to do it or are too intoxicated to do it.

At one point, Block O, back before the 'Shoe was actually renovated, went along the side of the field—the 20-yard line, the 30-yard line, moving around in there. And then it moved to the north end of the stadium for a long time. Then, after the renovation, they moved it to where it is now in the south stands.

—**Kyle Blizzard**, student, Trenton, Ohio

The only people who are eligible to dot the "i" are fourth- and fifth-year sousaphone players in the marching band. You have to march in the band for four years before you even are eligible to choose a game to dot the "i". We have to try out each fall. We're never guaranteed a spot in the band. Once you make it the first year, you're not guaranteed a spot the next year.

A tuba and sousaphone are basically the same thing, except the tuba is played in a concert band or an orchestra, and it sits in your lap and plays up and points upward, while the sousaphone is what marching bands use, for the most part. Sousaphones rest on our shoulders and form a big loop around the belt and point forward. They play exactly the same notes and fingering on the valves, so it's just a different shape.

You have to prove your spot for three years, and then, as a fourth-year senior, you get first pick in all the games of that season. Then whatever is left over the fifth-years get a chance to pick through. It all goes by rank order. We have 28 sousaphone players in the band, but in each game only 24 of us march, leaving out four extra guys. Each week, they get a chance to challenge for one of the 24 regular spots. So each week is kind of like a trial itself, because you can be challenged by any of those alternates for your spot. The tryout process is unbelievably competitive. My freshman year there were 60 to 70 sousaphone players trying out for the 28 spots . . . 24 of the 28 were returning from the year before. There were only four spots for about 50 players, so it was definitely a nerve-wracking experience.

—**Dan Wanders**, dotted the "i" in three epic
No. 1 vs. No. 2 matches

I never did get to meet Woody. My dad and I would always watch his TV show, where he'd get the players standing up there looking like they were in marine boot camp, standing there at attention. "Yes, coach." "No, coach." "Whatever you say, coach." He'd dissect the previous game with whoever it was. I remember Brockington standing up there just looking like he was about ready to mess himself he was so nervous, trying not to say the wrong thing, not because he was on TV, but just because Woody was the one asking the questions.

I'm 52 years old, and I'm still a huge Ohio State football fan. Most of my buddies are big NFL fans, too. I like to watch NFL games on Sunday if I'm not doing anything, but I'm mostly watching NFL games to see how the Ohio State alumni are doing.

—**J.K. Simmons**, Former OSU student, the voice of the
yellow M&M, actor (*Spiderman*, TV's *The Closer*)

There was a theater built under the stands. It's called Stadium Theater. It was under the stands, but it had no heat, so it was a summer theater. I spent the summer there doing shows. It was like a fun, kitschy thing to do in Columbus—to go to the shows under the grandstand at the stadium.

> "It was like a fun, kitschy thing to do in Columbus—to go to the shows under the grandstand at the stadium."

Socially, at 18, you could drink 3.2 beer. It was like tiger p---, we called it. It was horrifying. Horrifying. But we drank it, because we could! We thought this was great. We could actually drink something with alcohol in it—*to wash down all the marijuana.*

After I left Ohio State, I went back a couple of times to see people. Oddly enough, it wasn't anything to do with the campus—I went back because a friend of mine was in a musical. It was on tour and happened to play in Mershon Auditorium. I tour with Bette Midler and every time she played Columbus, I would go.

—**Bruce Vilanch**, Los Angeles, OSU Grad, comedy writer, *Hollywood Squares* panelist

When John Cooper was fired and Tressel was hired, I had two reactions to that. My first reaction was they were getting a guy from Division 1-AA to coach in the Big Ten and to coach at Ohio State. Is this gonna go well? Andy Geiger, the athletic director at the time, got that question right away. He said, "Well, as we examined everything, we noticed that at 1-AA, the football games were played on a field that was 100 yards long and 53 yards wide"—or whatever the number is—and just brushed that one aside.

One interesting thing, when they released the latest spring roster, there was no attrition. Nobody was gone due to academics or injury—that's unheard of at this level. No transfers. I went through the whole roster, and I was stunned. Their retention is pretty good. Their graduation rate is going straight up. Their academic profile is very good. Over time, those NCAA marks that people have lampooned Ohio State about are going to go up. It just takes time. A lot of it is attributed to the things—he's got a guy who secretly goes and checks on these kids to make sure they're going to class. That's how involved this whole effort is. If kids don't go to class, then they've got some consequences they have to deal with. Jim Tressel has changed the whole culture of Ohio State football.

—**Steve Helwagen**, Bucknuts.com

The first writing I ever did was when [my friend] and I were in seventh grade . . .

We called sports stars. Real sports stars. He would pick up the receiver on one phone/ I'd pick up the receiver on another—we'd switch houses in which to do it every month—and we'd make the calls. The one of us doing the dialing would have to yell to the other in another part of the house once the dialing was complete—you couldn't dial another phone if the extension was off the hook.

So one of us would dial, and then shout for the other to pick up—and when someone answered at another number we'd called, one of us (we worked this out in advance; we rehearsed it) would say: "Could I please speak to Jack Nicklaus?" Or "Could I please speak to Jerry Lucas?"

We were in seventh grade when we started this. Lucas was our first. He was in his initial year as an Ohio State basketball player—on the team that would go on to win the NCAA championship—and we decided (dreamed) that we wanted to interview him for the junior high school paper, the *Beacon*. But how do a couple of twelve-year-olds do that? We couldn't get into Ohio State basketball practice; we couldn't get into a postgame locker room.

We had read in ***SPORTS ILLUSTRATED** he was a member of the Beta Theta Pi fraternity. One night at dinnertime we each drew a deep

***SPORTS ILLUSTRATED** was first published in 1954 and its first swimsuit issue was in 1964. The *Sports Illustrated Swimsuit Issue* has 52 million readers, 16 million of them are females . . . 12 million more than normal. . . . In 1955, SI selected horse owner William Woodward as their Sportsman of the Year. Woodward's wife shot and killed the unfaithful Woodward before the issue went to press. SI then selected World Series hero, Johnny Podres.

breath, ran to a different room of Jack's house, looked up the number of the Beta house on the Ohio State campus, dialed, and when someone answered Jack said, "Could I please speak to Jerry Lucas?"

Amazingly, the fraternity member who answered didn't ask who was calling. He just yelled downstairs to the dining room in the chapter house: "Hey, Luke. It's for you."

Thirty seconds later in a deep voice:

"Hello?"

We did it just like we'd practiced beforehand. We wouldn't believe it was happening; we couldn't believe we'd gotten him on the line.

"This is Jack Roth," Jack said into his receiver.

"This is Bobby Green," I said into mine.

"We're from the Bexley Junior High School *Beacon*," Jack said.

And we asked for an interview.

And—miracle—*__JERRY LUCAS__ did not say no.

"I've just begun to eat," he said. "Could you call back in half an hour?"

Which we did, and we asked five or six questions (taking turns—we never wanted to do this alone, the whole idea was that if it was something we did together and when we turned in our interview, at first the faculty adviser to the *Beacon* thought we had made it up. We had to convince her—and it wasn't easy—that we had really talked to Jerry Lucas, that it wasn't fiction. We might as well have told her that we landed an exclusive interview with President Eisenhower.

After Lucas, we were hooked. We got Nicklaus, who lived in Columbus; we got Lucas's basketball teammate Larry Siegfried; we got Ohio State football fullback Bob Ferguson. We would scan the downtown papers to see when athletic banquets were being held in Columbus (the Touchdown Club was the big one) and on the day of the dinners we would call the two major downtown hotels, the Deshler Hilton and

> *__JERRY LUCAS__'s Ohio State teams were 40-2 in conference play. They never lost a Big Ten game until after the conference title was clinched.

the Neil House, knowing that the out-of-town stars being honored at the banquets would almost certainly be staying there. That's how we got Dick Groat, the shortstop of the Pittsburgh Pirates; that's how we got Bill Mazeroski, his second-baseman teammate; that's how we got the legendary retired Washington Redskins quarterback Slingin' Sammy Baugh. We never missed; once we set our sights, we never failed. "This is Jack Roth . . ." And they would talk to us. They would actually talk to us. . . .

The first teams you fall in love with you think are going to last forever. You learn soon enough that it's not so, but when you are young and those first teams do break up, you can't quite figure out the feeling. Jack and I had loved the Lucas-Havlicek-Siegfried-Nowell-Roberts Ohio State NCAA championship basketball team, when the seniors all graduated, when the new Ohio State team, with a player named Gary Bradds at center, took to the court at St. John Arena, it was disorienting to us. Especially when the crowd cheered just as loudly for that team as they had cheered for the Lucas team; especially when the Bradds team began to win consistently.

The first things that matter to you will not remain as they were; they can't. It's fundamental, and—once you learn it that initial time—you realize that it must be so. You look around the basketball arena and ask yourself if anyone else is thinking: Where is Lucas? If, even for a second, as the people in the crowd are on their feet and roaring for the newly constituted team, they are thinking the same thing you are: What happened to what was here before?

. . . If the receding away of the first great team is jolting for the spectators, what must it be like for those who play the games? How must Lucas and Havlicek have been feeling that first year out? If the people who had watched them with such passion and seeming devotion just a year before had moved on to new loyalties, what about them?

—**Bob Greene**, from *And You Know You Should Be Glad:*
A True Story Of Lifelong Friendship, reprinted
with permission of Bob Greene

YOU CAN'T GO TO HEAVEN UNLESS YOU'RE A BUCKEYE

FATHER KENNETH GRIMES

Father Kenneth Grimes wasn't shy about quoting Woody Hayes in a sermon. And he wasn't bashful about taking a few jabs at Hayes' least favorite school, either. The Ohio State grad shared friendships with two of OSU's Heisman Trophy winners and recalls the days when Hayes felt the kind of heat Earle Bruce and John Cooper would later be chased by.

I retired from the priesthood after 49 years in July of 2006, but I'll never retire from being a Buckeye fan.

I grew up in Columbus and was a native of Columbus. The Buckeyes were always No. 1. Going through a Catholic grade school and a Catholic high school, in the city of Columbus, still 80 percent of the people and the kids were Ohio State, 20 percent were Notre Dame. It's in the blood.

The first game I saw, my next-door neighbor had an extra ticket and invited me, and I saw Les Horvath play. It was in 1942. I saw Horvath play Michigan. There I was, an 11-year-old kid. Coming out of the place, that's where I learned to sing "We Don't Give a Damn for the Whole State of Michigan." Even my parents had no trouble with me singing that song. Back then, too, the Michigan game was a big deal—absolutely! Even at that young age, I can recall when **TOMMY HARMON*** was killing us. He beat us 40-0, and there was a pall over the whole town. I can remember that—it was 1940.

The game with Horvath was something. He was quick and the leader.

> Ricky Nelson and John DeLorean married daughters of ***TOMMY HARMON**.

I believe that was Paul Brown's second year as coach there. After that, I didn't get to go to games, but later in life I became a regular—had season tickets for a long time. I was chaplain for the Ohio House of Representatives for 22 years. In that role, I had the opportunity to buy tickets—I didn't get them free, and I didn't want them free. So all those years, from 1972 to 1994, I had season tickets to the games. Prior to that, I'd see four or five games a year. I was at the famous Snow Bowl in 1950.

I was one of the 500,000 people that said they were there at the Snow Bowl . . . but I *was* there. The same thing—I went with the next-door neighbors. As I can recall, the weather was awful. My dad was stuck in Akron—he was a traveling salesman. The neighbors called and said, "Do you want to go?" I said, "Yeah." Mom made me hot chocolate in a Thermos. I lived on a hilltop in those days. For the first time in my life, we drove right down West Broad Street, right down to High Street and made a left-hand turn at Broad and High. There was just nobody down there. Never before or after have I ever made a left-hand turn at Broad and High.

We went over to the stadium, and we stayed there until the end. It was a heck of a ballgame. Vic Janowicz punted the ball 17 times or something like that, and kicked a field goal. But it wasn't enough. Michigan made no first downs, but they had us bottled up down in our end of the field most of the game. At that game, I thought people

> **"I was one of the 500,000 people that said they were there at the Snow Bowl."**

would be talking about the game for a long time. That was in my mind, "Boy, we won't forget this one very soon." And that was true. Michigan won 9-3.

When I was a kid, Ohio State football was the only show in town. It was big. It was very big. Before Woody, it was the graveyard of coaches, and you had to win here or get out. I can recall the first couple of years of Woody's time, the airplanes would have trailers, "Good-bye Woody." They would come flying over the stadium on Saturday afternoons.

It took Woody four or five years to get his feet on the ground here. I can remember that, my God, we wanted Paul Brown back! There was a "Bring Back Brown" movement. Yeah, "We want Brown," but Brown was winning like mad with the Browns at the time. It took five years for Woody to get to the point where he became untouchable.

I got to know Woody pretty well later on. He was a great man. When I went to Portsmouth as the principal down there, we had good football teams. It was a small school. I wanted to get Woody to come down and give a talk. I was in Columbus for some occasion. I thought, "Well, I'll just go over to the center." I knew where his office was. I walked in unannounced, walked down the hall and knocked on the door.

Woody said, "Come in." "Oh, Father, how are you?" I told him what I wanted, and he said, "What's the date?" I told him, and he said, "I'll be there. No problem, Father." He came. He gave a heck of a good talk. We gave him $50 or something like that, and he said, "Father, I don't take any money. I like to do this kind of thing." That's how he was. He made the people feel like they were important and that he was so happy to see them, etc. And not just on that occasion—that's what Woody did.

I can recall that the Jai Lai was his favorite restaurant—of course, it was the favorite restaurant of a lot of people. I remember taking my mother and my aunt to the Jai Lai to celebrate their birthdays. Woody was there sitting across the restaurant. I saw him from a distance, so I said to my mom, "Do you want to meet Woody?" She said, "Oh, Kenneth. You can't do that." I said, "Well, I'll go see. I don't know." I went across the restaurant. Woody greeted me, "Father, how are you?" I said, "Woody, I don't want to bother you, but I've got my old mother and my old aunt over here. We're having a birthday party. When you leave, if you could stop by, I'd appreciate it." "Don't you worry, I'll be there."

Five minutes later, Woody came over, and he just charmed those women, "Oh, Mrs. Grimes. I'm so glad that you're here. You're looking so well. And your sister . . ." On and on and on—he just charmed them to death. He was just there two, three minutes and was gone, but while he was there, he turned on that charm and just melted them. That's the kind of fellow he was.

Because I knew Woody, and knew what kind of man he really was, and I'd been around athletics enough to know, his temperamental side didn't bother me. Some high school coaches are the nicest people in the world. But, my gosh, you put them on that field, and they're tigers. So, it wasn't just Woody. That's a part of it.

My favorite players over the years would have to come down to Vic Janowicz or Hopalong Cassady. I knew Vic very well. He was my parishioner at St. Agatha Parish. This was afterwards, of course, in later years. He never missed Mass. He was a fine gentleman. He couldn't have been friendlier. He was involved in the parish—good, good guy. I knew him well.

After some years, Vic was just another person. He was in the parish when I first transferred there. When I realized who he was, I was interested in the fact, but then, once you meet him, he's just like everybody else. There wasn't any adulation or that kind of thing. I did respect him. He was a good Catholic and a good citizen.

Hop I knew fairly well. Hop is about my age. In high school, I played baseball against Hop—didn't play football against him. Afterwards, I played against him in amateur ball—Saturday-afternoon leagues and that kind of stuff. Both were fine baseball players. Vic was a catcher, a heck of a player. Vic played for the Pirates at one time. He was not quite Major League caliber, but he played with the Pirates.

The funny thing about faith and football, when the team was winning, we'd have worse church attendance. They'd all stayed home to watch the ballgame. Of course, that's true all over Columbus. Saturday afternoon Masses during football season—they're down everyplace. It'll be up on Sunday morning then. A lot of them will come Sunday morning, but the regular Saturday Mass attendance is down. I know this year, the Ohio State-Michigan game was one of the biggest Ohio State-Michigan games ever played. Many of the parishes were down over half. Usually they're down maybe 10 percent, but for that game, they were down over 50 percent.

We have had Michigan fans in our congregation. They were treated fine. Jokingly, they walk out with their Michigan shirts on, and you joke, "What are you doing in here? Get out of my church." But it's jokingly. They understood, so no problem about that.

I would say people are in a better humor when Ohio State is winning. Everybody is jovial and jocular and happy when Ohio State is winning. After Mass, the conversation just bubbles. Everybody wants to talk. After a loss, though, people aren't very interested in talking.

As a pastor—not every Saturday, but if there was a big game—at the end of Mass I'd say, "Go in peace and love and serve the Lord. Thanks be to God. And, Go Bucks"—that kind of thing, but I wouldn't talk about it during Mass. Once in a while, some of Woody's sayings would fit in the sermon. "As Woody says, you've got to pay forward. You've got to take care of people." I never did quote any of the other Ohio State coaches.

And I still sing that song, "We Don't Give a Damn for the Whole State of Michigan" every blessed year.

If you're lucky enough
to be a Buckeye,
you're lucky enough.

TO BE CONTINUED!

We hope you have enjoyed the first *For Buckeye Fans Only*. You can be in the next edition if you have a neat story. Email it to printedpage@ cox.net (please put "Buckeye" in the subject line and include a *phone number* where you can be reached), or call the author directly at (602) 738-5889.

For more information on ordering more copies of *For Buckeye Fans Only*, as well as any of the author's other best-selling books, call (602) 738-5889.

NOTE: THERE WERE NO ACTUAL MICHIGAN FANS HARMED DURING THE MAKING OF THIS BOOK.

PHOTO CREDITS

OTHER BOOKS BY RICH WOLFE

Da Coach (Mike Ditka)

I Remember Harry Caray

There's No Expiration Date on Dreams (Tom Brady)

He Graduated Life with Honors and No Regrets (Pat Tillman)

Take This Job and Love It (Jon Gruden)

Been There, Shoulda Done That (John Daly)

Oh, What a Knight (Bob Knight)

And the Last Shall Be First (Kurt Warner)

Remembering Jack Buck

Sports Fans Who Made Headlines

Fandemonium

Remembering Dale Earnhardt

For Yankees Fans Only

For Cubs Fans Only

For Cardinals Fans Only

For Packers Fans Only

For Browns Fans Only

For Mets Fans Only

For Broncos Fans Only

For Georgia Fans Only

For Nebraska Fans Only

For Notre Dame Fans Only—The New Saturday Bible

For more information on these books, call (602) 738-5889.

Jack Buck (circled left) made his TV debut at WBNS, Columbus, Ohio in 1952. Also circled are WBNS staffers Jonathan Winters and Woody Hayes.